# The Pubs of the Malverns, Upton and neighbouring villages

# The Pubs of the Malverns, Upton and neighbouring villages

*by*
Tony Hobbs

**Logaston Press**

LOGASTON PRESS
Little Logaston, Logaston,
Woonton, Almeley, Herefordshire HR3 6QH
logastonpress.co.uk

First published by Logaston Press 2012
Copyright © text: Tony Hobbs
Copyright © illustrations as per Acknowledgments

All rights reserved. No part of this publication
may be reproduced, stored in a retrieval system,
or transmitted, in any form or by any means,
electronic, mechanical, photocopying, recording
or otherwise, without the prior permission,
in writing of the publisher

ISBN 978 1 906663 65 0

Set in Times New Roman by Logaston Press
and printed in the UK by
CPI Antony Rowe, Chippenham

# Contents

| | | page |
|---|---|---|
| Acknowledgments | | vii |
| Introduction | | ix |
| Chapter 1 | Alehouses, Taverns and Inns | 1 |
| Chapter 2 | Brewing & Breweries | 9 |
| Chapter 3 | Great Malvern | 21 |
| Chapter 4 | Malvern Link Top | 67 |
| Chapter 5 | Malvern Link & Newland | 79 |
| Chapter 6 | North Malvern | 99 |
| Chapter 7 | West Malvern | 107 |
| Chapter 8 | Malvern Wells | 121 |
| Chapter 9 | Barnards Green, Poolbrook, Guarlford & The Hanleys | 131 |
| Chapter 10 | Welland, Castlemorton, Birtsmorton Longdon & Rye Street | 149 |
| Chapter 11 | Colwall, Chance's Pitch & British Camp | 165 |
| Chapter 12 | Powick, Bransford & Callow End | 183 |
| Chapter 13 | Leigh Sinton, Storridge, Stiffords Bridge, Cradley, Mathon, Alfrick, Longley Green & Suckley | 199 |
| Chapter 14 | Upton-upon-Severn | 227 |
| Bibliography | | 257 |
| Index of People | | 261 |
| Index of Hotel, Inn & Pub Names | | 271 |
| Index of Breweries | | 275 |

# Acknowledgments

Where does one start? There are so many people who helped in providing information useful in the writing of this book that it is difficult to account for them all. They range from employees of organisations such as libraries and museums to landlords (typically tenants or owners) and customers of all the licensed premises visited, and inhabitants of properties converted from inns to private residences. Some people who simply heard what I was doing volunteered their own pub knowledge.

However, there are two people who helped me enormously along the way. Firstly, Brian Iles, the curator of Malvern Museum of Local History, helped establish a list of all the pubs and hotels in Malvern and surrounding district, provided a number of excellent prints of old pubs, and kindly agreed to edit and proof-read each chapter as it was finished. Secondly, Ann Utley, an inhabitant of Colwall and a personal friend, kindly accompanied me on trips to the hostelries of Malvern and further afield and joined me in a drink or two and a meal or so. Her interest and enthusiasm for all pub matters including real ale provided stimulating company. She also kindly took some photographs of pubs for me.

My main areas of research were Malvern Library (where staff members, particularly Catherine Lees, were always a great help); Malvern Museum; Malvern Tourist Information Centre; Malvern Civic Society; the History Centre, Worcester; Colwall Library and Cradley Heritage Group.

I am also indebted to the following: Roger Hall-Jones of First Paige, Malvern, who provided old pub prints and pub knowledge; Elizabeth Ranbridge of Malvern Girls College; Karen & Graham Ellaway-Bell (Moodkee); Steve Lewis (Cowleigh Arms); John Hurrell (Fir Tree); Diane Barker (Swan, Alfrick); Ron & Joanna Richardson (The Stable, Cradley), Mrs. Patricia West (customer, Malvern Library); Stan Jackson (customer, Green Dragon, Guarlford); Derek Rees (Colwall); Matthew & Jim Cooke (Malvern Hills Hotel); Tim Rowe & Anni (The Bell, Mathon); Lorimer Stodart (Swan Cottage, Alfrick); the late Trevor Marston (landlord, Brewers Arms, West Malvern); and Michelle Cairns (widow of the late Jim Cairns, landlord of Cross Keys, Suckley).

My thanks go to the following who assisted me in compiling the chapter on Upton-upon-Severn: local historian Simon Wilkinson, whose guide *Upton-upon-Severn Public Houses – Past & Present* proved invaluable, and who also kindly agreed to proof-read the chapter; Max Harris, who provided the information on the Crowne/King's Head/Queen's Arms in the High Street; Lavender Beard (Tudor House Museum), who provided numerous old prints; Jon & Chris Lear (White Lion Hotel); Graham Bunn (King's Head); and Upton Library.

A word of thanks too for my editor Andy Johnson.

# Introduction

Having gone north (from Herefordshire) into Shropshire with *The Pubs of Ludlow* and to the west with *The Pubs of Radnorshire*, it seemed only natural to take the next step to the east and into Worcestershire, and this is exactly what I have done with *The Pubs of Malvern and Upton*. What about Herefordshire itself, do I hear someone cry? Why haven't you written a book closer to home? My answer to this is that while I would be delighted to write such a book, Hereford City and the rest of the county has already been covered. So to continue this series it made sense to travel further afield and Malvern seemed as good a spot as any. Indeed, the locality itself couldn't be bettered. Set against the imposing backdrop of the Malvern Hills, one encounters the different elements which make up the whole – Great Malvern, Little Malvern, Malvern Link, West Malvern, Malvern Wells and North Malvern – all with their own individual identity. As the area didn't start to flourish until the opening of the spa amenities in the late 18th century, it is not surprising that most of the hostelries date from that period and later although there are a few of a more historic nature.

Broadening the scope of the book, I decided to include the various surrounding villages up to and just over the Hereford boundary to the west, up to the City of Worcester and in the area enclosed by the M5 and M50 motorways, stopping short of Ledbury, which has already been covered. This area includes Upton-upon-Severn, which for its size boasts a plethora of pubs, past and present, some of which date back to the 15th and 16th centuries.

Through the description of the individual inn and hotel, together with anecdotes including murder, mayhem and ghosts, hopefully I have managed to bring to the reader's attention the fascinating life and times of Malvern and the surrounding district; and also of the people who ran and drank in their hostelries.

My main concern has been the length of time it has taken to research and write this book and the missing of the deadline last year (2011). With independent bookshops closing at a faster rate than pubs, the number of outlets is dwindling all the time and electronic books haven't helped either. So I would imagine that you are more likely to have found this book in your local newsagent, tourist information centre, or garden centre, or even your local pub, than in a bookshop.

*The Pubs of Malvern and Upton* gives firstly a general overview of the inn and how it has changed over the ages and the changes that have taken place in the licensing laws, and then details of the growth of brewing and breweries, of which Malvern has seen quite a few, and the end product, real ale. Then follow separate chapters on the different Malverns and neighbouring villages.

CHAPTER ONE

# Alehouses, Taverns and Inns

The alcoholic drinking place, or inn, was probably introduced into this country when the first roads were formally laid out by the Romans. During their 400-year occupation of Britain, the Romans built something like 10,000 miles of road. Initially the roads linked places of military importance and broke up enemy territory, but eventually they formed a national network for all travellers. As G.K. Chesterton observed: 'Before the Roman came to Rye or out to Severn strode, The rolling English drunkard made the rolling English road'.

Alcoholic refreshment, mainly in the form of wine but also cider and ale, would have been served along these and other routes. There were usually *mansiones* and *diversoria* along the roads and *tabernae* in the towns. One of the commonest signs was a Chequer Board – of Roman origin, having been found on houses in Pompeii, and referring to a game such as chess or draughts. A bush of vine leaves, symbolical of Bacchus, the god of wine, was often displayed above the door of *tabernae*.

After the departure of the Romans in the early 5th century, the country descended into the so-called Dark Ages. There are no traces of Saxon ale houses, built of wood and wattle and daub, but it is certain that inns were a feature of English life in 600 AD, for there exist decrees of Ethelbert, King of Kent, in 616, and of Ine, King of Wessex, in 730, for regulating the number of ale sellers and for keeping the inns in better order. By 750 the Archbishop of York issued a Canon 'That no priest go to eat or drink in taverns', and there were so many inns by the time of King Edgar (959-75) that he issued a decree limiting their number to one per village.

In those times alehouses were indistinguishable from other domestic dwellings, and while customers, some clerical, drank indoors, off sales business was also conducted. Much brewing was done on a communal basis, as with the church ales. These were specially brewed ales sold to the public with the money raised going for church purposes.

Immediately after the Norman Conquest the country was parcelled out amongst the newcomers and numerous castles were built which in turn generated settlements outside their walls. These new towns with growing populations inevitably resulted in a sizeable increase in the number of inns and taverns. However, permanent alehouses only start to appear in significant numbers in the 13th century.

Various measures to protect the customer were introduced, including the 'Assize of Bread and Ale' in 1267. This enactment accepted the principle that both bread and ale were necessities of life and, for a period of some 300 years, it ensured that the retail price of ale was fixed according to the prices of corn and malt. At that time, ale was usually made from malted barley, or occasionally wheat, which was steeped in water and then fermented with yeast.

During the 13th century there was a gradual increase in the sale of wine, and a separation came into being between 'taverns' which sold both ale and wine, and 'alehouses' which sold only ale. In addition to these there were the wayside inns or 'hostels' that provided accommodation for pilgrims and other travellers as well as food and drink.

Outside the towns, the principal hospitality for travellers during the medieval period was provided by monasteries. The great monastic houses, especially those situated along main roads, were the halting places for all who travelled. During the 14th and 15th centuries, a gradual change occurred as merchants began to travel and the influence of the church began to wane.

*A 14th-century inn*

In the Malvern area, afforested by William the Conqueror as a hunting preserve and known as the Chase, the monastery at Great Malvern, with its great guesten hall where visitors could be entertained, would have shone like a beacon for weary travellers probably making their way to Wales.

The first formal licensing law at the end of the 15th century empowered Justices of the Peace to obtain sureties for good behaviour from landlords and, if necessary, to close alehouses. Some 50 years later the Justices obtained the power to both license and suppress alehouses – hence 'licensed premises'. Legislation continued, and 1553 saw an Act of

*A picture of an evergreen bush displayed outside a building to indicate that it was an inn, from a 14th-century manuscript*

Parliament curtailing the number of 'taverns', with most towns restricted to one, and thereby limiting the sale of wine. But there were still plenty of alehouses in which to drink, with about 44 alehouses for every tavern in the latter part of the 16th century. This was equivalent to more than one drinking establishment for every 200 persons, a far higher ratio than exists today. This number was far lower in Malvern where only a sprinkling of alehouses existed such as the Unicorn, British Camp, and the Swan at Welland.

*The misericord at Malvern Priory showing a bunch of grapes*

The priory, which underwent a 60-year-long redevelopment in the 15th century, contains a remarkable series of misericords (mercy seats) in the choir stalls, carved in the 14th and 15th centuries and illustrating medieval life. The earliest, dating from between 1350 and 1380, and after being broken reset upside down, probably depicts a drunkard being beaten by his wife. There is also a small, prone figure drinking out of a blackjack, or tarred 'leather bottel.' Another one, carved in about 1450 to 1480, depicts a man holding up two wine-cups and representing January – after Janus, the Roman god with two heads. A second carving from the same period shows a man with a bunch of grapes that looks more like a pineapple, representing September.

During the Civil War soldiers from both sides had to be sheltered and fed and no doubt hostelries in the vicinity would have benefited from the supply of victuals and liquor – if it was paid for. After the Restoration, the old ale-stake (the pole projecting from the front of an inn) outside licensed premises was replaced by the painted inn sign.

With the arrival of William of Orange, a Dutchman, on the throne in 1689, the distillation of gin, a Dutch drink, was encouraged. Exempt from duty it was much cheaper than ale and soon was being sold from every small alehouse. Until well into the 18th century there was what Monkton in his *History of the English Public House* described as 'one of the biggest orgies of over-indulgence our island history has ever seen'. The result was that consumption of spirits increased from half a million gallons in 1684 to over nine million gallons in 1743. While beer and ale were foods and part of the nation's diet, gin was a poison, as Hogarth's famous prints of the horrors of 'Gin Lane' and the prosperous 'Beer Street' illustrated. The various 'Gin Acts' that followed, together with increased duties and a strengthening of the powers of the justices,

**16    99**

*Whereas by the Laws and Statutes of This Realm*

# NOTICE

IS HEREBY GIVEN TO ALL

## INN KEEPERS, ALEHOUSE KEEPERS, SUTLERS, VICTUALLERS

*and other Retailers of*

# ALE and BEER

AND EVERY OTHER PERSON or PERSONS KEEPING A PUBLIC HOUSE
IN ANY
CITY, TOWN CORPORATE, BOROUGH, MARKET TOWN, VILLAGE, HAMLET, PARISH,
PART or PLACE IN THE *Kingdom of England*

*That, as from the* **24th** *day of* **JUNE, 1700**

THEY SHALL BE REQUIRED TO RETAIL and SELL THEIR ALE & BEER

*by the* **FULL ALE QUART** OR **PINT**

*According to the Laid Standard*

IN VESSELS DULY MARKED *with* W.R *and* CROWN

*be they made of*

**WOOD, GLASS, HORN, LEATHER** OR **PEWTER** etc.

*Any Person Retailing Ale or Beer to a* **TRAVELLER** *or* **WAYFARER** *in Vessels not signed and marked as aforesaid will be liable to a* **PENALTY** *not exceeding*

# FORTY SHILLINGS

FOR EVERY SUCH OFFENCE

By Act of Parliament ~ at WESTMINSTER
In the Reign of Our Sovereign ~ **WILLIAM III** by the Grace of God, King,
Defender of the Faith &c

*In 1700 it became a legal requirement that vessels in which ale and beer were served should be accurate and marked*

rapidly changed this trend and by 1758 excise duty was paid on less than two million gallons of gin consumed per year. The 'gin era' was over.

However, the means of regulating public houses continued to attract government interest, and from 1729 licences had to be renewed annually at Brewster Sessions.

The end of the 17th century saw the beginning of the new coaching era and with it the golden age of the inn, providing food and accommodation for travellers. As the poet Shenstone put it in *Written at an Inn*, Whoe'er travelled life's dull round/Where'er his stages may have been/May sigh to think how oft he found/The warmest welcome – at an inn'. And Boswell, in his *Life of Samuel Johnson*, painted a cheerful picture: 'No, sir, there is nothing which has yet been contrived by man, by which so much happiness is produced, as by a good tavern or inn'. This was not always the case as John Byng, who covered thousands of English miles and sampled the fare of hundreds of English inns between 1781 and 1794, put it: 'The imposition in travelling is abominable; the innkeepers are insolent, the hostlers are sulky, the chambermaids are pert, and the waiters are impertinent; the meat is tough, the wine is foul, the beer is hard, the sheets are wet, the linnen is dirty, and the knives are never clean'd.' But coaching was good business, and in the Malvern area inns like the Foley Arms and the Crown in Great Malvern, and the White Lion and Star in Upton-upon-Severn carried on a flourishing post house business.

*A late 18th-century painting by Joseph Farrington showing the sign for the New Inn on Belle Vue Terrace, which possibly later became the Crown Hotel, against a backdrop of Malvern Priory*

While the introduction of turnpike roads meant better and speedier travel for coaches, it also saw toll gates and charges. Modes of travelling were changing and soon the 'iron horse' made vast strides all over the country, reaching Malvern in the 1850s.

It was during the 19th century that most of the legislation that affects the present-day consumption and sale of alcoholic drink was enacted. The Alehouse Act of 1828 meant that the licensee no longer had to find sureties for his behaviour. However, he was bound to use the legal, stamped measures, not to adulterate his drinks, and not to permit drunkenness on his premises.

The Beerhouse Acts of 1830, 1834 and 1840 followed. The first allowed premises to open for the sale of beer, but not spirits, on payment of a simple excise licence; the second differentiated between 'on' and 'off' licences and made 'on' more difficult to obtain; whilst the third ensured that licences were issued only to the occupier of the premises. The first Act abolished all duty on beer and enabled any householder to sell beer on the purchase of a two-guinea licence from the Excise. As a consequence, a number of illegal drinking places became legal, and many craftsmen also sold beer as part of their business, naming their beerhouse after their craft – with resulting names such as the Three Horseshoes, the Mason's Arms and the Butcher's Arms. As a result, the number of licensed premises increased from about 50,000 in 1828 to 82,500 three years later. 1828 was the last year that alehouse keepers had to provide recognizances, a legal bond by which the innkeeper had to maintain an orderly house or forfeit the deposit that accompanied the bond. At the beginning of the 20th century public houses were, in general, still allowed to open for some 20 hours each day.

The first Beer Act was not to everyone's liking. Worcestershire Court of Quarter Sessions resolved that the Act ought to be amended, having, they opined, produced the worst consequences upon the morals of the county. A committee was appointed to draw up a petition to both Houses of Parliament and a memo to the Secretary of State. Ten Malvern landlords were fined either £2 or £5 for offences against the Beer Act.

Just before the Beer Act, tokens, usually to the value of three old pennies, were introduced and were immediately popular in Malvern, with a number of inns offering them to customers. Although there were no fixed rules about how they should be used, they were normally exchanged for a drink for advertising purposes, as games' prizes and as 'wet rent' (for the hire of a room, for instance). In Victorian times the popular games were skittles and bowls, which required alleys and greens to be built and maintained; bagatelle, which needed special equipment; and dominoes, cribbage and other card games. 'The laws against gaming were strict and strictly enforced,' said John Whitmore in his book *Worcestershire Inn Tokens*, 'and any publican who allowed even the most modest amounts of money to change hands at any of these pastimes would be in danger of losing his licence'.

It is not often realised that the regulations concerning licensed houses, alcohol and children are mainly of 20th-century origin. Although the 1872 Act made it an offence to sell spirits to those using licensed premises under the age of 16, it was not until the Children's Act of 1908 that children under the age of 14 were prohibited in licensed premises. It was only in 1923 that it became, in general, an offence to serve alcoholic drinks to those under 18.

Limited opening hours were instigated during the First World War and the situation was regularized by the Licensing Act of 1921 which defined 'permitted hours' as being eight hours between 11am and 10pm except for Sunday, when opening was limited to five hours. The Malvern Licensing Sessions of 1919 reported that for a population of 19,338 there were the following numbers of people licensed to sell intoxicating drink, namely 36 full licences (four for just six days a week), 22 on-beerhouses (two for just six days), eight off-beerhouses, one wine licence, four beer, wine & spirits off-licences, and three wine and spirits off-licences. The average number of persons to each licence was just slightly over 250.

The chairman of the Malvern Licensing Sessions of 1919, Dr. H.E. Dixey, said that at all licensing meetings a good deal was spoken about the decrease in drunkenness, and he hoped this would continue when the beer became a little stronger than it was then. Dr. Dixey later amended his comments by saying that from time there were cases of excessive drinking, especially among women coming to Malvern.

After the Second World War there were several minor Acts, culminating in the 1961 Licensing Act which encouraged the proliferation of off-licences and provided for 'restaurant' licences. It also gave the customers' grace – the ten minutes of 'drinking-up time'. A late 20th-century Act restored the situation to more or less what it was at the beginning of the century, by allowing inns to stay open throughout most of the day if they so wish, most commonly any times between 11am and 11pm.

The *Malvern Gazette*, of 4 February 1949, ran an editorial comment under the headline 'A Sober Town':

> Malvern residents can take a bouquet for sobriety. In spite of the town's rising population – now estimated at 24,000 – there are fewer cases of drunkenness than ever, and last year there were only two convictions, three less than in the previous 12 months. No wonder Mr. R.O. Allen, chairman of the licensing justices, this week commented that the position was very satisfactory, while we have reason to believe that Supt. W. Adams considers us all a good, sober lot ...
>
> Cynics and Government critics might suggest that the decline in drunkenness is only to be expected from weak and expensive beer, but certainly those who feared the invasion of the town by youth and by the soldiers can be reassured. Perhaps drinking is no longer an end in itself it seemed among a certain section of the community, but merely a pleasant, and now unabused, adjunct to the pleasures of conversation and company.

By the late 1980s the big six national brewers – Allied, Bass, Courage, GrandMet, Scottish & Newcastle and Whitbread – owned more than 30,000 pubs, over half the pubs in Britain. The regional breweries owned 11,500. Following an investigation by the Monopolies Commission, the government decided to break this stranglehold. The 1990 Beer Orders set a ceiling of 2,000 pubs and told all brewers who owned more than that number to sell half of the surplus. This had the result of wiping out the big six with the exception of Scottish & Newcastle. Most of the pubs were gobbled up by pub chains (pubcos) and, led by Enterprise Inns and Punch Taverns, in a few years they owned 30,000 pubs.

New licensing laws came into effect in 2005, enabling pub owners to choose longer or more flexible opening hours if approved by the licensing authorities which in theory meant they could stay open all day. However, this never really materialised and most pubs stick to 11am to 11pm opening hours. A ban on smoking in pubs and bars was introduced in 2007 and was immediately accepted by the general public.

# CHAPTER TWO

# Brewing & Breweries

'Ale's the true liquor of life'. (From a 17th-century ballad)

Ale, or beer, has been the staple drink in Britain since the introduction of grain. It was central to life, on an equal footing to bread, if not higher. The Romans found the Britons drinking fermented liquor made from barley and wheat. The Saxons and Danes who followed were great beer drinkers and brought more sophistication to the art of brewing. The Normans built castles and abbeys all over the country and every monastery had a brewery for the refreshment of monk and traveller. Brewing, like baking, was an essential part of housekeeping and ale was brewed in farmhouse, inn and tavern.

Those engaged in brewing then were female, and ale-wives or brewsters, as they were known, were not held in very high esteem. And God help the brewster who brewed bad ale or adulterated it. This heinous crime was punished by the ducking stool or even worse. An ale-conner, or ale-taster, tested the quality and strength of beer and, or so the story goes, they did this by sitting in a puddle of it. Beer was poured onto a wooden bench and the conner, clad in leather britches, sat in it. Depending on how sticky it was felt to be when he stood up, he was able to assess its alcoholic strength and impose the appropriate duty. Later, when the profits to be made from brewing began to increase, men took over the role of brewster.

In the late Middle Ages ale was the only safe liquid to drink, and people drank it all day. For breakfast it was 'small beer', a weaker beer made from a second boiling of the barley mash, and at other times, strong ale. There was no alternative to ale (or its companion, beer) until tea was introduced in the country as a whole at the end of the 18th century.

For perhaps 1,000 years ale had been the basic drink but a fundamental change occurred with the introduction of hops. The hop, *Humulus lupulus,* belongs to the *Cannabinacene* family of plants and was used by the Romans and throughout the medieval period as a delicacy (young hop shoots being prepared like asparagus) or for medicinal purposes. Its value for preserving and flavouring beverages was known by the 12th century; its use in beer is probably of German origin. An anonymous rhyme dated 1520 observes 'Hops and turkeys, carp and beer, Came into England all in one year'. However, most authorities favour the year 1400 for the commencement of the use of hops to make English beer, for a consignment of hops was received in this year from Holland. There were many people who objected, with a variety of reasons. Coming from the Low Countries it was considered by many to be a Protestant plant. Thus Andrew Boords, a physician, in his *Dyetary* of 1542 wrote: 'Beer is the natural drink for the Dutchman and recently it is much used in England to the detriment of the Englishman ... it killeth those who are troubled with collic and the stone ... it makes a man fat as shown by the Dutchman's faces and bellies.'

*A 14th-century brewhouse*

Henry VI is said to have prohibited brewers from using hops, and many towns in England tried to prevent the brewing of beer by forbidding the use of hops – including Shrewsbury, where the use of the 'wicked and pernicious weed' was banned in 1519. Hops, it was said, not only spoilt the taste of the

*A brewhouse of 1756*

drink, but endangered the lives of the people. However, the improvement made in the liquor by the new constituent came at last to be generally recognised, and several hop gardens had been set up in Kent by the mid-16th century. The hop not only gave the new drink a more bitter flavour, it was also of considerable importance for its preservative properties, enabling the beverage to be kept much longer than ale before 'going off'. For well over 100 years brewers produced both ale and beer, but the popularity of the former gradually declined and beer eventually became the accepted drink, although cider was still popular.

Burton upon Trent, Staffordshire, was home to some of the country's finest brewers such as Ind Coope and Allsop; its brewing tradition, aided by the calcium sulphate content of the local water, dated back to brewing by the Benedictine monks of Burton Abbey, founded in 1002. By the mid 18th century, the Burton breweries were producing prime quality beers which were lighter and more bitter and began eroding the popularity of the London porter beers.

The Protestant Reformation and early Nonconformism had very little influence on the old links that had been forged between beer and religion. The early peripatetic preachers were given a 'beer allowance' and the 'beer of the cause' was always drunk at monthly meetings. The earliest prayer meetings and services in some areas were held in pubs.

Until the beginning of the 19th century nearly all the landlords made their own ale in small brewhouses behind their inns. However, many of the small inns and beer-houses that opened during the first half of the 19th century had no brewing facilities and were dependent on other inns or on the growing number of breweries for their supply. This change accelerated as breweries bought public houses whenever they came onto the market, a process that resulted in a substantial decrease in the number of 'free-houses' and independent breweries.

Adulteration of beer was apparently a fairly common practice, more often perpetrated by the publicans than by the brewers, and quite often making a difference of 50% in the alcohol content. Dr. Normandy, an analysing chemist, told the Malvern Licensing Committee, as reported in the *Malvern Advertiser* of 28 July 1855, that the only substances that could be detected as adulteration were common salt, used to increase thirst, and sulphate of iron, which created vomiting and colic – like any other poison. He went on to explain that *cocculus indicus* (a south-east Asian climbing plant the fruit of which is both a stimulant and a poison), foots sugar (a dark brown sugar syrup), sulphate of ammonia and extract of gentian were constantly sold by druggists for the purpose of adulteration:

> Some go by the name of 'beer druggists' but they should be called 'beer brigands'. *Cocculus indicus* contains two and a half per cent of poison.

It produces the same effects as the alcohol which ought to be found in the beer, causing intoxication. It is added to supply the strength of the beer, which is reduced by the quantity of water added; and, for the same reason 'foots sugar' is used, because the beer has been rendered less sweet; the sulphate of ammonia being added to restore the colour lost by the adulterations. Then, instead of hops, the extract of gentian is used because the adulterated beer would not be so bitter as it should be.

Malvern has had a long tradition of brewing, with as many as a dozen breweries operating in the area at different times during the 19th century. All of these have since closed, others sprouted up and fell by the wayside, but today there are two relative newcomers which are trading successfully.

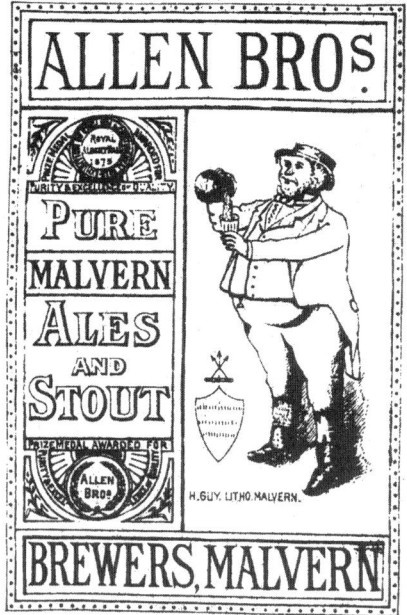

Two of the main brewers were Allen Bros Brompton Brewery, which brewed beer in Newtown Road, Malvern Link Top and Howsell Road, and the Royal Well Brewery in the West Malvern Road. The former started off as the Brompton Steam Brewery with offices at 5 Holyrood Terrace, Great Malvern run by James Allen, Senior, and Son, but by 1868 it had moved to Link Top and was run by the Allen Brothers. At that time the Royal Well Brewery was a rival enterprise, but the two firms later amalgamated, and when the Newtown brewery closed down, the brewing equipment was moved to West Malvern.

Brompton Steam Brewery tokens were discovered when parts of the old buildings of the Royal Well Brewery were demolished in 1986. These tokens were similar to inn tokens which could be exchanged for a drink, but probably functioned in a different way. John Whitmore wrote in *Worcestershire Inn Tokens*, 'The range of four values, from penny to sixpence, suggests something akin to a replacement coinage, but the manner in which they functioned can only be a matter of speculation. On the

*Brompton Steam Brewery tokens (Brian Iles)*

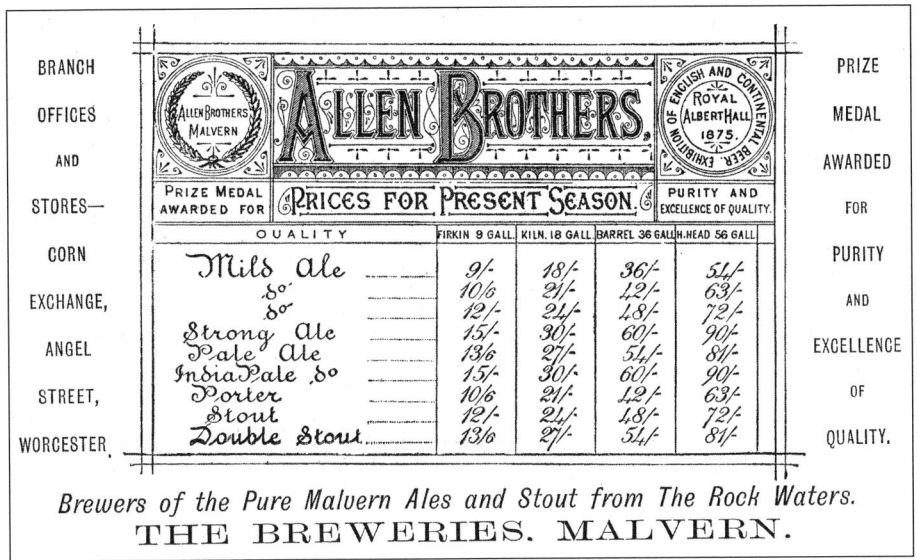

*An Allen Brothers price list for 1879 showing that a firkin of mild ale cost 9s (the equivalent of 1s a gallon), strong ale 15s, Pale Ale 13s 6d, India Pale Ale 15s, Porter 10s 6d, stout 12s and double stout 13s 6d. (Brian Iles)*

obverse of the coins was "Brompton Steam Brewery, Malvern", while on the reverse were 1D, 2D, 3D & 6D, all surrounded by a laurel wreath.'

By the 1870s Allen Bros was a well established brewery on land behind the Retired Soldier public house in Newtown Road, Malvern Link Top. The white house which still stands next to the Retired Soldier was the residence of the manager of the brewery. The way at the side of the house is terminated by gates, which were the entrance to the brewery grounds. A lithographed engraving, from a directory of 1879, indicates that this was an extensive enterprise, although a certain artistic licence must be allowed for. On the north side were the stores for pop and non-alcoholic drinks. Prizes were won by Allen Bros, including a medal for Purity and Excellence of Quality at an exhibition at the Albert Hall, London in 1875. The purity of the Rock Water used was stressed in the firm's advertising.

According to Elsie Godsell in her book *Reflection on Colwall*, the Brewery in West Malvern Road was renamed the Royal Well Brewery in about 1850 after the Princess Royal asked for a drink of water at a thatched cottage nearby.

In 1891 the brewery was owned by Mr. J.H. Tyler, of Worcester, with 'the exclusive right of brewing from the Royal Well water, which is particularly noted even among Malvern waters, and the excellence of the ales and stouts brewed, prove both its suitability for the purpose and the superior methods employed in the process'.

One satisfied customer from near Bristol wrote: 'The cask of beer which you sent me has proved quite a boon ... I take about 1 pint to 1 quart per evening. My doctor wishes me to stick to it, and I think it is the best cure I can have for my nerves and general debility.'

The Royal Spa Hall, a grand but ill-fated enterprise which only ran for a few years before closing, was built in 1883 next to the brewery. It had a large hall with a domed roof, capable of seating 2,600 people, an art gallery and extensive pleasure grounds, complete with a grotto, fountains and croquet lawns. Nicknamed Ryland's folly after the builder Mr. W.H. Ryland, the hall saw the last public performance of Jenny Lind, the 'Swedish nightingale'. However, after the Malvern Assembly Rooms opened in 1885, the Well Spa became something of a 'white elephant', and it closed down in 1895. The Hall was used as a storage space by the brewery, which had several pubs in the area, until the 1930s when the brewery went into liquidation. The hall became derelict and subject to vandalism, and was demolished in 1939, with a house built on part of the site.

*The Royal Well Brewery (Brian Iles)*

*An advert for Allen Brothers' products of 1889, stating that they had been tested and found clear of lead and other potential 'pollution'*

The *Malvern Advertiser* of 8 December 1901 reported that the Royal Well Brewery had been acquired by Messrs. R.W. Blackwood-Wileman and Francis J. Blackwood from Messrs. Homfray Ltd., who said that

> ... every effort will be made to continue to meet the requirements of customers to the very fullest extent, and the high standing of the new firm is a guarantee that everything that emanates from the establishment will be of the very best.
>
> We observe that the services of Mr. H.G. Rashleigh have been secured as brewer. He is a gentleman well known in the district and held a similar position for several years at the Brewery under a former proprietor, Mr. J. Tyler, and gave the highest satisfaction. In addition to ales and stouts (which we may add are brewed from the finest malts and hops with the famous Royal Well water, noted for its purity), the wine and spirit business will also be continued.

Elsie Godsell also noted in her book that Mr. Blackwood-Wileman was a friend of Mr. Cave-Brown-Cave, who helped put Colwall on the map. 'The two men were returning from the hunting field one day along the Ledbury Road, when they bet £5 on who would first get to Barton Court by jumping all the hedges in a straight line,' she wrote. 'Unfortunately Blackwood-Wileman fell

**Blackwood-Wileman**
**and Blackwood,**

Royal Well Brewery, Malvern.

**Brewers of Fine Ales & Stouts**

FROM PURE MALT AND HOPS.

☞ Exclusive right to Brew from world-famed Royal Well.

|  |  | Per Gall. | Kild. 18 Galls. | Firk. 9 Galls. |
|---|---|---|---|---|
| X | MILD ALE | 10d. | 15/- | 7/6 |
| PA | BITTER ALE | 1/- | 18/- | 9/- |
| PAS | BITTER ALE (Stock) | 1/2 | 21/- | 10/6 |
| PAK | BURTON BITTER | 1/4 | 24/- | 12/- |
| IPA | INDIA PALE ALE | 1/6 | 27/- | 13/6 |
| XXX | MILD STOCK ALE | 1/4 | 24/- | 12/- |
| *IDS | INVALID DOUBLE STOUT | 1/8 | 27/- | 13/6 |

* Brewed expressly for Invalids, in Pins of 4½ Galls., **7/6**.

**BOTTLERS OF BASS AND STOUT.**

**Wine and Spirit Merchants,**

WHISKY BONDERS & BLENDERS,
BONDERS OF CHAMPAGNES AND OLD BRANDIES.

Extract from Report of Rural District Council Meeting, Ledbury,
*Tuesday, March 26th, 1901:*

"The Sanitary Inspector said he had had a Sample of Beer analysed from the **Royal Well Brewery**, Malvern; and the Analyst reported he had made a careful analysis, and found it **Free from Arsenic**, and not contaminated with Lead or Poisonous Metals. **He had also tested it for any probable injurious constituents, but could find no trace of any present.**

Blackwood-Wileman and Blackwood,
ROYAL WELL BREWERY, MALVERN.

*An advert for the Royal Well Brewery of 1901, stating that their products are 'free of arsenic'*

at the first jump and broke his neck – and lost the bet! There is a memorial stone in the field.'

An outbreak of poisoning occurred in the Manchester area in 1901, with the deaths of two women from supposed arsenic poisoning due to drinking beer. Another 20 cases were reported with the likelihood that none would recover, which sent alarm bells ringing all over the country. The *Malvern Advertiser* of 6 January 1901 stated: 'The poisoning has not been traced to any one brewery, and the measures taken by the local brewers will ensure no more poisoned beer being made.' In the event, arsenic was discovered in the sulphuric acid used in producing sugar supplied to brewers.

As a result of the scare, an advert was run which stated: 'Absolutely Pure Ales – Analyst's report on Allen Brothers Ales, The Brewers, Malvern'. It contained the information that samples of beers and brewing materials had been analysed by Frank Thatcher at The Laboratory, West Drayton, London, who had found them 'entirely free from arsenic or any other deleterious matter injurious to health'. A similar advert proclaimed that Cecil Duncan, the County Analyst, had examined Lewis, Clarke and Co's Ales (of Worcester) and found them 'absolutely pure'.

The 'Beer Scare' was taken up by Malvern Urban District Council, which reported that a communication was received from the Local Government Board relative to the illness in different parts of the country alleged to be caused by arsenic in beer, and calling attention to the powers which local governing bodies possessed under the Foods and Drugs Act for testing beers on sale. The *Malvern Advertiser* of 6 January 1901 reported that Dr. H.E. Dixey (chairman of the Malvern Licensing Sessions) said the county council had already taken this matter in hand, and had tested over a hundred samples.

In 1971 the site of the former Royal Wells Brewery had become a builders merchants, W.F. Bailey. Then, in April 1989, the *Malvern Gazette* carried an advert announcing the sale of the brewery, mineral water site and buildings for development, and the buildings have since been converted into apartments.

Other breweries in the 19th century included the Royal Malvern Well Brewery, then owned by A. Bennett & Co, who advertised in the *Malvern Advertiser* of 6 January 1883, begging 'respectfully to invite attention to their Malvern Imperial Pale Bitter Ale made with especial reference to meet the increasing demand for a light tonic beverage, which they particularly recommend for family use; price 1s per gallon ... This ale is sparkling and contains an unusual amount of nutritive element'. Malvern Imperial cost 1s a gallon, while their Crown beer ranged from 1s to 1s 4d, and it was sold in casks holding between 9 and 54 gallons. The brewery, also known at one time as Hilliar & Bennett, was located in Spring Lane, Malvern Link.

In 1850, Mr. J.W. Harrop founded the Link Family Brewery (also known simply as the Link Brewery), behind the Vaults in Worcester Road, offering 'genuine home-brewed ale, beer and stout', and, according to adverts which appeared in the *Malvern Advertiser* from 1855 to 1860, 'families [were] supplied at the shortest notice'.

At a later date the Link Brewery was taken over by Jones & Davis who renamed it The Malvern Hill Brewery and produced 'nourishing sparkling Malvern ales and stout in cask and bottle', as well as ginger beer. They also

*The Royal Malvern Well Brewery after it had been sold in 1971 and become the builders merchant, W.F. Bailey (Malvern Museum)*

> # The ROYAL MALVERN WELL BREWERY,
> ## MALVERN.
>
> ## A. BENNETT AND Co.
>
> BEG respectfully to invite attention to their MALVERN IMPERIAL
>
> ## PALE BITTER ALE,
>
> made with especial reference to meet the increasing demand for a light tonic Beverage, which they can particularly recommend for Family use: price 1s. per gallon.
>
> In its manufacture only the best Malt and Worcester Hops are used in combination with what is now recognised as the *purest* known water, from the *Celebrated* ROYAL MALVERN WELL, they having secured the *sole* and *exclusive right*, and which from careful analysis has been found to be entirely free from all trace of organic matter.
>
> It has for a considerable time past been the aim of MESSRS. BENNETT & CO. to produce a light Table beverage that should fulfil the conditions which are most generally sought after in the best manufactures; and they have, after a series of carefully-conducted experiments, attained these results, which they invite the public to test. This Ale is sparkling and contains an unusual amount of nutritive element.
>
> It may be not out of place to offer a suggestion or two for preserving to Ale its bright and sparkling properties. It should be kept in a place of moderate temperature—neither hot nor cold; it should stand at least a week before using; and should not be *vented* unless absolutely necessary. When not convenient to have a large supply at a time, a good plan is to give an order as soon as the last cask is tapped, and not wait until quite out so as to be obliged to use the fresh cask as soon as delivered.
>
> A. BENNETT & CO. deliver their productions free to any Railway Station in England and Wales.
>
> PRICE LIST.
>
> |  | s. d. |  |  | s. d. |  |
> |---|---|---|---|---|---|
> | Malvern Imperial | 1 0 | per gal. Bitter. | 4—CROWN | - 1 2 | per gal. Bitter. |
> | 1—CROWN - | - 1 0 | ,, | 5—CROWN | - 1 4 | ,, |
> | 2—CROWN - | - 1 2 | ,, | Porter - | - 1 2 | ,, |
> | 3—CROWN - | - 1 4 | ,, | Invalid Stout - | - 1 6 | ,, |
>
> Sold in 9, 18, 36, and 54-Gallon Casks.

*An advert for The Royal Malvern Well Brewery*

ran a grocery and general provisions shop in Church Street, Great Malvern. They sold out to Lewis Clarke's of Worcester who in turn were taken over by Marston's in 1937.

In 1856 Henry Orgee began business as a wholesale brewer on premises adjoining the Belvoir Hotel, North Malvern. In an advert in the *Malvern Advertiser* of 25 October 1856, Mr. Orgee 'respectfully solicits the Patronage of the Inhabitants of Malvern and Neighbourhood, and to call their attention to the fact that the Water used in his brewery is of the purest kind, being supplied from the Tank. The Ale and Beer is of the most genuine quality, and cannot fail to ensure for him that extensive custom which it will always be his study to deserve.'

Mr. James Broad, of the North Malvern Brewery, advertised in the *Malvern Advertiser* of 23 June, 1860 'Genuine Home-Brewed Ales,' also cider and porter. And in the same edition of the paper it was reported that Mr. Broad was granted an application by Malvern Petty Sessions for a licence for a house he had recently completed at North Malvern. He had formerly held a licence for a house opposite to his present brewery.

Other breweries included Berkeley's Brewery, Royal Well; Homphreys Brewery at the Express Inn, Malvern Link; the Old Brewery in Church Street, Great Malvern; William Essington Webb in Malvern Link; and William Ivey at Hanley Swan.

During the 20th century, breweries throughout the country closed at an alarming rate. In 1900 there were some 6,390, a number which steadily fell until 70 years later there were fewer than 200 in the country. Pasteurised sterile beer, known as keg, and lager were taking over, and together soon accounted for the majority of beer sales. Malvern followed the national trend and the old breweries either closed or were taken over, so that by the end of the 1970s there were none left. However in the 1980s two micro breweries opened up nearby, one in Leigh Sinton and one in Upton-upon-Severn. Michael Fass opened the Malvern Chase Brewery at Sherridge, Leigh Sinton in 1981, and two years later was selling his Chase Ale to 27 freehouses within a 25 mile radius and celebrated the sale of 250,000 pints of his beer. In 1983 the Chase Brewery found itself challenged by Bailey's Brewing Company, of the Old Pig House, Crowcroft, started up by Tim Bailey, an independent brewing consultant who had actually helped start the Chase Brewery. Chase's new owner Peter Norbury, a farmer, claimed two local ales would flood the market and feared both would fail.

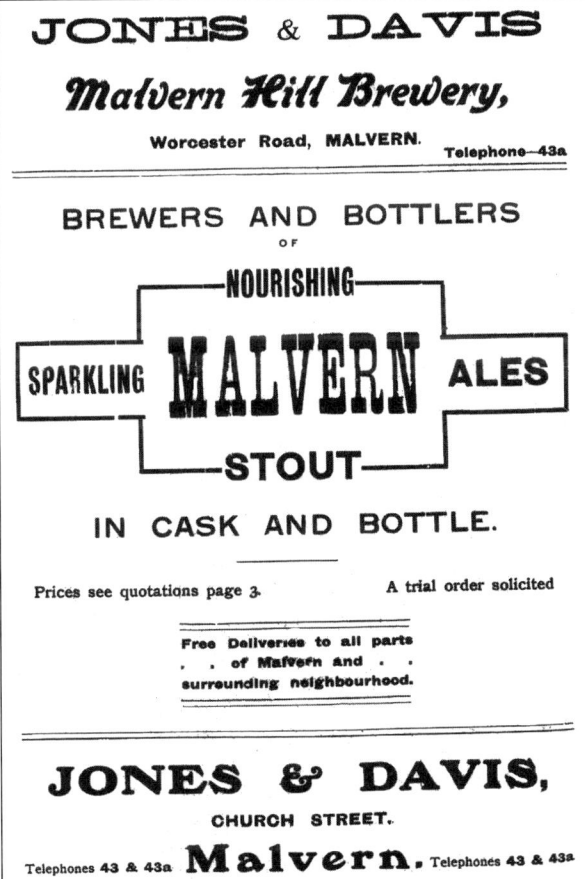

At the Somers Arms, Leigh Sinton's only freehouse, Bailey's Best Bitter soon outsold its local rival, but landlord Dave Henshaw decided to stock both and get rid of his national brews. Regulars hoped the row between the two brewers would be ended with a drink called Diplomat, half a pint of each brew. However Tim Bailey took umbrage at a Chase beer mat claiming it was the only working brewery in Worcestershire in the last 50 years. He called in the Trading Standards office and that so annoyed Chase boss Peter Norbury that he took his beer away. The Chase Brewery closed in 1984 and Bailey's the following year.

Meanwhile another brewery was opening in Upton – the Jolly Roger at the back of the Olde Anchor Inn. Run by the landlord's son Paul Soden, helped by his brother Martin, four barrels were brewed a week of three different strengths and sold mainly in the pub itself. After operating for four years the brewery moved in 1987 to Worcester, where it continued trading until 1996. The Upton brewery became the Old Anchor Brewery, now also defunct.

However, two new breweries set up business in 1998 – the Malvern Hills Brewery, or MHB, housed in an old quarryman's gunpowder store at West Malvern Road, and St. George's Brewery in a former bakery in Callow End – and both are still very much in business. MHB's brewer and owner, Julian Hawthornthwaite, initially brewed beer as a hobby, but after winning several awards he decided in 2005 to quit his job in the heating systems trade and concentrate on making and selling his beers. In 2011 MHB celebrated its 1,000th brew by releasing a special beer called Cyneweard, after the last Anglo-Saxon sheriff of Worcestershire. The beers often take their names from local luminaries and events.

A family called Foden originally started the St. George's Brewery at premises which used to be Brickell's bakery in Bush Lane, with the brewing equipment coming from the Anchor in Upton-upon-Severn. They ran the business until 2001 when David Butcher and Brian McCluskie bought it. David stayed for only a year, but Brian kept it going until 2006 when the brewery was purchased by Duncan Ironmonger, who owned the Nag's Head and the Chase and leased the Swan at Newland from the Madresfield Estate. He therefore had a ready-made outlet for the St. George's range of beers, including three main regulars – Friar Tuck, Charger and Dragon's Blood. Andrew Sankey has been the brewer for the last nine years.

With the virtual demise of the national brewing industry, following a series of mergers and takeovers, has come a significant increase in the number of independent breweries, over 800 and still counting, with the future for real ale looking very buoyant.

# CHAPTER THREE

# Great Malvern

When the Benedictine Priory of Great Malvern was built in the 11th century on the lower slopes of the Worcestershire Beacon, Malvern itself was nothing more than a wilderness of woods and bracken. Even by the 16th century, it was only a group of cottages at the junction of the main Worcester to Ledbury road and the lane from the valley, the 'Spital Way', now called Church Street. Following Henry VIII's dissolution of monasteries, local people bought the Priory for £20 in 1541 to save it from destruction, and since then it has been Great Malvern's parish church. The population at that time was 105 families.

While the quality of the local well water had long been appreciated by the villagers, it was not until Dr. John Wall, born at nearby Powick, and other writers started to praise the waters that what had been the village of Malvern started to expand in the first half of the 19th century. After analysing the water of Holy Well, St. Ann's Well and Chalybeate Spring, Dr. Wall concluded that 'the efficacy of this water seems chiefly to arise from its great purity, with very little mineral matter.' This led to one humorist remarking 'The Malvern water, says Dr. John Wall, is famed for containing just nothing at all.'

The fortunes of Great Malvern took a dramatic turn for the better with the arrival of two more doctors, both trained in the new wonder treatment of hydropathy. First to arrive in 1842 was Dr. James Wilson, who studied under Vincenz Priessnitz in Grafenberg in Silesia, one of the leaders of hydropathic cures. Wilson renamed the Crown Hotel Grafenberg House as the first centre of the hydropathic spa. He then moved to the newly built Hydropathic Establishment, later to become the County Hotel. Dr. James Gully soon followed his friend and set himself up in what became the Tudor Hotel, and Great Malvern became known as the English metropolis of hydropathy.

The water cure attracted the famous and the rich including Gladstone, Macaulay, Dickens, Carlyle, Tennyson, Darwin, Wilberforce and Florence Nightingale. 'After four weeks of anxiety and exertion, I was told my life was not worth 24 hours purchase – and I knew it too,' wrote Miss Nightingale in 1850. 'I owe three years of (not useless) life to the water cure at Malvern.'

Further stimulus was provided by the opening of the railway line from Worcester to Malvern in 1860. This meant that one could travel from London to Malvern in six hours as against the best part of two days that it previously took travelling by coach. This in turn led to more building work, including the building of the Imperial Hotel (now Malvern St. James) adjacent to Great Malvern station, and the Malvern Link Hotel (demolished, with blocks of flats since built on the site) at that station. A further 60 hotels were also constructed. Malvern College opened as a private school in 1865 and more followed.

For the best part of 200 years from about 1740, the manor of Malvern was held by the Foley family, who had bought it from the Bromleys. The Foleys were noted iron manufacturers and acquired their wealth during the Industrial Revolution. They were also on good terms with Queen Victoria. The most redoubtable family member was Lady Emily, who survived her husband's death in 1846 by over half a century. She spent the summer in Malvern, staying at the Foley Hotel, from where she managed her estate with a 'typically Victorian benevolent despotism'. The Malvern Hills Conservators have been lords of the manor since 1884.

*Lady Emily Foley*

With the increase in population and visitors, the Assembly Rooms were built in 1885 and some of the leading lights of the day subsequently appeared on stage there, including Clara Butt, Albert Chevalier, Jenny Lind, Marie Lloyd and Anna Pavlova. It was later converted into the Malvern Winter Gardens and Festival Theatre and opened in 1929 for the start of the first Malvern Festival with homage paid to George Bernard Shaw. Those who performed at the Festival were among the best known actors of the times.

Meanwhile Malvern's popularity as a spa town gradually waned. Dr. Gully became involved in the 1870s in an international scandal and then in the early 1900s typhoid broke out in the old Hydropathic Establishment building then run by Dr. Ferguson and renamed the County Hydro. Quarrying, from the mid-19th century onwards, had already marred the hills, and Malvern was in danger of becoming a quarry town with all the associated noise and dirt of daily blasting of tons of stone. Fortunately, this never happened, although quarrying rumbled

*The Hydropathic Establishment in about 1878; it included baths and a covered promenade, and later became the County Hotel (Brian Iles)*

on until 1977. During the Second World War much of the town was sealed off as British and, later, American scientists flooded into the town to continue their work on radar in relative safety from German bombers.

Today, Great Malvern is not just a town for the retired and genteel. It has a thriving town centre with a revitalised theatre and industries such as QinetiQ, which replaced the radar establishments, and now carries out non-military research, and the Morgan Motor Company, the last wholly British owned carmaker in the country. And providing inspiration, solace and healthy exercise are the Malvern Hills, attracting walkers like bees to a honey-pot.

Travelling along the Worcester Road towards Great Malvern one comes across, on the left hand side, the 200 year-old **Foley Arms Hotel**, with an impressive frontage with cast-iron verandahs and a royal Coat of Arms above revolving doors. The hotel was built by local entrepreneur Joseph Downs on an orchard owned by the Lord of the Manor, Lord Foley, in anticipation of an increase in visitors to Malvern as it developed as a spa town. Built to a plan drawn up by architect Samuel Deykes on traditional Georgian lines, the new **Downs' Hotel** (as it was then called) opened its doors for business in 1810. Opposite was the gabled half-timbered smithy of Thomas Martin.

Business was so brisk that Downs added a new wing in 1812 and a second one in 1817. Good post horses with closed and open carriages and pony traps were kept, while stabling at the rear was provided for horses and livery. Families boarded in private apartments for £2 2s a week, with daily tea and sugar costing

7s, while a servant's board was £1 2s including tea. The name was changed to the Foley Arms in the 1820s, when it was described in a local guide as 'this very spacious hotel, which abounds with every comfort, as well as every elegance'.

*An advertisement for Downs' Hotel (Malvern Museum)*

*An engraving of the renamed Foley Arms Hotel*

It was also for a while called the **Royal Kent and Coburg Arms**, a reference to the time when the Duchess of Kent and her young daughter Princess, later Queen, Victoria stayed in Malvern in 1831. They did not stay at the Foley Arms, but at Holly Mount, a private house opposite. In 1833, Conservative statesman Sir Robert Peel, later to become Prime Minister, stayed at the hotel.

*The Foley Arms when under the management of the Archer family*

Later the hotel was acquired by the Archer family, whose portfolio of businesses included the Mount Pleasant Hotel, the Abbey Hotel and a wine shop adjacent to the Foley Arms.

In 1849 Charles Darwin and family stayed at **Archer's Royal Kent and Foley Arms Hotel**, as it was then called, in order that he could try Dr. Gully's water treatment for his chronic ill-health. He later rented a villa for his wife, Emma, and family in Worcester Road, and took his 10 year-old daughter, Annie, for treatment with Dr. Gully. Unfortunately, Annie died, probably from tuberculosis, and was buried in the Priory churchyard, with the inscription 'A dear and good child', on her memorial.

Princess May of Teck, who was Queen Consort as wife of George V, visited Malvern in 1891 with her parents the Duke and Duchess of Teck, and members of the German court, and enjoyed her six week stay at the Foley Arms so much that she kindly bequeathed the Teck family coat of arms to the hotel, still

*An advertisement for the Archers' wine shop which was next to the Foley Arms*

*The garden front of 'Archer's Royal Kent & Foley Hotel'*

proudly displayed above the front entrance. Teck then lay in the kingdom of Württemberg. On one side of the coat of arms is a lion, on the other a unicorn, and below is the motto *Treu und Fest* (Faithful and Firm).

Having inherited the Malvern estate when her husband died in 1846, Lady Emily Foley spent the summer in Malvern, invariably staying at the Foley Hotel, which she owned. Her arrival was a sight to behold, driving up in a bright yellow landau drawn by white horses and attended by servants in the family livery of scarlet coats and white breeches and stockings. At the hotel she was greeted with great deference by the vicar, churchwardens and chairman of the town commissioners, while servants had arrived earlier to ensure her ladyship's every comfort. Throughout the morning the Priory bells were rung. Lady Foley continued her 'benevolent despotism' until the new century, dying at 2.40am on New Year's Day 1900 at the age of 95.

On the death of the proprietor, John Archer, his son Edward took over the running of the hotel together with the wine business, originally sited in the old coach office and later in a block of buildings built by Edward on the south side of the hotel. In 1900 they offered champagne at 3s a bottle and Chelona wine, a tonic of port and turtle, at 3s 6d a bottle. An advert in the *Morning Advertiser* in 1900 proclaimed that the Foley Arms was patronised by the Royal Family, served 'Table d'Hote at Separate Tables and had Perfect Sanitary Arrangements'.

*The garden front of the Foley Arms as engraved in March 1874,*
*showing that extensive alterations and additions have been made*
*(Malvern Museum)*

Around the time of the First World War, Malvern had at least two sewer-gas lamps, supplied directly by sewer gas (methane), which never went out. One of these lamps was situated outside the Foley Arms, which then had a yew hedge in front of it. During the Second World War, when American servicemen were based at various army hospitals in the Malvern area, they had their own club in town opposite the hotel, called the Donut Dugout.

In 1949 the Foley Arms was acquired by Mr. Harry Lowis, who previously owned the White Hart at Uttoxeter. At that time, a stay of five days or more was priced at from 27s 6d with B & B from 20s. In the 1950s, when Mrs. Esca Reeves was the managing director, the rates were £2 to £2 10s for days or longer (inclusive), with B & B from 25s 6d to 27s 6d. Luncheon cost 7s 6d, tea 3s and dinner 10s 6d.

In the early 1970s the Foley Arms was managed by Robin Pagan, who left to become a minister with the United Reformed Church. It was then bought by the Wallimans, a family from Switzerland who also owned the Savoy Hotel in Cheltenham. On a Saturday night in September 1976, customers came in for a rude shock. According to the *Malvern Gazette*, during a torrential rainstorm a torrent of water cascaded along the Worcester Road and burst into the lounge bar, packed with customers. 'The force of the water pushed the bar door in and sent sticks of wood and other debris straight at our unsuspecting customers,' said the manager, Brian Comerford. The hotel's wine cellar and food store were flooded to a depth of three feet. However, the hotel resumed business on time at midday the following day.

In 1978, Mr. Comerford resigned and the hotel was sold for about £150,000, with the Walliman family returning to Switzerland. After short spells of owner-

*The Foley Arms in the 1950s (Brian Iles)*

*The Foley crest still stands above the street entrance*

ship, it was bought in 1991 by Helen and Nigel Thomas and marketed under the umbrella of Best Western. The connection with Darwin was renewed in 2001 when members of the far-flung family held a reunion at the hotel to commemorate the 150th anniversary of the death of Charles's daughter Annie. It also coincided with the publication of a book called *Annie's Box,* based on a box of keepsakes and Darwin. The Thomases sold the Foley Arms to a property company, Allied Investment Partners, in 2007 but stayed on as managers.

Then in January 2010, the owners dropped a bombshell by suddenly closing the hotel. Mr. Thomas was told to hand the keys over and leave immediately, together with the 25 staff, despite there still being guests at the hotel. After a protest sit-in, the hotel was eventually closed and the windows boarded up. Just when the people of Malvern thought they were about to lose one of their finest hotels, J.D. Wetherspoon, the national pub chain, came to the rescue. Malvern Hills District Council approved plans for internal alterations and after a £2.2 million refurbishment, the Foley Arms Hotel reopened its doors for business in December 2010. The ground floor is now a spacious bar, lounge and eating area with another bar downstairs. The loos are palatial, but then Wetherspoon were winners of the Loo of the Year Award, 2010. Upstairs are 23 en-suite bedrooms. All the fixtures and fittings are of the highest quality and meals are available all day, with breakfast served from 7am.

*The White Horse Hotel in the early 1900s (Brian Iles)*

Across the road from the Foley Arms used to be the **White Horse Hotel**, in a building which is now home to a firm of chartered accountants with apartments above, next to the Bengal

*A hunt meet outside the White Horse some time between the two World Wars*

restaurant. In 1900 the landlord was Mr. E. Probert who, on Boxing Day night, was nearly assaulted by a drunken bricklayer when he prevented him from entering the house. The man was later fined 7s 6d for being drunk and disorderly. For some 10 years Herbert Jones was the licensee and in 1916 James Jones, possibly the son, was in charge. The hotel had two bars on the ground floor with special glass in the windows through which customers could see out, but people outside could not see in. The windows were decorated with beautiful patterns and the words Bar and Saloon. Upstairs were several bedrooms. The English Impressionist painter Dame Laura Knight would meet the theatre director Sir Barry Jackson, George Bernard Shaw and T.E. Lawrence at the White Horse.

While the road continues on to St. Ann's Well and the Malvern Hills beyond, a quiet courtyard on the right-hand side is home to the **Red Lion Inn,** which originally was the middle of three cottages with a blacksmith's to the right, all built about 200 years ago. Over the years, these other buildings were incorporated into the Red Lion. *Robson's Commercial Directory* of 1838 states that Mr. H. Lane was landlord, followed in the 1850s by Thomas Lane, possibly his son. It was Thomas who was instrumental in offering the specially made beer tokens during this period. The token, or check as it was also called, had the figure of a lion walking with raised paw and tail under Thomas's name. On the reverse were the words 'ales wines & spirits/check', and '3D' (three pennies) with oak sprays. Mr. Lane was also president of the Loyal Hope of Malvern Court of the Ancient Order of Foresters.

By 1870, the proprietor was Mr. J.W. Lee who, in the *Malvern Advertiser*, advertised the Red Lion Inn as having 'Genuine Wines and Spirits, Home Brewed and Burton Ales and Good Stabling'. Another later advert, when Mr. C. Oakley was proprietor, stated: 'Every accommodation for visitors. Spirits, wines, ales, porter, etc. of the finest quality. Bagatelle.'

By the turn of the 20th century the courtyard must have been quite a lively place with the Red Lion providing stabling for its B & B guests, home-made beer for its customers, and entertainment by way of pub games including bagatelle, the precursor of the pinball machine. Adjacent to the Red Lion was

Welch's Dining Rooms, now an antique shop, and on the opposite side the Central Temperance Hotel.

During the Second World War, the Red Lion's functions room, a separate two-storey building, was frequented by American servicemen based at several camps in the area looking for 'a good time'.

At the beginning of the 1970s Marston's, the Burton-upon-Trent brewers who owned the Red Lion, decided that the way forward for beer sales was with pressurised, or keg beer, and started removing hand pumps in their pubs. But they met resistance at the Red Lion in the form of landlord Ron Gould. 'I tried to save them [the pumps] then, but the brewers were adamant,' Gould told the *Malvern Gazette* in 1975. His customers organised a petition to the brewery while Gould, after turning down an offer of £5 for the pumps, stored them safely in his cellar and waited. 'Then in 1974 public interest in real ale boomed,' added the *Gazette*. 'The brewery relented and Ron triumphantly refurbished the brass and ebony pumps to serve real ale again.'

In 1982 the *Malvern Gazette* played an April Fool's day hoax on its readers by announcing that drinking habits in Malvern would be in disarray for at least 12 months following a recent discovery. The *Gazette's* story said that historians at Oxford University had carried out tests on an ox-hide document found recently at Little Malvern Priory, and confirmed that it was the authentic work of St. Wulstan, 11th-century Bishop of Worcester. 'The document, very battered but clearly bearing the bishop's seal and signature, prohibits use of alcohol within a five-mile radius of the priory, except on holidays and saints' days.'

*The Red Lion in the late 1950s or early 1960s (Malvern Museum)*

The paper added that it would probably take 12 months before a private member's bill rescinding the law could be introduced. Ron and Paddy Gould immediately saw through the prank, but decided to play along with it. They put up a notice on the front door explaining that 'Due to recent legal findings' no alcohol would be sold on the premises until further notice. Inside, towels were draped over the pumps and optics. For half an hour shocked customers were served soft drinks only. 'It was a great joke,' said Ron. 'It really livened up the day and gave people something to talk about. I wish it could happen every week.'

Unfortunately the pub went through a bad period when it was allowed to become just a 'drinking hole', but this was to change in the late 1990s with the arrival of Steve Hickman who introduced what was described as 'proper food'. It soon became known as *the* pub in Malvern for food, attracting celebrities such as Roger Bannister, Jim Davidson, Nicholas Lyndhurst and Prunella Scales.

In 2008 a fire which started in a fat fryer in the kitchen literally took the roof off. It had to be removed and rebuilt, and the whole of the inside had to be gutted and refurbished. Deciding to leave, Hickman sold out to a Thai couple who ran a restaurant in Bromyard. He worked with them for a year before moving out altogether in March 2010. A patio with heated jumbrellas and a heated conservatory are new additions at the front, while the functions room is now a Thai restaurant.

*The Thai Connection restaurant in a separate building belonging to the Red Lion in 2011*

At the junction of St. Ann's Road with Worcester Road and Belle Vue Terrace stands the **Unicorn Inn,** a black and white building generally recognised as being the oldest pub in Malvern, dating back to the 16th century. Behind the 18th-century front are the remains of timbering which shows it was originally a timber-framed building similar to Worcestershire cottages built in the 1500s. The Unicorn may have started life as **le Taverne**, which was kept by John Green in 1540 and by another John Green, probably the son, who was an aleseller in 1604, though not licensed by the local magistrates as were four others. He died in 1623 when his alehouse contained 'a table board, benches, forms and stools, a malt mill, several hogsheads, barrels and a large amount of cheap earthenware dishes and mugs'. He was also a farmer with two head of cattle, 13 sheep, a mare and £4 worth of corn.

The name Unicorn was probably chosen after James VI of Scotland became James I of England in 1603, and the mythical creature replaced the Welsh dragon in the royal coat of arms. Originally it had a sign that stretched across the road welcoming the traveller. During the 18th century, mail coaches travelled through Malvern on their way to Gloucester and stopped at the Unicorn.

The Unicorn's skittle alley was turned into an emergency hospital to deal with casualties from one of the worst accidents that ever occurred in Malvern. In May 1866, the *Morning Advertiser* reported that Robert Wallis, a Worcester haulier, was transporting 12 carboys of highly rectified sulphuric acid, or vitriol, to the Holy Well in Malvern Wells where it was to be used in the manufacture of Malvern Seltzer. Being the Whit Monday holiday he took with him his wife and 7-year-old daughter, Ellen, and 3-year-old son, Frank. His dray was an open one with two horses. After passing the Foley Arms, the breeching tackle of the shaft horse gave way and it was impossible to stop the dray from careering down the incline. Wallis intended to stop on the flat road at Belle Vue Terrace, but a heavily laden carriage turning the uphill corner near the Post Office crossed his path and diverted his dray down the even steeper Church Street. The dray crashed into a lamp-post and dumped the Wallis family on the pavement amidst the broken carboys and gallons of escaping burning vitriol.

Badly burnt, as were passers-by who helped drag them out of the wreckage, they were taken to the Unicorn Inn where beds and linen were set up in the skittle alley and treatment was given. Both children later died from their injuries, while Robert Wallis was left totally blind and his wife retained only partial sight in one eye. One of the horses had to be destroyed. The accident did have one positive outcome – the setting up of Malvern's first hospital, funded through public subscription.

According to an advert in the 1870s, the pub was described as the **Unicorn Commercial Hotel** with William Attreed as proprietor, adding 'Visitors, commercial gentlemen and excursionists, will find this one of the most convenient, comfortable, and economical houses in Malvern. British and foreign wines, spirits, etc. of the purest description. Table d'Hote at 1.30 p.m. prompt. Good stabling and coach through houses'.

On Unicorn tokens appearing around this time was the name of the landlord, W. Page, who was listed in *Kelly's Directory* of 1864, but had gone by 1868. Although no proprietor is shown on another token, the probability is that it was

*Landlord Harold Trigg at a meet of the North Ledbury Hunt outside the Unicorn circa 1935 (First Paige)*

issued by Page's successor Charles Harris, who was present in 1868, or a Mr. Attreed, present in 1872.

At the beginning of the 20th century, the Unicorn was run by Edwin Trigg, also jobmaster and farmer, the start of a long association with the Trigg family. He hired out horse-drawn carriages and charabancs for trips around the Malvern Hills. They were kept alongside the inn, where a garage was later built; it is now an Italian restaurant. Rum and coffee was served at the pub from 5am to men going to work – quarrymen and drovers, and sometimes shopkeepers, for they had a long day, from 8am to 8 or 9pm.

Edwin's grandson, Harold Trigg, was the next landlord, from the 1930s until about 1947. He was also involved with other Malvern pubs, while another Trigg, Thomas, Edwin's brother, owned the Lamb and was involved with the Lygon Arms. Harold had the habit of blowing a fanfare on a hunting horn at midday, to remind his customers that the pub was open for business. In 1933 he and his wife, Gladys, formed the Festival Club, which met regularly at the Unicorn and attracted many distinguished visitors. This followed the formation of the Malvern Festival, originally dedicated to the works of George Bernard Shaw, and a Film Festival which ran concurrently. Gladys kept an autograph album which included the names of luminaries such as James Bridie, Evadne Price, Emile Littler, Alastair Sim, George Arlis, James Hayter, Ernest Thesiger, Charles B. Cochran and Alexander Knox.

In the 1940s it was literary rather than theatrical figures who were attracted to the Unicorn, in particular two up-and-coming authors, C.S. Lewis and J.R.R. Tolkien, who would meet up before or after walks in the Malvern Hills. As they were walking home from the Unicorn one night, it started to snow. They saw a lamp post shining out through the snow and Lewis turned to his friend and said, 'That would make a very nice opening to a book'. *The Lion, the Witch and the Wardrobe* later used that image as the characters enter the world of Narnia.

*A plaque on the Unicorn commemorating the visits of C.S. Lewis*

In 1960 the owners, Whitbread, appointed John Jolley as manager, a position he retained for the next 21 years. With Carl and Melanie Shirley at the helm, Whitbread Flowers, as the owners were now called, spent £30,000 in 1983 on making a considerable number of improvements to the Unicorn. The public bar was opened up to form one lounge bar, central heating was installed and the kitchen modernised. To provide an 'olde worlde' atmosphere, the walls of the bar were decorated with antique agricultural tools, copper brasses, old golf clubs, alpine sticks and riding crops.

*The Unicorn in the 1970s (Malvern Museum)*

In 2009 the pub, now owned by Enterprise Inns, was taken over by Sue Warrener with her husband Dave as chef. It was shut for three months while further refurbishment was carried out and reopened in September. Food now plays an important part in the pub's business and all age groups are encouraged with activities ranging from karaoke to a knitting club.

Almost opposite the junction of St. Ann's Road and Worcester Road is a lane, Edith Walk, running steeply downhill. Here, at an unknown location, there used to be a beerhouse called the **Stanhope Cottage** named either after a person or, more likely, after a stanhope carriage, a light phaeton, itself named after Capt. Stanhope (1754-1828). According to the *Stevens Annual* of 1909, the pub was run by H.W. Denman, while in 1914 the proprietor was J. Fiskins.

The *Malvern Gazette* of 22 May 1914 reported that the Malvern Petty Sessions agreed that the licence of the Stanhope Cottage be transferred from James Fiskins to Albert Bosley. Owned by Mrs. Mary Clarke of the Chestnuts, Hanley Castle, and let to the Royal Well Brewery, West Malvern, the beerhouse, which operated a six day licence, continued to trade during the First World War. But just before the end of the war, in August 1918, it closed for the sale of intoxicants. At the Malvern Licensing Sessions in February 1919, it was stated that no application for the renewal of the licence would be made.

Further along Belle Vue Terrace one comes to a series of shops in a building which used to be the long established and well regarded **Belle Vue Hotel**.

*An early advertisement for the Belle Vue when Mr. Beard was proprietor*
*(Malvern Museum)*

Although becoming obsolete, it avoided demolition and instead sprouted shops and offices, and its coach entrance was turned into a shopping arcade. Still to be seen, however, high up on the front wall is the name Belle Vue and underneath a blank space where once was the word Hotel.

Built in 1816 or 1817 to a design possibly by John Deykes, son of Samuel, architect for the Foley Arms Hotel and the Library (now Barclays Bank), by 1825 it had Mr. Beard as proprietor and comprised 'various suites of airy and commodious apartments'. It was an elegant three-storey building with a projecting porch, a coach entrance leading to a spacious stabling yard, and metalwork balconies. It was of substantial construction; one of the walls exceeded 3ft in thickness. At the back, narrow, winding passages led to the pantries and old tap-room, while the beamed kitchen boasted a vast cooking range. Also to the rear was an unusually large, lofty and comfortable billiard room, to reach which it was necessary to climb some steps.

One of the three billiard tables, noted for its carvings and inlaid wood, was shown at the London Exhibition of 1862 and was owned for a while by Lord Dudley. In 1903, Mr. H.W. Stevenson, champion of the world at English billiards, played two games with Mr. W. Smith at the Belle Vue. Special accommodation was made available for ladies desirous of witnessing the games.

Families were boarded there in private apartments. As John Chambers wrote in his *History of Malvern*, the Belle Vue 'possesses all the advantages of a house with modern construction, fitted up with corresponding taste. Here is no table d'hote.'

*The Belle Vue as depicted in 1876 (Malvern Museum)*

Later a *Visitors' Guide to Malvern* included the passage: 'There are two excellent first class hotels, the Royal and Foley Arms Hotel and the Belle Vue, which are generally crowded with persons of rank and fashion during the season.' The Belle Vue offered good post horses with closed and open carriages, excellent stables for horses and livery, and commodious coach houses. At one time up to 30 coaches passed in and out every day.

In about 1838, the latest proprietor, George Matthews, was advertising the Belle Vue as a 'family hotel and boarding house. Now replete with every accommodation for visitors. Private and public coffee rooms.'

Various functions, including banquets, concerts and auctions, were held at the hotel. For instance, in June 1855 a sale was held in the yard of carriages, horses, dogs, harness etc., while in September of the same year Mr. W. Haynes, organist of the Priory Church, gave a grand concert. With the arrival of the railway in the 1860s, travel by carriage considerably lessened, which led to the stables and coach houses being replaced with two-storey buildings. An open passage to the billiard room was covered in.

In 1904, the Belle Vue was owned by Frederick Moerschell, who also owned the Imperial Hotel, but both hotels were fated to close down in the coming years. Suffering from gradual decline, the Belle Vue was reduced in size, with the ground-floor rooms being converted into several shops and the rooms above the main entrance becoming offices. The hotel retained an entrance through what is now Oliver's, the wine bar, and continued to trade.

*An unusual view of the Belle Vue. Note the impressive porch which has since been done away with*

In 1911 the Freemasons of Malvern took a lease on an area of the hotel including the main entrance with its columned porch, kitchen, dining room and billiard room. The Masonic Hall, or Lodge, was established in the billiard room, while the dining room, originally a refreshment area allocated to commercial travellers to entertain their customers, continued as the Oak Tree lounge and remained open to the public until at least 1928.

Mr. H.B. Tipping became proprietor in 1916 and stayed there until 1930 and the hotel closed three years later when it was known as the **Residential Hotel Ltd** with Miss E. Willis as proprietor. Remarkably the three main shops survive to this day, with hardly any loss to the original frames, doors, curved glass windows or tiled lower fascia. Even some of the mosaic flooring in the doorways has been retained.

The former Belle Vue hotel entrance now leads into **Oliver's** wine bar, a room with a long bar on one side. Originally it was the restaurant for Warwick House before opening as a wine bar and restaurant in the 1970s known as **Edward G's**, after its joint proprietor Ted Underhill, whose first names were Edward Graham. Then, in 1984, Mr. Underhill decided to change it into a 'fun pub', telling the *Malvern Gazette*: 'It's more of a meeting place than an ordinary pub, with disco music and dancing. Latest attraction is a laser disc, first in the country, which plays videos which are synchronised with perfect stereo sound.'

The owner introduced a new real ale brewed by Bailey's in Leigh Sinton called Underhill's O.P., or 'Over Pretentious', as Ted disliked snobbery surrounding real ale. Open seven days a week, the renamed bar particularly appealed to the 18 to 35 age group. In the 1990s, Oliver's was extremely popular, with DJs operating four nights a week, occasional live bands, quizzes and theme nights, but with the opening of a night club, the dance floor became redundant. Owned by Tony Wilkinson for the last four years, Oliver's opens from 3pm until midnight.

Right next to the former Belle Vue Hotel is Lloyds Bank, built in 1930 on the site of the former **Crown Hotel** which had been demolished. It may originally have been the **New Inn**, as this name appears on its sign board in a painting of Malvern in the 18th century. The inn made way for the Crown Hotel, built in the 1750s by William Mence, and it soon became Malvern's social centre as the town's post house. In addition to the mail coach service, coaches ran to London three days a week and seven coaches a day to Worcester. From 1760 annual venison feasts were being held there. A huge Crown signpost stood in the street in the 1780s.

After running a school for several years, George Roberts turned in 1796 to the more profitable occupation of keeping the Crown Hotel, which he altered considerably. Nevertheless, after a few years the hotel was taken over by Mr. J. Beard, who enlarged it considerably between 1802 and 1810, and then by

*The Belle Vue with the Crown beyond in the early 1800s*

William Harrison, who built and owned the Belle Vue Hotel next door in 1816 or 1817. One negative point was the state of the Crown's stables, situated near Abbey House, which were described by John Chambers in his *General History of Malvern* as 'a disgrace to this charming village'.

According to Mary Southall, in her book *A Description of Malvern*, part of the Belle Vue Hotel was attached to the Crown and used as 'a coffee and subscription newspaper room'. By 1838, the Crown, described as a family hotel, had been bought by John Archer, owner of the Foley Arms.

In 1842 Dr. James Wilson arrived in Malvern by coach and put up at the Crown Hotel. Fresh from his studies on hydropathy from its leading exponent, Vincenz Priessnitz in Grafenberg, the doctor was keen to put these miraculous water cures into practice. He managed to obtain the lease of the Crown, renamed it Grafenberg House, and opened it as Malvern's first hydropathic spa. Soon patients were flocking to his rooms and within three years he had made enough money to pay for a purpose-built hydropathic centre for 50 guests.

The old Crown building soldiered on into the 20th century, but there was no public outcry when it was eventually pulled down and Lloyd's Bank built in its place. To commemorate the 150th anniversary of the water cure, Malvern Civic Society in 1992 placed a plaque near the entrance to the bank with the words: 'Site of Crown Hotel (Grafenberg House). Dr. James Wilson established the water cure here in 1842'.

Next door to Lloyd's is the **Mount Pleasant Hotel**, still open after 200 years and seemingly standing in guard of its prime position, next to Rose Bank Gardens and overlooking the Priory.

*The Mount Pleasant Hotel with the Crown alongside*

*The Mount Pleasant, Crown and Belle Vue*

Originally a private residence, described as an elegant mansion, built about 1730 and often inhabited by aristocracy including Prince and Princess Esterhazy, the Mount Pleasant became a hotel in about 1810. One memorable occasion was a day in September 1843 when the Dowager Queen Adelaide and her sister-in-law, Queen Victoria's mother, the Duchess of Kent, came to Malvern. 'Flags were raised on the church, bells pealed and canons roared throughout the day, and banners fluttered from the hotels and prominent houses,' reported the local paper. A large party of aristocracy were staying at the Mount Pleasant, which had been decorated for their reception by Edward Archer, of the Foley Arms Hotel. After lunch, with crowds of people and musicians lining their route, the entire party rode to the top of the hills, all on donkeys except the Duchess of Kent, who took a small open carriage. At about 4 o'clock the party descended the hills to take tea at Mount Pleasant before returning to Great Whitley, where the Dowager and Duchess were staying.

The hotel's appeal to the aristocracy continued with, in 1851, the ex-Queen of France, Marie Amelie, taking up residence there. In her retinue was an old man called General Comte Dumas, who was the father of the great novelist Alexandre Dumas.

Edward Archer, who had succeeded his father William as owner of the Foley Arms, became the new owner of Mount Pleasant and just before the First World War the hotel was run by Blackford Tipping, with Ada Tipping, his wife, still there in 1916. A pre-Second World War advert proclaimed: 'This hotel – bedrooms with running water – offers comfort and individual attention by the resident proprietors ...'.

During the 1930s Dame Laura Knight, the Impressionist painter, and her husband Harold, stayed and painted at the Mount Pleasant. At the outbreak of

*The Mount Pleasant Hotel, showing the Orangery to the left (Brian Iles)*

*The Orangery at the Mount Pleasant Hotel (Malvern Museum)*

the Second World War the hotel was commandeered as a hostel for scientific workers, and when it was returned to the owners, it was in such great disorder that they put it up for sale at £10,000. Mrs. Gertrude Mitchell, owner of Warwick House, the department store opposite, fearing that Debenhams or Marks and Spencers would buy it and turn it into a store to compete with Warwick House, formed a company with some other local business people and bought the hotel, which was then modernised and refurbished. It was reopened a year later with accommodation for residents.

High in the gardens above the hotel was the Orangery, an elegant summer house built at the beginning of the 19th century, and now a Grade II listed building. By 1967 it was in such need of repair that it was threatened with demolition. The owner, Mrs. Kathleen Lancaster, set up an Orangery Restoration Fund and with the help of the Friends of Malvern more than £1,000 was raised to pay for the restoration work.

A few years earlier, in 1964, a ghost was seen in the empty Orangery by two female guests in separate incidents. According to folklore expert Roy Palmer, a guest in the main building woke at 2.30am to see an old woman in a long black dress standing by the window. 'She felt not fear, but puzzlement, as the figure turned towards her, then vanished. At breakfast she related her experience to another guest, who confirmed that at about the same time she too had awakened, and been paralysed with terror for some 15 minutes. The two women made enquiries,' Palmer added, 'and found that the adjoining rooms they had occupied were once a single bedroom in which, many years earlier, a mother had smothered her young daughter.'

No doubt in an attempt to recapture something of the 19th-century allure when Malvern was one of the leading spa towns in the country, in 1971 the Mount Pleasant Hotel introduced the Malvern Hydro, where 'tense muscles, tired tissues and ragged nerves are in turn relaxed, rejuvenated and soothed'. Treatment, under the personal direction of the actress Sue Nicholls, included sauna or steam with body massage, vacuum suction, sun-ray, and facials. And going even further back into the realms of history, romantic candlelight banquets were held in the Orangery with tables set with 'trenchers, tyg cups and bifurcated daggers. ... Food and drink are prepared from recipes of four centuries ago. Comely wenches in period dress wait on tables and assist the minstrels who sing and play music from the time when England was said to be "a nest of singing birds".'

It was a very different story by 1979 when the hotel was fined £400 for 16 offences under the Food Hygiene Regulations, and was enjoying possibly the worst reputation of all the establishments in Malvern. As new managers Pat and Marie O'Driscoll told the *Malvern Gazette*: 'There's no point in trying to hide the fact. The Mount Pleasant is on the absolute rock bottom – but that means that from now on it can only go up.'

'And "up" they fully intend to go!,' the paper added. 'They have already banned all scruffs, trouble-makers and rowdies who were contributing to the bad reputation and such characters will be kept out – for life if necessary. Those wanting to go into the Spa bar or the main part of the hotel will be expected to be well-dressed and not wearing scruffy jeans or leathers. There's a full time bouncer employed on the premises to carry out the new policies. They want to turn the Orangery into a place where regular discos are held and run on a club membership basis.'

Pat and Marie believed they were the hotel's last chance. If they couldn't make it work, the owners, Nicholls & Hennessy Hotels Ltd, of Wolverhampton, would close it down. 'But they don't want to close it down if they can help it because they have a very soft spot for Malvern and the Mount Pleasant – it was their first hotel,' said Marie. 'In fact, they've poured money in to try and make it as comfortable as possible. They've put central heating in throughout, put on a new roof and renovated all the rooms.'

The Georgian Bar was to be turned into a games room for young people with a pool table, added the *Malvern Gazette*. In addition the restaurant was to be restored to its 1920s Palm Court image with live music and a dance floor, and the Hydro refurbished as an up-to-date beauty parlour where men and women could spend a whole day with sun beds, saunas and baths. Facilities for electrolysis, massage, waxing and slimming were to be provided. Afternoon cream teas would return in style, and conferences, business meetings and wedding receptions would be encouraged.

It appears that things didn't go quite according to plan, however, as a story in the *Malvern Gazette* five years later stated: 'The Mount Pleasant Hotel has reopened for the 1984 season with a new image. While the historic building itself has been carefully restored in character, the new proprietors, Alison and Richard Downing, plan to alter the old formal hotel image by adopting a more modern, progressive approach. "Frankly we felt sorry for it – it was so badly in need of some love and attention," said Alison.'

*The Mount Pleasant Hotel in 2011*

The couple moved into the hotel in October 1983, since when the building has been rewired and replumbed, eight bedrooms redecorated, a new bar-restaurant opened in what had been the hotel dining room, and the functions room refurbished. Yet more refurbishment work was carried out after the hotel was bought in October 2003 by Marinder Bains and Aamer Gull, who also jointly run a hotel in south Wales.

Just south of the Mount Pleasant Hotel and adjacent to the '99 steps' alongside Rose Bank gardens is believed to have stood the **White Lion Inn**, long since demolished. According to *Kelly's Directory* of 1860, James Newsome was the landlord. The *Morning Advertiser* of 1 September 1860 reported that the White Lion applied for a spirit licence, urging its claim upon the growing necessities of the locality, but the Bench declined to grant it following objections.

There is in existence, according to John Whitmore in *Worcestershire's Inn Tokens*, a token with the name J. Neesam, White Lion, Malvern. Mr. Whitmore concluded that the spelling discrepancy was probably an error by the token manufacturers. The only other directory entry to the White Lion or a Mr. Neesam/Newsome is in 1864, and in 1870 the inn's contents were sold by auction with an advert in the *Malvern Advertiser* stating that brewing plant, billiard bagatelle table, household furniture and effects were to be sold by J.B. Harper and Sons. A week later another advert stated that stock-in-trade comprising six capital hogshead and other casks, about a hogshead and a half of beer, and a five pull beer engine were also up for sale.

Just the other side of Warwick House, now turned into apartments, at the beginning of Wells Road stands the former **Tudor Hotel**, which over the years has been allowed to fall into disrepair and also suffered severe damage from a fire in February 2010. The Victorian Society has warned that unless the build-

*Dr. Gully's water cure establishment at Tudor House and Holyrood House, later to become the Tudor Hotel, as engraved in 1852*

ing's fabric is maintained, its gothic façade, spiral staircases and turrets won't survive.

Originally there was just the one building, a private residence called Holyrood House, which was bought in 1842 by Dr. James Gully to use as a base for his new water cure therapy. So successful was his business that he built, on land next door, Newbie House, later renamed Tudor House, to accommodate the extra demand for his hydrotherapy. It was designed by the distinguished Victorian architect Samuel Teulon. At first Dr. Gully lived in Holyrood House and the patients stayed in the new building, with a bridge in between. Later, female patients were housed in Holyrood House and male patients in Newbie House, and the bridge became known as 'The Bridge of Sighs'.

*The 'Bridge of Sighs' that was built to connect Holyrood House, where female patients were housed in Dr. Gully's establishment, and Newbie House, where male patients stayed*

Dr. Gully helped build up Malvern's reputation as a spa town, with his urbane manner attracting famous visitors such as Gladstone, Darwin and Florence Nightingale. At the height of his career he was enjoying an income of £10,000 a year. A typical day's treatment began with patients being woken at five in the morning, wrapped naked in wet sheets, and then covered in blankets. An hour later, buckets of water were thrown over the patients, who then went on a five mile walk, stopping at wells for the waters. After breakfast of dry biscuits and water, they spent the rest of the day taking a variety of different baths, or in some cases wearing a wet sheet called the 'Neptune Girdle' round their middle at all times, apart from meal times. Dinner of boiled mutton and fish was served at 3 o'clock. For this treatment, a weekly fee of four guineas was payable.

After 30 years carrying out his water cure, Dr. Gully left Malvern in 1872 having met a young married woman, Florence Ricardo, to whom he became a secret lover, and getting involved in a mysterious death. The hydropathy clinic at Holyrood and Tudor Houses was sold and converted into the **Tudor Hotel**. Soon an advert was proclaiming: 'Billiard and smoke rooms. Bath rooms (hot and cold). The object of the Management is to combine the atmosphere of home life with the plentiful accommodation and resources of a large hotel. Inclusive daily tariff 7s 6d.'

Another advert, in the *Malvern Gazette,* dated 7 June 1901, stated: 'The **Tudor Hotel** has been redecorated and artistically furnished, and will be found a comfortable and well ordered establishment. Sanitary arrangements perfect.

*An advertisement showing the rear of the Tudor Hotel when the McHales were the proprietors in the 1970s (Brian Iles)*

The water, celebrated for its purity, is pumped direct from the Hay Wells. Resident proprietor – Mrs. Henry Young.' Mrs. Young was still in charge in 1916. In 1910, Queen Amelia, the last Queen of Portugal, and her brother, the Duke of Orléans motored from Wood Norton, where the Duke lived, to Malvern and after visiting the Priory had tea at the hotel. During the Second World War women of the WAAF and WRNS were billeted there. It was left in a ruinous state, but was sold in 1945 for £4,000 to a man from Blackpool.

Damage estimated at £1,500 was caused to the hotel during a weekend of torrential rainstorms in September 1976 (which also caused problems at the Foley Arms, as noted above), with part of the ceiling in the third floor bar and

*The main entrance to the Tudor Hotel is on the left of this photo. A wrought-iron archway and a battlemented addition to the adjacent property have been added by the time the photograph opposite was taken (First Paige)*

*The Tudor Hotel (Brian Iles)*

ceilings in some bedrooms collapsing. Mr. and Mrs. Bernard McHale were then running the business.

Mr. and Mrs. B. Lovell were the last proprietors before the **Tudor Hotel** was sold in 1989 for £900,000 to a company called Amescourt, which then went into liquidation. The building was empty for over a year until it was bought by David Southall in 1992. Originally offers of £500,000 were sought, but it probably went for half that amount. Builders started work on a £100,000 renovation programme with the new owner wanting to locate the original spa well in the basement and use it as the focus for facilities such as a health club, jacuzzi and gym and even a swimming pool. Later the same year it was announced that part of the hotel, which has 31 en suite bedrooms, would be converted to bed-sits.

However, at the beginning of the new millennium the hotel closed and was used as a DSS hostel for a while, then again remained unoccupied for several years. In 2006 permission was granted to convert the building into 14 luxury apartments, but no work was carried out at that time, and the building fell into further disrepair. It then suffered serious damage during a blaze in February 2010, possibly started deliberately according to a fire services report obtained by the *Malvern Gazette*. The Victorian Society started a campaign to save the building, Kristian Kaminksi of the Society stating, 'The Tudor Hotel is an attractive and important part of Malvern's history and must not be left to rot.' Fortunately, it has now been restored to its former glory, having been converted into apartments by David Habershorn, himself from Malvern, who described the project to the *Malvern Gazette* on 25 June 2012 as a labour of love.

*The Abbey Hotel (First Paige)*

Set against a backdrop of the Priory Church and with its front façade covered in Virginia creeper, the **Abbey Hotel** makes an impressive landmark right in the heart of Great Malvern. It is on the site of the prior's house, and its car park covers the ruins of the monastic buildings, a reminder of pre-Reformation days when there was a thriving Benedictine priory dating back to 1085.

Around 1600 the prior's residence was replaced by a large three-storey stone house, which by the mid 1700s had become a lodging house called Abbey House. Apparently this was built in the style of domestic architecture of the reign of Elizabeth I and James I and boasted a venerable long room lined with varnished oak. Kept by John Dugard, who charge 15s a week for full board, it was Great Malvern's only lodging house. It was also the social centre of the village, and Dugard provided somewhat entertaining and energetic breakfasts. 'At ten o'clock every Wednesday, during the season, will be a public breakfast, at 1s 6d each person at Dugard's Assembly Room,' an advert proclaimed, 'after which the Shepherd's Lottery will be played here. Music will be in waiting, in order to perform, if the company shall be disposed for a dance.'

In the early 19th century, Abbey House was kept by Mrs. Richards and her son, Mr. R. Richards, and was comfortably fitted for the reception of visitors as borders. It later came into the hands of William Archer who, in 1848, tried to sell it to the parish for £3,000. Failing to do so, he had it demolished and built in its place the present Abbey Hotel. A few years earlier, the historic timber guesten, or guest hall, was also demolished, in what some people have declared an 'act of vandalism'. It had originally provided accommodation for the prior's guests, including, it is thought, Henry VII, his wife and sons, Arthur and Henry, but had long been in use as a barn. Some of the ancient carved oak window heads are now in the nearby Malvern Museum of Local History.

Mr. Archer, whose son Edward was proprietor of Mount Pleasant, the Foley Arms and the adjacent wine shop, also owned the room over the Priory's north porch, said to have been used 'for drinking, feasting and dancing', which in 1849 he sold to the parish for £100, together with another small room inside the church. Later the hotel, still under the ownership of Mr. Archer, underwent extensive alterations and was 'entirely rearranged,' as an advert explained, adding 'It is in every respect suitable for the reception of First-class families.'

Another advert, this time in the *Morning Advertiser* of 6 January 1901, proclaimed: 'Most comfortable Family Hotel, plentifully supplied with soft water from the celebrated Hay Well, and thoroughly warmed throughout the colder months of the year. Billiard and reading rooms. Perfect Sanitary Arrangements.' The hotel was now being run by a Swiss family called Schneider, with Miss L. Schneider as manager. One important guest was Haile Selassie, Emperor of Ethiopia, who spent part of his exile (1936-1941) in Malvern.

During the Second World War, the hotel was converted for use by the Ministry of Information, followed later by the Belgian Army and then the RAF.

In 1958 the hotel was bought by Mr. Reginald Manley, together with his mother Mrs. N.R. Manley, and two years later it underwent extensive alterations and improvements, including the addition of a new wing on the south side. Four years later the hotel changed hands again, this time to De Vere Hotels, who appointed Mr. Cave-Brown-Cave as manager.

One of the staff taken on was Terry Gillon, who started as a pastry cook and later became head chef, remaining at the hotel for 40 years until he retired in 2000. As related in *Malvern Voices – Work and Leisure,* edited by Gill Holt, to start with he slept in the Abbey Gateway, used as staff quarters and later

*The Abbey Hotel as several postcards have portrayed it, wreathed in creeper and with formal gardens (Malvern Museum)*

given by De Vere Hotels to the Malvern Museum Society for use as a museum. Mr. Gillon recalled a supper party attended by the Prince of Wales to celebrate the 50th anniversary of the Malvern Festival. The event was organised by Mrs. Helen Boehm, from America, who owned the Boehm porcelain works in Malvern.

In the 1970s the Elgar Suite was built on the site of the gardener/handyman's house to provide modern conference facilities with more bedrooms above. In 1998, the hotel was given a £1 million upgrade by the new owners, Sarova Hotels. It now boasts 103 en-suite bedrooms, including four-poster and executive rooms. There are also banquet, restaurant and bar facilities.

Going down Church Street and just past the entrance to the Priory are some modern shops including Clarks, the shoe shop, standing on the site of what used to be the **Fermor Arms**, the smallest pub in Worcestershire consisting of possibly just one room and also known as the **Hole in the Wall**. Though the building was erected in 1815, the earliest reference to the Fermor Arms is in *Robson's Commercial Directory* of 1838, when William Harrison was landlord. Where did the French-sounding name come from? Well, the French word for farmer is fermier, but then fermor in Old English was a collector of land taxes. Intriguingly Easton Neston, a country house near Towcester, Northants was built by Sir William Fermor, later created Lord Leominster in the early 18th century.

*Two views of the Fermor Arms (Brian Iles)*

Malvern Licensing Sessions were told in February 1918 that the Fermor Arms, holding a six day licence, had only one room – the front bar. There was no lavatory or urinal accommodation, and men using the house seemed often to go to a passage close by and commit a nuisance there. The police commissioner told the meeting: 'I have received complaints with regard thereto. In my opinion these premises are structurally unsuitable for the sale of intoxicants.' Despite these threats, the pub was given a reprieve and happily soldiered on.

Some years later the Fermor Arms was in trouble again, according to Frederick Covins in his book *Malvern between the Wars*. A friend, John Rae, recalled the day a 36-gallon barrel of beer rolled off the back of the dray making a delivery to the pub, trundled down Church Street at an alarming rate and crashed head on into Fishy Davis's open front shop. 'The shop was ankle deep in beer and fish floated in a sea of brown ale.'

After the Second World War, Frank Paine was for many years the landlord. In the 1950s the proprietor was Tom Southgate who gained a certain notoriety for declaring in 1957 to a French magazine that 'The women may govern, but

*In 1957, a French magazine carried an illustrated article about Malvern in which it highlighted the number of women in prominent positions, including the deputy mayor, a police sergeant, the director of the Festival Theatre, and the editor of the Malvern Gazette. Tom Southgate, proprietor of the Fermor Arms and depicted above with his wife, behind the bar, told the magazine: 'Les femmes peuvent bien gouverner Malvern, mais elles ne me gouvernerant jamais!' (First Paige)*

they will never govern me'. This followed national and foreign press coverage of Malvern's claim to be a town run by women. Ladies did indeed hold most of the key jobs including, for the first time, the chairmanship of the Urban District Council, the editorship of the *Malvern Gazette*, and ownership of the only theatre and cinema. There was also a female police sergeant, and the chairman of the Malvern Hoteliers' Association was a woman.

But the men didn't seem to object. As Mr. D.R. Andrew, secretary of the local Rotary Club, said: 'The women take a lot of hard and unpaid work off our hands. "Never do today what you can get a woman to do tomorrow" – that's my motto.'

According to customers who used to frequent the place, the Fermor Arms was indeed very small, though larger than the one room mentioned above. There was a narrow entrance with the door and a window to the left. The bar was on one side as you entered, with sliding doors leading to a lounge, while at the back was a crib room, described as always damp, and part of the church gardens. Opening hours were from 10 to 2 and from 6 to 10. It was the last pub in Malvern to obtain a licence to open on Sundays as it was on church property. Very steep steps led down to the gent's loo which was partly under the pavement. One customer is said to have broken his neck after falling down the steps. It is not known whether the man was tipsy at the time, but the incident was probably very much frowned upon by the local authorities. A Marston's house, the pub was very handy for staff from the nearby post office and also popular with theatrical people from the local theatre.

Landlords for over 15 years from the early 1960s were Wally and Daisy Jones, who in 1970 celebrated their silver wedding anniversary. Wally, described as a very smart man who always wore a cravat, would invariably be found together with Daisy behind the bar. A less welcome celebration occurred in July 1976 when they had to ring last orders for ever, with the pub consigned to the scrap heap. 'The regulars turned out in force for the final night,' reported the *Malvern Gazette*, 'and towards closing time, with all but one of the beer pumps dry, engaged in a bit of a sing-song led by Daisy.' The following week the Jones had taken over the Bakery pub in Malvern Link. The Fermor Arms and several shops were demolished for redevelopment, but work did not start. The result was an empty and scruffy site for several years. Eventually a Yorkshire development company bought the site and quickly built four new shops.

Almost opposite in the alley alongside the current Three Cooks bakery shop, used to be the **Brewery Inn** and also a brewery. The inn appeared in *Tilley's Directory* of 1860 when Richard Leighton was landlord, but by 1909 it had disappeared. The brewery well is still in a cellar under one of the shop units at the rear.

Further down Church Street on the opposite side of the road and on the corner with Graham Road is the Halifax Bank which occupies the site of what

was once the main entrance to the **Beauchamp Hotel.** Although cut down in size and with the entrance on the other side of the building in Graham Road, it still operates as a hotel, but now called the **Great Malvern**.

In 1864 it was described as a family hotel and boarding house with extensive stabling, coach houses and out offices. On the ground floor along Graham Road towards Church Street was a commercial room, three sitting rooms, private shop or booking office and coach house. At the rear, with an extant archway entrance in Church Street, was a coffee room, bar, waitress pantry, still room, smoke room, tap room and servants' room. In a separate building across the yard was a brewhouse, harness room and six stall stables with lofts above. There were 28 bedrooms and numerous little rooms where commercial travellers laid out their wares for shopkeepers to come and buy them.

The hotel was named after the Beauchamp family of Madresfield Court, who owned much land in Malvern. Of particular interest was Henry, fourth Earl Beauchamp, who by the time he succeeded to the title at the beginning of 1853, was in his 69th year and only had 10 years still to live. One of the first to introduce mechanised farming to Worcestershire, Henry, who was also a general, bought one of the first steam-powered tractors and drove it through Malvern to display it behind the Beauchamp Hotel. It was rented out to farmers on his estate for ploughing and reaping.

An advert in the *Malvern Advertiser* of 28 June 1856 stated: 'Beauchamp Hotel and family boarding house. Terms moderate. Good stabling and lock-up coach houses.' The proprietor was Mr. E. Fielders. Four years later another advert added: 'Wines and spirits, bottled ales, stout, perry and cider, all of the best quality. Good stabling and lock-up coach house.' In 1870 William Hilliard

*This photograph was clearly taken in the early days of photography: everyone is standing still, posing for the photographer (Malvern Museum)*

was in charge of the hotel, described as being for families and commercial gentlemen. An advert in the *Malvern Advertiser* stated: 'Visitors and Resident Families supplied with wines and spirits, by the gallon or bottle, at wholesale prices. Orders left at the bar of the hotel promptly attended to.'

By the 1880s the Beauchamp had been sold to David Kendall, a linen draper who also kept the hotel. The shop was extended into a small department store, which he named Kendall's, stretching right round to the Church Street entrance. The hotel then seems to have been run by the Chapple family, first by William in 1883 and then, in 1904, by Mrs. Jane Chapple, when *Kelly's Directory* said that the principal commercial house in Malvern was the Beauchamp Commercial Hotel, which had been considerably enlarged for the reception of families. In the 1916 *directory*, Charles Chapple was named as proprietor. In the 1920s, frequent visitors at Festival time were the famous trio of George Bernard Shaw, Edward Elgar and Barry Jackson, the festival organiser.

Between the wars the hotel was a regular place for 'commercials' and was happy to put on display in the foyer their guests' samples for potential buyers. In May 1945, a group of prisoners-of-war, repatriated to their homes in Malvern and District, were feted at the Beauchamp Hotel at a dinner provided by Mr. and Mrs. H.T. Trigg, of the Unicorn Hotel.

In 1947 William Burton became proprietor and stayed at the hotel for the next 17 years until his retirement in 1964, during which time he played a prominent part in both the national and local Licensed Victuallers Association. He was for 11 years a member of the General Council of the Licensed Victuallers Defence League of England and Wales, a member of the Midlands District for 16 years (chairman for the previous three years), and member since 1947 of the Malvern LVA, including holding the offices of chairman and president. The hotel was then bought by Welcome Inns Ltd, Hereford, and Ralph Southwood was appointed as manager.

It was about this time that the stables and yard were sold off, and the stables were demolished when the supermarket Somerfield was built.

Kendall's department store closed in the 1970s when the premises were taken over by Courts the furnishers. In 1981 the property was again sold and divided into small units including a shoe shop, butcher and the Halifax, then a building society. In the same year, the hotel's former coach house was transformed

*Two views of Kendall's department store and the Beauchamp Hotel*

into an up-market fashion shop with a new frontage, but retaining the internal exposed beams.

Sometime after 1995, new owners changed the hotel's name to the **Royal Malvern Hotel**; more recently the Royal was dropped from the title and replaced with Great. In 1999, the hotel was bought by Jeremy Sutton who, with the assistance of his father Roger, is carrying on the hotel's traditions, including its long association with the theatre. The number of bedrooms is now only 14, but all are en suite; the main change was to turn the cellar into a bar called the Great Shakes, used for private hire.

Approaching through the Church Street archway leading into the stableyard at the rear of the Beauchamp Hotel, one comes to large plate glass windows behind which used to be the **Beauchamp Vaults**. It seems likely that when the hotel was built in the 1840s, a bar was created at the rear of the premises to cater for the ostlers and servants of visiting guests. An internal wall kept it separate from the rest of the hotel. However, it appears to have become a popular drinking hole with local customers and became known as the Beauchamp Vaults. Josh Davies was the last landlord when it closed down in about 1970, after having been there for several years. The cellar and ancillary equipment still survives.

Going straight across the traffic lights into Grange Road one comes to an impressive Victorian Gothic building housing a large bar and restaurant called **Priors Croft**. Situated immediately opposite the Malvern Theatres complex and built on land once owned by Malvern Priory, it was previously known as Reginald's Tower. For many years it was the office of a firm of solicitors as well as acting as headquarters for the Malvern Hills Conservators.

*An advertisement for the Beauchamp Hotel in the 1950s when the proprietors were Mr. and Mrs. Burton (Brian Iles)*

*The Great Malvern Hotel in 2011*

*Priors Croft in 2011*

The building was bought in 2004 by developer Jonathan Roe, who invested about £250,000 in creating a downstairs bar and restaurant for up to 100 people and a formal restaurant upstairs for a further 100 diners, later used as a functions room. In May 2008, planning permission was granted for a 300 capacity function room consisting of a stage and dance floor area with new toilets and office at the back of the existing building. Mr. Roe hoped to attract well-known performers to Priors Croft in a bid to reestablish Malvern's history as a live music centre. From the 1960s to the 1980s, the Winter Gardens – now Malvern Theatres – had hosted scores of well known bands.

However, by April 2011 the functions room had not materialised and, although some live music was provided, the music at present comes from a DJ, who officiates from a disused church pulpit. Part of the dining area behind the bar is now used as a pool room.

On the junction of Grange Road and Abbey Road is a large apartment block known as Park View, formerly the **County Hotel**, a popular hotel during the Malvern festivals. It started life as the first purpose-built water cure establishment in the United Kingdom having been built by Dr. James Wilson in 1845 at a cost of £18,000. He called it the Hydropathic Establishment,

*'The Establishment', above, and below with the two wings added by John Ferguson, as the County Hotel sometime after the First World War*

having been inspired by his master, Dr. Priessnitz, the Czech who invented hydrotherapy. The original building was the central block only, set in its own grounds.

Known locally as the Establishment, it contained 72 rooms including a 30-metre-long dining room and a 23-metre-long drawing room. There was also a gymnasium 'for the application of Swedish Medical Gymnastics under a professor from Berlin'. Over 60 invalids would be treated there at a time.

Dr. Wilson died in 1867, and by the end of the 19th century the house had been taken over by Dr. John Ferguson, Malvern's last water cure practitioner, who added a large wing on either side of the building, which he renamed the County Hydro. In 1905 the water supply to the Hydro became contaminated and three patients caught typhoid, creating a great deal of bad publicity. The establishment managed to stagger on for another eight years before bankruptcy finally forced it to close.

After the First World War, the building became a hotel, although its baths were retained and continued to be used by patients, trading under the name of the Hydro. In 1929 the property was purchased by the Honywood Hotel Company, with Lady Honywood as managing director. The company owned a number of large hotels in London and the provinces, including the Queen's at Cheltenham. No licence to serve alcohol was possessed, however, necessitating in guests having to 'send out a page or servant for what was required'.

This was something of a stumbling block for Lady Honywood, who wanted a licence before spending £50,000 on a major refurbishment and transforming it into the new County Hotel. The following year, she applied for a new publican's licence before the Malvern Licensing Committee, who objected to the opening of a public bar. On being satisfied that a full hotel licence was requested, not a bar, the Committee eventually agreed to grant the licence. Work then went

*The rear façade of the County Hotel*

*The County Hotel's dining room in the mid 1930s (First Paige)*

ahead in carrying out a great deal of structural alterations, including refitting and refurnishing.

Later an advert appeared stating the County Hotel 'had been entirely built and furnished to comply with every comfort and convenience. Beautiful suites of rooms, bedrooms with private bathrooms, running hot and cold water, and central heating in all rooms.'

Later a brochure proclaimed: 'The most up-to-date establishment in Worcestershire. Risen to five storeys at rear overlooking hotel grounds, with croquet lawn and other attractions. Banqueting hall and conference room. 80 bedrooms.' Prices were given as double room 37s 6d, single room 21s, breakfast 4s 6d, luncheon 6s 6d, dinner 7s 6d. Fires – whole day 7s, half day 5s, evening 3s 6d.

The brochure also pointed out: 'The Management will appreciate it if visitors will bring to their notice any act of inattention or incivility, in order that it may be dealt with. The finishing touch, which ensures complete satisfaction, is provided by the superb cooking supervised by an accomplished chef, and by the dainty and swift service. The staff are specially trained in civility.'

A local inhabitant recalls that the County Hotel 'was a very grand hotel before the war with a large ballroom. This was very often hired out for dances and parties – often for charity.' During the Second World War the hotel accommodated American scientists working on radar. Afterwards, no longer a paying proposition, Honywood Hotels sold it to Western and Midland Hotels. It was then offered for auction in 1950, but there was no bid, and in 1951 it was bought by the Ministry of Supply for use as a hostel for apprentices at both the scientific research establishments, TRE and RRDE. Under the name Park View, it accommodated 100 or more apprentices. Since 1983 it has been turned into privately owned apartments, retaining its name.

Retracing one's steps to Church Street and travelling along Avenue Road, one comes to a grandiose Gothic building by Great Malvern Station which houses Malvern St. James school for girls, but was originally built as the **Imperial Hotel**. It was the inspiration in 1861 of architect E.W. Elmslie, who was originally from London but settled in Malvern, and also designed the railway station and the Link Hotel. The Malvern Hotel company, chaired by Dr. Gully, was formed and bought land not only for the Imperial but also to lay a tree-lined approach to both hotel and station by way of the appropriately named Avenue Road.

When it first opened, the Imperial, built to attract a high class clientele, could boast that it was the only hotel in England lit with incandescent gas, and

*The Imperial Hotel showing its close proximity to the station (First Paige)*

it also had its own baths for the water cure, a dining room to seat 100 guests, and a covered way, nicknamed the Worm, which ingeniously connected it to the station. The *Illustrated London News* described the hotel as 'a truly magnificent building'.

Built of red brick with stone dressings in a Continental Gothic style, the building was six storeys high surmounted by a commanding tower and situated in three acres of land. It

*The entrance to 'The Worm' which led from the station to the hotel*

was described as a 'palatial and sumptuously fitted hotel' with 100 bedrooms, all lofty and well ventilated and said to have had a window for every day of the year.

The hotel was abundantly supplied with water from a special spring in the tunnel of the Great Western Railway at Malvern Wells, whence it was conveyed by mains direct to the hotel. The sanitary arrangements had great attention paid to them, and were considered perfect. Baths were erected to provide guests with 'every advantage afforded by the most celebrated establishments of hydropathic physicians, combined with the comfort of a first class hotel'.

*The conservatory in the Imperial*

In her book *A Description of Malvern*, dated 1822, Mary Southall wrote '... we find ourselves at length looking up at a vast palatial pile of building, the Imperial Hotel. ... fabulous sums of money have been lavished thereon: it is fitted up, and its general arrangements are said to be of a complete character.'

The *Malvern News* for 21 August 1869 carried the following item: 'Everybody has heard of the Aptommas, whose harp recitals are the admiration of all who hear them. Well, this said Aptommas, the King of Harpists, assisted by his daughters, who are very clever, is to give two recitals in the Imperial Hotel.'

The *Morning Advertiser* for 10 February 1883 reported that new baths were to be built at the Imperial, at the rear, with a swimming pool adjacent. Baths included Turkish, saline and hydropathic. The paper added: 'The Imperial will become one of the most delightful and desirable hotels, not only in England, but in Europe. A speciality of the new Baths is the Droitwich Saline Bath. The brine is pumped from the never-failing springs at Droitwich, and is conveyed to Malvern, by railway, in vessels constructed specially for the purpose.' A railway siding led into the hotel's cellar.

On 28 April 1883 the *Advertiser* ran an advert stating: 'Imperial Hotel – Sanatorium and Bathing establishment – the new bath buildings are now open, and comprise Tepid Swimming bath, 80 ft. long by 27 ft. wide. Brine from Droitwich, administered as at Droitwich. Turkish Bath, heated and venti-

*The Imperial is now part of Malvern St. James girls' school*

lated on the most approved principle. Hydropathic baths of every kind including Vapours, Douches etc.'

In 1892 the hotel became for a while a school, with the evacuation there of Wellington College following a diphtheria epidemic. In 1898 a dinner was held at the hotel to celebrate the formation of the full Malvern Urban District Council with the Earl of Beauchamp as chairman.

Around the turn of the 20th century, the Imperial was taken over by the German hotelier Mr. F.A. Moerschell, who had previously managed the Queen's and the Grand Hotel in Manchester. Among the attractions highlighted at the hotel were tennis courts and an archery range, while 'forming a species of square with the main building of the hotel are the Imperial Baths with Turkish bath and swimming bath, warmed in the winter'. The Droitwich saline cure was also advertised.

In 1919 the hotel was sold for £32,500 to Malvern Girls' College and improvements were made including the installation of central heating and electric lighting. The hotel baths were adapted for the teaching of science and art, the old brine baths removed, and the dining room turned into the assembly hall. A new wing, York Hall, was opened by the Duchess of York (later the Queen Mother) in 1934; the spire and top of the tower were removed. The Edinburgh Dome, a sports hall, was opened by the Duke of Edinburgh in 1977. Following the merging in 2006 of the College with Lawnside, the Abbey and St. James's schools, the building is now Malvern St. James, an independent boarding and day school for girls.

On the other side of Avenue Road is Manby Road, where there once was a pub called the **Imperial Tap**, now a private house. It probably ceased trading around the turn of the 20th century, having been used by coachmen and staff from the hotel.

Other pubs which existed in Great Malvern at one time or another were **Ye Boars Head**, the **Angel** and **Talbot** (both 18th century), and the **Cob and Castle**, in Worcester Road, allegedly about where Beacon Books until recently stood.

# CHAPTER FOUR

# Malvern Link Top

Link Top is situated at the western end of Malvern Link at its boundary with Great Malvern and North Malvern. It is centred around a sharp bend in the Worcester Road at the junction with North Malvern Road, Hornyold Road, Newtown Road, and Lygon Bank. Most of the shops, and pubs, are in the Worcester Road and Newtown Road area. Dominating the centre of Link Top is Holy Trinity Church, the parish church of North Malvern.

Travelling westwards along the Worcester Road one comes to a short row of shops on the right hand side, just before the traffic lights, including a small block of flats which until 2010 was a pub called **The Morgan** and which originally was known as the **Lygon Arms**. Built sometime before 1855, it was a commercial inn run by Cecil McCann on land owned by the Beauchamp Estate. Lygon was the family name of Earl Beauchamp, whose family lived in nearby Madresfield Court, and were the inspiration for the Marchmain family in Evelyn Waugh's *Brideshead Revisited*. The inn's sign probably portrayed the family coat of arms – two lions *passant*. In 1856 the branch of the Friendly Society known by the convoluted name of the Loyal Hope of Malvern Court of the Ancient Order of Foresters held their first annual dinner at the inn 'under the able presidency of Mr. Thomas Lane, of the Red Lion Inn. Catering and wine were excellent being creditable to Mr. McCann.'

In June 1857, the *Malvern Advertiser* reported two less salubrious events. James Pugh, 22, and Sarah Pugh, 25, were sent to prison for seven days each for having stolen two ale glasses, value 9d, from Mr. McCann. Then one day after this incident Alfred Phipps, a carriage worker employed at Macarte's Circus (which probably was appearing on Link Common at the time) assaulted PC Spiers at about 2 o'clock in the morning at the inn, as he was endeavouring to stop a fight. The report added: 'Some of the roughs attempted to rescue Phipps after he was in custody, but PC Staunton and PC Ludlow prevented it, although they got roughly handled.' Phipps was fined 10s and 15s 6d expenses; in default 14 days hard labour.

But an advert which appeared in the *Malvern Advertiser* in January 1860 painted a much rosier picture: 'Superior accommodation at moderate charges' with dinner at 1s, tea 9d', and offering 'good beds, stabling and coach houses, and a room 42 ft by 22 ft (having extensive views of the surrounding country), for the accommodation of large parties'. Home brewed ale was served, together with wine and spirits. Closed and open carriages were available for hire, with carriages to the station priced at 6d each person from livery stables at the rear of the premises.

William Brewer was landlord at the beginning of the 20th century and served beer from Allen's Brompton Brewery in Newtown Road. Mr. Brewer was succeeded in about 1908 by Thomas Trigg, whose price list at the time included pale ale at 1s 6d a gallon, gin at 13s 6d for the same quantity and Scotch whisky at 3s a bottle. Allen's brewery was taken over by the Royal Well Brewery at West Malvern, which in turn was swallowed up by Flowers, of Stratford-upon-Avon. In 1942 the licence of the inn, now owned by Flowers, was transferred from Fred Bond to James Dunn.

*The Lygon Arms around the turn of the 20th century (Brian Iles)*

In 1957, the Lygon Arms, now described as a hotel, was taken over by Dennis Campbell, who had been in the hotel trade all his life, starting as a page boy in London. The following year he transformed the billiards room into the Warwick Lounge, to accommodate parties, wedding receptions and reunions. Several Malvern licensees were among the guests at its official opening. Mr. Campbell was instrumental in carrying out other modernisation projects including a new grill room, which was officially opened in May 1960 by Col. Sir Fordham Flower, OBE, chairman of Flowers, the owners.

The year 1976 saw some radical changes to the property, now reverted to inn status and owned by Whitbread, who had absorbed Flowers; not only were major alterations carried out internally but the name was changed to **The Morgan**, after the internationally known sports car produced in Malvern since 1910. The face-lift was the idea of the new tenants, Tony and Lynne Wood, and Tony's brother Bill, but the name change came about by chance.

Tony told the *Malvern Gazette*: 'There were only small, poky bars and doors everywhere. We had to do something. So we knocked out a few walls and opened the whole place up. A new name also seemed appropriate.' The premises then included a large through bar in front, a saloon bar in the back, and a party room in the basement. When the change of name came up, a Whitbread representative suggested The Morgan; the car company was approached and managing director Peter Morgan readily agreed. A splendid new sign soon replaced the old Lygon Arms one. On the Great Malvern side, it showed a 1919 Morgan three-wheeler with the late Henry (H.F.S.) Morgan at the wheel, and his wife Ruth beside him; and on the Malvern Link side the latest 1976 model with Peter Morgan driving. In addition the walls of the lounge bar were decorated with framed photos of Morgan cars and the workshops, provided by Mr. Morgan.

In the summer of 1980 Lynne Wood and 14 Morgan regulars rolled a 35-gallon beer barrel from Chase End to West Malvern car park to raise money to buy equipment for Malvern Hospital. Their fund-raising efforts earned The Morgan the Boozer of the Year award of 1981 in a national newspaper competition that involved 400 pubs. They also won £2,500 to go towards their hospital equipment fund, and another £500 to throw a party to celebrate the pub's success.

The Morgan was later bought by Enterprise Inns, who in 2007 decided – in their wisdom – to close the pub and sell it, with a restrictive covenant preventing it from being used as a pub, restaurant or hotel. Despite strong objections from CAMRA (Campaign for Real Ale), who were particularly against the covenant, it was sold by auction for £180,000 to Prime Restorations, who applied for planning permission to turn the property, empty for over a year, into four flats. In December 2008 the property was bought by Pegasus Restorations. The application was turned down in April 2009 by Malvern Hills District Council, but their decision was overturned by a planning inspector in October 2009 and work proceeded.

*The Wine and Spirit Vaults in the early 20th century (Brian Iles)*

Further along Worcester Road, just by the traffic lights, is **The Vaults**, now lying empty but latterly a night club and originally a public house. According to Anthony Collis in his book *The Inn Signs and Pub Names of Worcestershire*: 'The name was originally a synonym for cellars because a medieval cellar was normally vaulted. It came to mean a place where wine or spirits were not only stored, but also sold straight from the barrel.' So presumably when the Wine and Spirit Vaults opened in Link Top some time in the latter part of the 19th century, customers would have been served their wine and spirits from the barrel. The car park was the site of the Jones & Davis Brewery, known partly for their bottled beer. It then became the Vaults Inn, essentially a drinking pub with a stone floor single bar, housing a darts board surrounded with numerous trophies. To the rear was a garden with a children's play area. At some point it became owned by Banks's brewery, which later took over Marston's, but retained the name.

In 1947 Harold James became licensee, but he died less than two years later, aged just 48. Mr. J.R. Roberts was the landlord in 1960 when a Harvest Festival auction was held which realised £42 5s for the boys of St. Peter's Lodge, North Malvern. Customers provided gifts which were auctioned, followed by harvest supper.

In 1969 Percy Dunn and his wife Mary took over, but they retired in December 1974 due to Mr. Dunn's ill health. 'He had been ill for the last three and a half years now,' Mrs. Dunn told the *Malvern Gazette*, 'and during this time I have had to run the pub and I was finding it a bit much.'

At the beginning of the 21st century, Julie Allsopp was the landlady and during her time at The Vaults she began to do research into the burial of her uncle, Havelock Hipwell, a Merchant Navy seaman who was killed after his ship was torpedoed near Newfoundland, Canada, during the Second World War.

In 2004, The Vaults was taken over by Karl Crangle who turned it into 'something different, a bar with cocktails, DJs and a dress code'. In October 2005, Mr. Crangle took his 'different' image even further by applying for, and getting, a license for adult entertainment, specifically performances of podium and lap dancing. He was also allowed to keep The Vaults open until 3am at weekends. There were no objections from residents to the application. When adult entertainment was put on, door staff were employed and no under 18-year-olds were allowed in.

But in December 2005, London-based Mountside Estates, which owned The Vaults, wanted to convert the property into a mixtures of houses and apartments and in so doing create a terrace facing Oxford Road. This time local residents objected to the scheme, which never materialised.

Then in January 2011, Mr. Crangle, who now owned The Vaults, said he was closing the business for the last time. He planned to sell the property to a developer, feeling unfairly blamed for drinking and anti-social behaviour problems in the town. In February, the licensing sub-committee of Malvern Hills District Council reduced the establishment's licensing hours to between 10am and midnight, with no extra late opening hours. The sub-committee felt that shorter opening hours would give some measure of protection to local residents should any future owner of The Vaults want to run it as a pub.

Continuing along Worcester Road, and down Moorlands Road on the right, one comes to Bank Street where the **Nag's Head** is prominently situated. The inn was in existence in 1847 when Thomas Berry was the licensee and, according

*The Vaults, latterly a night club, lying empty in 2011*

*The Nag's Head in 1900 (Brian Iles)*

to Daphne Drake in her *Story of Malvern Link*, might have existed in 1841 when William Berry was a beer seller at an unspecified address in the Link. The building itself is much older, however, as it originated as three cottages.

From the 1890s for the next 40 years until 1938, the proprietor and licensee of the Nag's Head was Frank Rudd, a sporting enthusiast and well known in the boxing world. Both Jack Hood, who retired undefeated as European welter-weight champion, and Owen Moran, a championship bantamweight boxer who Rudd sponsored, trained at the Nag's Head. In July 1908, a large number of people visited the Nag's Head to see the championship belt, presented to Moran the previous week, which Mr. Rudd had proudly put on display.

In his book *Malvern Between the Wars*, Frank Covins recalled that fairs were held three times a year on Malvern Link Common. 'The fair covered the whole common, from the Nag's Head down to Pickersleigh Road,' he wrote, 'with steam driven roundabouts, side-shows, boxing booths, beer tents, swingboats, jugglers and fortune tellers.' He added that children exploited the situation by minding bicycles by the Nag's Head for 2d a day.

Towards the end of the 1930s Frank Bridges was at the helm and in 1939 the licence was transferred to Clifford Blackburn. At some point the Nag's Head became owned by brewers Mitchells and Butlers.

Soon after his arrival in 1974, new landlord Ted Garmston set about making improvements to the inn costing £2,000, that included turning two bars into one large room and the installation of new bar counters. The Nag's Tail, a room adjoining the pub and used as headquarters for several local organisations including the local Folk Club, also underwent improvements with the provision of a new bar and extra space created by the removal of several cupboards.

Mr. Garmston continued making improvements including structural alterations inside the pub and an extension to the Nag's Tail providing more space for functions, together with a new dance floor and separate bar and servery. 'I have known this pub for 25 years,' Harold Elliston, chairman of Malvern Hills District Council, told the *Malvern Gazette* in July 1975, 'and always considered the tatty old tin hut on the end as a bit of a nonsense. Now it is really going to be the palladium of Malvern.'

But in 1976 Mr. Garmston became bankrupt and left the pub. He told Worcester Bankruptcy Court that he had been 'very foolish' in spending more than £7,000 of his own money on improvements to the property – without any return.

After Mr. Garmston's departure a number of landlords came and went, and the Nag's Head became rather tatty and was frequented by what might be termed 'undesirable' customers. However, in 2000 the property was purchased by Duncan Ironmonger, who turned its fortunes right around, and as a former professional soldier banned no fewer than 1,086 people from the pub over the next five years. He later acquired The Chase in Upper Colwall and the Swan Inn at Newland and also opened the St. George's Brewery in Callow End. The whole pub was upgraded, redecorated and refurnished, while the Nag's Tail was converted into a restaurant with at one end the building of a connection to the pub and at the other an extension.

The patio area leading to the main entrance became festooned with hanging baskets bulging with a variety of gorgeous and colourful plants which led to several Malvern in Bloom first places in the Licensed Premises category. At the rear is a heated beer garden.

*The Nag's Head in 2011*

In 2004 the Nag's Head was Worcester CAMRA pub of the year, and then in 2006 it gained another accolade, being named Town Pub of the Year for Britain by the *Good Pub Guide*. It was the first pub to receive the award, which was devised after the editor noted that most town pubs were 'fairly grotty, smoky, somewhat shabby and very blokey'. The judges found the Nag's Head 'is a warm-hearted and an interesting pub with good food, drink and service. They keep an astonishing range of 16 real ales on hand pump.'

The following year, the pub went one better and was named as the best in Britain by the *Good Pub Guide*. On the back of this success, the Nag's Head was featured in the *Daily Telegraph* in December 2007 with a complimentary piece written by Chris Arnot.

*'Our friend Bill Watson 1944-2007'*

The Nag's Head, which now has a manager in charge, houses an interesting collection of memorabilia in its several bars and snugs with stone flagged floors and nooks and crannies on different levels, and settles and antique chairs. Items include 'Our Friend Bill Watson – 1944-2007', a photograph of one of the pub's longest serving customers, whose wife worked in the bar in the 1990s; a camel saddle and a picture of Trevor whisky (in honour of a customer called Trev) in the restaurant. Perhaps best of all, in the snug, in the glass-covered cellar revealing a skeleton and mugs lying on the cellar's floor.

Above the bar are two flats in one of which lived Mr. Ironmonger's parents, who ran the pub for a few years before the death of Mr. Ironmonger Snr.

Up until the 1890s there used to be another pub in Bank Street called the **Oddfellows Arms**, so named because it was the meeting place for members of the Friendly Society which provided benevolent and social help. The landlord in the 1860s was Thomas Powell whose name appeared on tokens given out by the pub in exchange for drinks or as prizes for pub games (see chapter 2 on Brewing and Breweries). On the reverse side of the token, or check as it was also called, was the name of the token's manufacturers in Birmingham. Mr. Powell had left by 1872 and the inn disappears from directories after 1892, when it was demolished. However, the name lived on, with another Oddfellows Arms being established in Malvern Link.

Situated just off Oxford Square is No. 8, a square house with bay windows either side of the front door. This was once the **Oxford Arms Hotel**, which probably closed sometime after the Second World War. The house next to it is reputed to have been lived in by the hotel manager. The property became the Oxford Coffee Tavern, then, coupled with adjoining land, a garage, and later a launderette. For many years it housed the spares department of the adjacent garage and car dealership of S.E. Walker. In due course out-buildings were knocked down and replaced with a row of new houses which now comprise the new Oxford Square.

*The building that was once the Oxford Arms*

Returning to Worcester Road and crossing over to Newtown Road, a short way down one comes to **The Retired Soldier**. Built sometime before 1855, its name may have originated from wounded soldiers returning home from the Crimean War (1853-6); the sign shows a Chelsea Pensioner and a soldier in khaki uniform. But another explanation for the name might be that many retired soldiers spent their savings in a pub. At the rear of the house next door was the site of Allen's Brompton Brewery, and The Retired Soldier was probably the brewery tap house. The lounge bar was once the cellar. In 1901 Mrs. H. Limerick was the proprietor, while in 1914 the licence was transferred from Charles Evans to Geoffrey McCann. In 1930 Jack and Doris Davies took over the pub and ran it for six years before moving to the North Malvern Hotel. Then in 1942 the licence was transferred from James Dunn to Archibald Cotterell.

In 1967 the pub was taken over by Donald and Corinne Maund and it continued operating as a quiet watering hole mainly for local clientele until it suddenly made the headlines in November 1975. Police found the body of the landlady, Corinne Maund, aged 44, stabbed to death in the kitchen, and her husband, Donald, 52, was charged with her murder. The following May at Birmingham Crown Court, Maund was found guilty of manslaughter, but not of murder, and was sentenced to three years imprisonment.

The jury was told that the killing was the culmination of several months of tension and scenes of violence between the couple. Mrs. Maund had moved out to live with her lover a month before the fateful day, though still helping to run the pub. At 12.45pm on the day of her death she went into the living quarters to make a sandwich for a customer and was followed shortly afterwards by her husband.

According to the prosecution in the court case which followed: 'After about five minutes Mrs. Maund was heard to scream. A customer went to the kitchen and saw Mrs. Maund lying on her back on the ground with Mr. Maund sitting or kneeling astride her aiming what appeared to be light blows at her chest. The customer, thinking it was a domestic scene, returned to the bar. But in fact it was not blows he saw but Mr. Maund stabbing his wife with a knife.'

Minutes later Mr. Maund returned to the bar, helped himself to a large whisky and dealt with other customers. This continued until about 1.30pm when he asked the remaining customers to leave. He then telephoned the police and told them he thought he had killed his wife. The defence counsel told the court that it was not disputed that Mr. Maund killed her, but that the issue was one of provocation.

*The current sign for The Retired Soldier*

Graham and Clare Paul then ran the pub not once but twice, then in 2000 the pub's owners, Wolverhampton and Dudley Breweries, included it in a group of pubs that they sold to the Royal Bank of Scotland. Described by a bank spokesman as being 'in poor shape', The Retired Soldier was closed while improvements were carried out.

It was later given a more complete refurbishment in about 2005 including a new bar counter, fixed seating along the walls, and a new entrance into the lounge bar. For about two years it was known as **The New Recruit**, but the recruit obviously did not live up to expectations and the old soldier was brought out of retirement again, but with a new inn sign.

Now owned by Admiral Taverns, the pub has since 2008 been run by Steve East, who believes another murder was committed on the premises, involving a person being pushed down the stairs. He also admits that a spiritualist recently carried out an investigation of The Retired Soldier for ghosts and found several, including one in the kitchen, one in the cellar and one in the bar. 'It doesn't worry me,' said Mr. East. 'You have got to believe in them, haven't you?'

Just a stroll down the road but on the other side at the junction with Hospital Bank is the **Prince of Wales**, which was probably built in the mid-19th century and named after the eldest son of Queen Victoria, who later became Edward VII. It is the end building of Gloster Place, a terrace of houses with the date mark 1863, and is believed to have been built as a club for staff from Malvern's newly constructed first hospital in Hospital Bank, which closed in 1911. Later a coach house was built in order that the inn could accommodate travellers and their carriages.

The stables, now used as an outhouse, still retains its double front doors, a hay rack, a trough and a farrier's pit used for shoeing the horses. What was once the courtyard at the back is now used as a smoking area with a barbecue in what was the old Gents. The inn itself has seen several changes. The existing main bar area was originally used as private living accommodation and its bar counter came from The Morgan when that pub closed down. On the other side of the main door, where once was an off sales section, is another bar with a pool table which used to have a separate entrance and was divided into two rooms, a snug and a bar. Upstairs was a meeting room and a snooker room, which were still in operation in the 1970s.

From 1922 the proprietor was William Lane for a number of years, while another long serving licensee was Dave Boycott, who took it over in the late

*The Prince of Wales in 2011*

1960s and ran it for nearly 30 years, first with his wife, Barbara, until her death in 1979, and then with Pat, his second wife, after their marriage in 1983. After retiring, he was steward of Malvern's Town Club for three years. Then in the summer of 2001 Mr. Boycott, aged 73, died rescuing his wife's dog after being struck by a train at a pedestrian crossing near Jamaica Road, Malvern Link. He was described as a man who would 'do anything for anyone'. The dog, a nine-year-old German Shepherd, Shanty, escaped and survived.

    Brian Lynch was landlord for about five years up to 2000, followed by Chris Brace and then by the present incumbent, Ian Randall, who has run the pub with his partner Khamala Baylis for the last three years. Ian is also a retained fire fighter. For many years owned by Marston's, the pub is now owned by Piccadilly Licensed Properties. On display by the door into the lounge bar are two brass and iron beer engines with patterned ceramic pump handles, which are believed to be the pub's original hand pumps.

CHAPTER FIVE

# Malvern Link & Newland

Malvern Link was part of the manor of Leigh, under the ownership of Pershore Abbey, for several hundred years until after the Norman Conquest when the Link became a separate part, or walk, of Malvern Chase with its own deer keeper responsible to the forester at Hanley Castle. After the dissolution of the monasteries, Leigh manor passed to the Crown. Elizabeth I gave it to Edmund Coles, Justice of the Shire, and the Link was later sold separately. The area became a centre for brick making with five works there in the mid-19th century. Link common today divides Malvern Link from Great Malvern.

The name 'link' may have originated from the linking up of more horses to carriages from Newland for the pull up the hill on what is now the A449, or it may refer to a ridge in the slope of the Malvern Hills on which it is situated.

With the opening of the railway station in 1859, trainloads of Black Country trippers descended on the Link, which was quickly developing along Worcester Road with residential areas growing northwards during the 1920s and 1930s. The *Link directory* of 1841 lists one beer seller, but by 1860 there were four in addition to 'the highly respectable inn,' the Royal Oak.

Travelling down Worcester Road towards Worcester one comes to Albert Park Road along which the fourth road on the left is Quest Hills Road. At the junction stands a block of flats called Portobello Court, on the site of which once stood the **Portobello Inn**. The name refers to the capture of the Spanish naval base at Porto Bello in Panama in 1739 by Admiral Vernon, who became a national hero. He was also the first man to issue rum to the Navy.

The inn was probably built in the mid-19th century. The proprietor was Mrs. Caroline Hill in 1901, in which year her husband, Albert, wrote to the *Malvern Gazette* complaining about an exaggerated accusation regarding Sunday drinking in Malvern. Mr. Hill described as an invention a passage in the published letter to which he took exception which stated that 'no less than 14 persons staggered out of a public house, one after the other, some staggering, and others just about able to keep straight'. He also disliked the term 'dens' being used for respectable licensed houses.

Frederick Stafford was in charge in 1922 and in 1930 it was run by Mr. W.J. Rayner, who remained the host until 1946 when he handed the business over to his son-in-law, Rex Kilford, and daughter, Evelyn. Mr. Rayner, however, continued to work behind the bar and later he and his wife celebrated their Golden Wedding at the pub.

The Kilfords spent the next 30 years at the Portobello before retiring in 1977, when a 400-day clock was presented to them by Banks Brewery, the owners, and a standard lamp with matching table lamp by the customers. Rex also retired from the Malvern Licensed Victuallers Association, after being connected with that organisation for 30 years, serving for 25 years as secretary, and for three years as chairman. Evelyn was prominently associated with the Women's Auxiliary of the Association. About six years ago, the Portobello was demolished and replaced with a modern block of flats.

Another block of flats, called Aspen Court, in Osborne Road, and adjacent to Malvern Link railway station, is the site on which the **Railway Hotel**, later called the **Malvern Link Hotel**, was originally built in 1861 to a design by Mr. E.W. Elmslie, who was also the architect for the Imperial Hotel in Great Malvern. The building was more like a grand château and in the mid-Victorian period enjoyed a certain amount of refined society with the names of its summer visitors communicated to the social register published every week by the *Morning Advertiser*. But the hotel, with its ballroom and bars, was really intended to accommodate Black Country trippers who arrived at the newly built station and invaded the town. It had extensive gardens for the meetings of public societies and pleasure parties.

*The Railway Hotel portrayed rather idyllically in 1861 (Malvern Museum)*

*The same building as that opposite, now as the rather more austere looking Malvern Link Hotel*

An early advert proclaimed: 'Visitors can be received as boarders during the winter months at two and a half guineas per week, including attendance. Bath, billiard and smoking rooms.' But despite the introduction of trains, it still provided 'First class stabling with lock-up coach houses' for customers who still chose to travel by horse-drawn carriages. The proprietor was Geoffrey Parsons.

Another advert stated: 'The prices are moderate – single beds 1s 6d, 2 6d and 3s. Sitting rooms – 2s, 3s and 4s per day. Attendance 1s per day. Families and gentlemen boarded by the week at £2 10s each person, including attendance.'

Unfortunately the hotel was not a viable proposition and in 1873 was sold at a knock-down price to Mr. H. Wilson, who ran a coaching establishment, or crammer's, and the building was converted into a boys' preparatory school. The Link continued as a school for many years, although the building had a troubled history, suffering from a fire in 1925 and being bombed by the Luftwaffe during the Second World War. It closed as a school in 1965 and was demolished in 1967 to make way for the Aspen Court apartments. The original hotel railings and gates can still be seen alongside the station platform.

Further along Worcester Road, on the right hand side, is Lloyds TSB Bank and adjoining shops on the site of which once stood the **Railway Inn**, built at about the same time as the nearby Malvern Link Station, which opened in 1859. For many years a concert party involving Pierrots, French panto type characters dressed in floppy white costumes, performed annually in a back room.

*In this photograph of the early 1900s, the Railway Inn is in the foreground; the Bakery Inn a few doors further along and on the white-painted wall further along still just visible is the word 'inn' of the Fir Tree Inn*
*(Brian Iles)*

In 1870 the landlord, William Dutson, charged a Mr. J. Hicks with assault. The latter was found guilty and fined 40s with costs. In 1901 the licence for the Railway Inn was transferred from Miss Elizabeth Dutson, for the late William Dutson, to James Dee, of the Wyche.

In 1922 the landlord was Alfred Wagstaff, while in the 1950s the licensee was Mr. C. Morris, who in 1959 raised £20 4s 3d for Father Hudson's Homes (which provided homes for otherwise homeless Catholic children) at a harvest supper with customers contributing an assortment of gifts which were auctioned. In the late 1960s and early 1970s, the landlord was Geoff Bartlett, who, it is understood, kept budgerigars and canaries. The Railway Inn was demolished in 1973.

Just a few buildings further along stands **The Bakery Inn**, the premises of which, as the name suggests, were originally used for that purpose. It was in existence as a pub, with probably only a beer licence, by 1874 when the licence was transferred to Nathaniel Wade, who was also a baker. The two trades must have carried on for several years with bread being sold there until after the turn of the 20th century. The original baker's oven was still in place in 1978 and was probably removed during alterations in the 1980s.

Still in existence, though, is the inn sign showing a baker preparing the daily bread, while still clearly visible on the windows of the public bar are the finely etched words Lewis-Clarke, referring to the Worcester brewery (1895-1970), which owned the Bakery at some stage.

In 1922 the manager was Mr. J. Cotton, in 1942 Edgar Shiers was landlord, and in 1976, when the Fermor Arms in Great Malvern closed down, it was taken over by Wally and Daisy Jones, who were still there in 1984. Mr. Jones was also chairman of the Malvern branch of the Licensed Victuallers Association.

*The Bakery Inn in 2011*

*The inn sign for the Bakery Inn*

A Marston's pub, the Bakery is now run by Chris Evans, who also owns The Bell in Cheltenham. The pub is divided into two bars, the lounge and the public bar, which has a pool table. To the rear is a beer garden and a large car park. A meat raffle is held every week.

Not far from the Bakery is a small shopping arcade called Fir Tree Walk, which used to be the **Fir Tree Inn**. Earliest deeds relating to the property are dated June 1857, when it was sold by William Reeves, a lodging house keeper of North Malvern, to William Wilder, described two years earlier as a tailor, for £400. The property was then licensed but was not referred to as the Fir Tree until documents dated 1876. Mr. Wilder offered tokens for his customers to exchange for drinks. On the obverse side was his name and the name of the pub, while on the reverse were the words 'Ale, wines, refreshments' and its value of 3d. In 1883, Samuel Wilder, son of William, owned the property and in 1899 he sold it to George Foster and Henry Watley, who in turn sold it to Spreckley's Brewery, of Worcester, in the same year. A photograph taken in 1908 shows the Fir Tree Inn with a sign advertising 'Spreckley's Celebrated Worcester Ales'.

In 1917 the landlord was James Hickinbotham, who the following year was in trouble with the police. Supt. Sherriff told the Malvern licensing Sessions that it had been brought to his notice that during the past year Mr. Hickinbotham had allowed a number of women, apparently soldiers' wives, to frequent the premises. There was a piano and singing took place, but he didn't know whether that was the attraction. So far as he was aware, Mr. Hickinbotham was the only licensee in the whole of the Malverns who allowed such a thing. The inn's music licence was withdrawn.

Herbert Hill married Mr. Hickinbotham's daughter, Sarah, who had been at the Fir Tree since the age of 14, and eventually took over the licence, which he held for a number of years before his death at the early age of 38 in 1939. The licence was then transferred to Sarah Hill. During the Second World War, what is now the Pizza Parlour was used as a Sergeants' Mess and anti-aircraft guns were positioned in the car park. In the winter, a billiard room at the rear was used by the local football team as a changing room, with buckets of cold water used as showers.

In 1954 Jack and Doris Davies took over as mine hosts and stayed there until 1966. By this time ownership of the pub had changed with Spreckley's becoming part of West Country Breweries, which in 1963 became part of the Whitbread Group.

The licence was then taken over by Frank Dean, previously a master carpenter, helped by his wife, two daughters, and son-in-law. By 1973 exten-

*The Fir Tree Inn in its new existence as a shopping arcade*

sive alterations had been completed, resulting in a pub with a large public bar, a smaller cosy lounge bar, and a skittle alley also used as a party room. Always a popular games pub, the Fir Tree boasted three skittle teams, two darts teams and two crib teams. Weekly meetings were held there by the Firm Lodge of the Royal Antediluvian Order of Buffaloes, another Friendly Society. Mr. Dean was in charge for about 25 years until the Fir Tree closed its doors in 1991. The pub remained empty for a while as Whitbread sought a buyer until an offer by local entrepreneur, John Hurrell, was accepted in 1993. He decided the Fir Tree had no future as a pub and turned the building into a shopping arcade with a variety of different shops taking residence following alterations.

Just a few buildings along is the **Beauchamp Arms**, named after the Earls Beauchamp who were important landowners in the area with their seat at Madresfield Court. Built probably in the mid-1850s, the inn was originally a beerhouse, but, as reported in the *Morning Advertiser* of 1 September 1860, the licensee, Mr. W. Taylor, had just applied for a spirit licence due to the rapid increase in the size of the neighbourhood. However, some adjoining beerhouse keepers and others in the locality opposed the application, and the licence was refused.

The following week the *Morning Advertiser* ran another story about the Beauchamp Arms reporting that Mr. Taylor was charged by PC Griffin with keeping his house open for the sale of beer and cider at 10.45pm on the night of 31 August. At the resulting court appearance Mr. Taylor said no beer had been drawn after 10 o'clock, the official closing time, and on being fined £1 and costs, said he would sooner go to gaol than pay the money. After the magistrates said they would distrain his goods if he so insisted, Mrs. Taylor paid up and they left the court.

According to John Whitmore, in his book *Worcestershire Inn Tokens*, there is a drinks' token to the value of 3d in the unattributed section of the British Museum collection, which bears the name Beauchamp Arms and W. Taylor. This quite likely refers to the inn at Malvern Link, where Mr. Taylor appears as landlord from 1860 to at least 1864. The inn disappears from the directories between 1876 and 1896, but has a permanent presence from then on.

In 1904 the landlord was William Lane, in 1916 Edward Haywood was in charge, and in 1922 Mr. W.C. Oliver was the proprietor with Mrs. Lily Oliver, presumably his widow, at the helm in 1928. Steve Chadwick was landlord in the 1950s or 1960s, and in 1977 Wally Jones was in charge; he was also vice-chairman of the Malvern branch of the LVA.

Coaching facilities were originally available at the rear of the inn with a courtyard and two large gates, which still exist, in Pickersleigh Road. There was also a blacksmith. However, the courtyard is now the garden of a private dwelling built later. The pub was owned for a number of years by Mitchells and Butlers, the Birmingham based restaurant and pub chain.

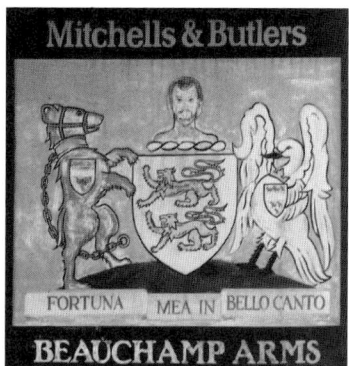 

*The Beauchamp Arms in 2011, with its inn sign, unaltered from the days when it was owned by Mitchells and Butlers, showing the Beauchamp coat of arms*

In about 1990 the Beauchamp Arms was bought by Dave Griffiths, who also owns pubs in Shrewsbury and Telford, and he made his son-in-law, Steve Newson, the landlord. With work having to be carried out in the main bar, Steve started trading from a small bar at the rear. Originally there was a corridor from the main entrance leading to a smoke room and bar on either side with an off-sales area at the end. Now it is all open-plan with the walls having been knocked down. Original bench seating remains under the bay windows and along other walls, complete with their individual service bells, though these are no longer in use. At the back of the pub is a large games room with, on one side, a bar and a skittle alley. Skittles is still a popular pub game locally, having the biggest pub sports league in Malvern with 30 plus teams in three divisions and 20 ladies' teams.

The inn sign bears a design based on the Earl Beauchamp coat of arms, with the words *Fortuna Mea In Bello Canto* underneath.

On the other side of Worcester Road, just past Malvern Link station, is Howsell Road leading to Quest Hills Road, on the corner of which stands **The Express Inn**, which was already in existence by 1874 when the licence was transferred at the local petty sessions court. It was originally called the Express Vaults and owned by a Salford brewery, Walkers and Homfrays. The building next door was once part of Allen's Brewery.

Thomas Wormington was the occupier in 1884 when tokens were available for exchange of drinks. On the obverse side of the token was: T.A. Wormington, Express Inn, Malvern Link, and on the reverse the name of the manufacturers and the value, 3d, of the token. In the early 20th century the landlord was Arthur Harrop.

*The Express Inn in 2011, with its inn sign*

By the 1970s the licensee was Jeff Stubbs, who, in 1977, became chairman of the Malvern branch of the Licensed Victuallers' Association. From 1991 to 2005 it was run by Anne and Gerry Deegan, who now run the Malvern Link post office. During their tenure a regular customer for 20 years, Michael Brooks, died at the age of 40; he was a big man both physically and personality-wise. A memorial plaque to him is displayed in the bar. Another customer, Jimmy Mason, actually dropped dead in the pub, from natural causes, about a year after the Deegans had left.

The Express is a two-roomed pub, owned by Marston's, with a split-level public bar with a pool table and large screen TV, and a separate lounge where food is served. At the back is a skittle alley, also a smoking area and a large car park. On the Howsell Road side is a gate leading to out-buildings at the rear of the pub. The inn sign for some reason shows a North American train, complete with cowcatcher, rather than the 'express' that one might expect. The pub is now run by Donna Stimpson, who at one time worked behind the bar when Mr. and Mrs. Deegan were in charge.

Further along, Howsell Road becomes Upper Howsell Road, where at the junction with Yates Hay Road, on the left, is **The Anchor**, built more than a

*The Anchor Inn in the 1930s (Brian Iles)*

hundred years ago. The choice of name is not immediately obvious, with no nearby sea or river, but it was possibly derived from the ancient word anker, meaning barrel, or that it was once owned by a retired sailor.

It started out as a beerhouse and even up to 1922 the landlord, William Hill, was described as a beer retailer. At some later date it was granted a spirit and wine licence. The pub also boasted a Brewery House which, in the 1920s, was owned by the Royal Well Brewery of West Malvern. The inn was bought in 1930 by the Stratford firm of Flowers Ltd, who were later taken over by Whitbread.

Leonard Grant was in charge in the early 1950s, but in 1958 the licence was transferred to Ernest Clewer. The following year he organised an auction of gifts provided by customers including two pigs' heads, a chicken and a huge harvest cottage loaf; the auction raised £17 4s 8d for the boys of St. Peter's Lodge, North Malvern. Mr. Clewer and his wife Laura stayed at the Anchor until 1970, when they retired.

The Anchor was basically a one-room pub with a small smoking room and it was later described as being a 'ramshackle place'. A feature was an open fireplace, now sealed up, around which pokers were provided so that customers could mull their own cider. One regular customer in the 1960s was Danny, a pig farmer who collected pig swill with his horse and cart. When he went into the pub for a bevvy, if he stayed too long the horse would go home on its own. Another occasional visitor was the super-star in the making, Ozzie Osbourne.

*The Anchor Inn in 2011*

Whitbread Brewery, owners of The Anchor, bought land at the pub for a car park in the 1960s, but did not proceed with the development. In 1970 Geoff and Carrie Bartlett, who previously ran the Railway Inn, took over the licence and it was their idea to modernise the place. In 1973 plans for a new car park and alterations, including moving the main door to the side of the building and altering the front windows, were approved. After several months of building and extension work, the Anchor reopened in January 1974 with a large car park, accessible from both Yates Hay Road and Upper Howsell Road, and with the whole of the outside painted in brilliant white, reminding visitors of a seaside pub according to a report in the *Malvern Gazette*.

Internally, there were two bars, lounge and public, where once there was only one. In the public bar a new elm wood counter was installed and there was a new games extension, which used to be the pub's bottle store, for darts and cribbage. A nautical atmosphere prevailed in the lounge bar including fishermen's ropes set into the counter, ship lantern-style lighting and partitions made of rowing oars.

Since 1998 the landlords have been Del and Jane Peters, who enlarged the public bar into a bigger games area with pool table and darts and about five years ago built a separate skittle alley further to the rear which doubles up as a functions room. The nautical atmosphere in the lounge bar has disappeared. Ownership passed from Whitbread to Avebury Taverns which in the early 21st century was taken over by Punch Taverns.

Returning to Worcester Road and continuing towards Worcester you turn up Hampden Road on the left and shortly afterwards right into Merton Road to find the **Gloster Arms**, a cosy back street pub. According to Daphne Drake in her book, *The Story of Malvern Link*, it started life as a cottage in that part of Merton Road known as Gloucester Terrace until 1884 when the owner David Bullus, a chain and rivet maker, was granted a licence to open an alehouse. In 1907-08 he was succeeded as licensee by his widow and in about 1916 by Samuel Bullus, presumably the son, while a Louisa Bullus was in charge in 1928.

According to tradition the bar was in the back parlour of the cottage and was very strictly managed by Mrs. Bullus, who would admit no women. The names of regular users were engraved on brass plates above their customary chairs, which have long since disappeared. A brewery later bought the Gloster Arms and the adjoining cottage, which had been bequeathed by its owner to a cats' home; all the cottages were originally built as service quarters for the big houses on the other side of the road. The two buildings were then converted into the present Gloster Arms. In 1947 Mr. and Mrs. Ernest Clewer became licensees and stayed at the Gloster Arms until 1958, when Stephen Chadwick took it over. Even so, up until 1975 there had only been six licensees.

In 1990 the then landlord, Neil Finch, presented the pub's 12th dog to the Guide Dogs for the Blind Association after raising £12,000 in the previous six years. He presented at least another six dogs. The present landlord, Richard Forrester, took over the pub in 2007 and before that was manager for a year.

*The Gloster Arms in 2011*

A customer for the past 65 years, Dave Collins, aged 81, admits to often popping round to the pub in his slippers as he lives nearby. He first came to the Gloster Arms when he was 16 but even on the day before his 18th birthday, Mrs. Bullus refused to serve him 'as he was under age.' He recalls that Trophy beer was sold and when it went up from 1s 10d to 2s some of the regulars walked out.

Although called the Ancient Arms of Gloster, the coat of arms on the inn sign is made up and does not actually represent the arms of the city of Gloucester, after which Gloucester Terrace was probably named. Interestingly, Gilbert de Clare, Earl of Gloucester, was given Malvern Chase as part of the dowry when he married Joan of Acre, daughter of Edward I. He also built the Red Earl's Dyke, running along the crest of the Malvern Hills.

At the junction of Worcester Road and Lower Howsell Road is a white house which once was the **Oddfellows Arms**, built in the 1870s. It existed for a short while at the same time as the Oddfellows Arms in Bank Street, Link Top, until the latter closed down in the 1890s. The name comes from the Oddfellows friendly society, lodges of which held meetings at pubs. One of the earliest licensees was William Jones, who rented out cabs to passengers from Malvern Link station wishing to go to Great Malvern. By 1880 Mr. Jones was also providing a horse-drawn bus.

In 1930, Lewis Thomas applied at Malvern Petty Sessions for the transfer of the licence to Henry Israel, which was granted. Other landlords afterwards were Frank Dunne, Emma Porter and Jimmy Dunne, who was the last licensee. The pub later became the headquarters of Malvern Rugby club for about 10 years. The building was finally de-licensed in the 1970s and became a private house. Owned by Ansell's Brewery and later by Flowers, the Oddfellows Arms had comprised a smoke room and a bar, and front lounge. On becoming a private dwelling the two front doors were taken out and converted into windows with the main door at the side.

*The building that was once the Oddfellows Arms at the junction of Worcester Road and Lower Howsell Road*

*The New Inn and its sign in 2011*

Continuing some distance along Lower Howsell Road one comes to the **New Inn**, which was first mentioned in a local directory in 1884. The sign shows an architect starting to draw a plan of the proposed 'new inn'. Arthur Tennyson, brother of the Poet Laureate, is reputed to have lived at a house called Sherbourne next door to the New Inn.

In 1901 the landlord was Thomas Morris, described as a beer retailer, and he was still there in 1922. A number of other landlords followed. About five years ago the owners, Marston's Pub Company, decided to make the New Inn more of a restaurant than a pub and carried out a major refurbishment to make it open plan. A wall dividing the two bars was knocked down and an extension built at the end of the lounge providing table space for many more covers. The front door, now an emergency exit, was closed and a new main entrance was entered from the car park. On the other side of the building is a large beer garden.

On the other side of the road, less than a hundred yards from the New Inn, is a low, white painted wall, behind which is an overgrown empty plot on which once stood the **Carpenters Arms**, a black-and-white listed building which was demolished in the mid-1990s. A nearby cottage was also knocked down. This was the scene for a controversial plan to build a vast housing estate here and on the adjacent field.

Although it was only first mentioned in a local directory in 1901, the inn may have existed before as an unnamed beerhouse run by George Knapton and later by his widow, Dinah, who were licensed to sell beer in Lower Howsell Road from 1876 to 1892. At the turn of the 20th century Robert Haynes was in charge but during the First World War he joined the Army and the licence was transferred to his wife, Nellie.

Roland Trigg held the licence in the 1950s and 1960s. In 1958 a turkey weighing 30lbs was carved in the bar on New Year's Eve, the gift of Mr. Trigg and his wife to their customers. In February 1960, Mr. Trigg applied for a full licence, the present one covering beer and wines only, as there had been considerable housing development in the area and he found there was now a demand for spirits. There were no objections and his application was granted.

Arthur Todd later ran the Carpenters Arms for several years until 1978, when Mr. and Mrs. Mario Bresclani bought the inn from the owners, Courage Breweries, and ran it as a free house. The couple carried out several improvements, including the building of an extension as a new bar cum games room. When the extension was being built, Mr. Bresclani filled in a 24ft by 6ft well which still had 13ft of water in it. The well pump was put on display at the entrance to the pub. Renovation was also carried out to the cellar, living room, toilets and kitchen. In February 1979, the *Malvern Gazette* reported the opening of the new Tudor Bar, with pool table and dart board, to complement the Malvern Lounge and the Link Bar.

In the 1980s, the Bresclanis sold the inn to a private buyer who was unable to make a go of it and it was run as a private house before being bought by the Trustees of Madresfield Estate, who then demolished it. They also demolished a nearby cottage to gain better access to the Lower Howsell former allotment site, which they owned, and which they wanted to redevelop for housing. Bovis Homes submitted plans to build no fewer than a hundred houses on the site, but following a public inquiry, the land was declared to be 'public open space'. Bovis subsequently withdrew their option to purchase the land and then withdrew their planning application.

Returning to Worcester Road, one soon comes to, on the left, Royal Oak Gardens, the site of the former **Royal Oak Inn**, which closed in the late 1990s and, after lying empty for a couple of years, was turned into residential dwellings. The name 'Royal Oak' is usually derived from the legend of Charles II hiding in an oak tree at Boscobel near Shifnal, Shropshire, to escape Roundhead soldiers after his defeat at the Battle of Worcester in 1651. However, there is a closer legend regarding the ancient Mitre Oak on the A449 between Worcester and Kidderminster where Charles is also supposed to have hid.

Built some time before 1851, the date when it first appeared in a directory, the Royal Oak lived up to its reputation as being a 'highly respectable inn' and proved a favourite watering hole over the years. The first recorded landlord was Mr. R. Bennett, who appeared in the *Lascelles Directory of Worcester and Neighbourhood* in 1851.

Thomas Ashmore had a long occupation as landlord lasting at least 12 years from 1864, when the licence was transferred to him following his marriage to Miss Bennett, the then incumbent. In 1873 he placed an advert in *Littlebury's Directory* of 1873 which described the Royal Oak as a family and commercial hotel with 'well aired beds' and 'wines and spirits of the choicest description'. It also offered excellent stabling and lock-up coach houses. Like many another licensee, Mr. Ashmore also offered the facility of special Royal Oak tokens, to the value of 3d, which could be exchanged for drinks.

The building itself was quite impressive with railings round a front terrace and porch with two fluted columns leading into the square-shaped brick building. In 1901 James Parsons was the proprietor, with the livery stables run by Mr. C. Merriman; in 1904 Charles Baines was at the helm, while Thomas Evans was in charge in 1916.

Another advert, this time in the *Malvern Gazette* dated November 1919, described the inn as having 'every accommodation for visitors' and also boasted a bowling green at the rear of the premises. This space was later converted into a skittle alley. 1958 saw alterations being carried out and sometime afterwards its regal claims were dropped and it was named simply the Oak. However, the old sign showing Charles II in his legendary hiding place was preserved on a side wall.

In the Worcester branch of CAMRA guide, *Real Ale around the Malvern Hills*, of 1996, the Oak was described as 'one of the original "converted" pubs still going strong as a rustic gardener's woodshed complete with old handles for hand pumps'. Games included darts, skittles and table tennis, with seven teams.

For a while owned by West Country Breweries, taken over by Whitbread in 1963, the inn was sold to Trent Taverns who in turn sold it to the Punch Taverns. In about 1998, when Mr. Taylor was the landlord, they decided to close it with a view to its redevelopment. Although a Grade II building, the inn was boarded up and allowed to remain empty for two years, the semi-derelict premises being described as an 'eyesore'.

In November 2001, a Solihull company submitted an application for listed building consent to convert the pub into three apartments. The plan also involved a pair of semi-detached houses to be built next to the Oak, fronting onto Worcester Road, while a terrace of three houses and two chalet bungalows would be built on the rest of the site at the rear. The skittle alley and storage building would be destroyed.

Two local brewers, Malvern Hills Brewery and St. George's Brewery, put forward a rescue scheme to turn the Oak into an outlet for their real ale, but the developers won the day and the housing plan went ahead. This was confirmed

*The Royal Oak has been converted into three flats, but a reminder of the past is retained in the name of the cul-de-sac which serves the new houses built on part of the site*

as converting the pub building into three flats, conversion of the coach house into a private dwelling and building more houses in the grounds. Still proudly displayed by the front door of the former inn is a colourful ceramic plaque boasting a castle, or tower, with the words 'West Country Ales. Best in the West.' These plaques were put up by West Country Breweries on their pub walls from 1958 to 1967.

Continuing along Worcester Road towards Worcester one comes to the parish of Newland and, just off the main road, the **Swan Inn**, a former coaching inn dating from the 18th century which is believed to have had an earlier history, having housed the troops of Oliver Cromwell on the eve of the Battle of Worcester in 1651. Older buildings still are believed to have once stood on the site. According to the late Canon Hunt in *A History of the Parish of Newland*, a building where the Swan now stands is mentioned in the Domesday Book of 1085. In the Norman Chronicles, William of Malmesbury (1095-1143) described the hamlet of Newland, some 800 acres, a mile from Malvern, as a 'wilderness'. It was not until 1100 that Gilbert, Abbot of Westminster, gave the land which comprised Newland and Guarlford to the priory at Malvern, and the monks set to work felling trees, draining the land and building cottages for woodsmen and hunters. For several centuries the population was sparse, and even in 1562 the hamlet consisted of just 13 families – Malvern itself only having 105 families at this time. Even now, apart from the Beauchamp community, there are very few houses in Newland, including the Swan, Grange Farm and Ashbeds.

According to A.W. Gwilliam in *Old Worcestershire Inns*, the Swan had links with the church. 'In Victorian days, church people visited there because it had a Holy Thorn in the garden,' he wrote. 'This tree came from the parent tree at Glastonbury where, tradition has it, part of the Crown of Thorns was brought over to this country by Joseph of Arimathea; and planted; it took root, and blooms at Christmas. F.E. Morgan, who was librarian at Malvern, found it blooming on Boxing Day, 1922.' But, it is believed, the Holy Tree stopped growing in the garden of the Swan prior to the Second World War.

The Worcester Turnpike Trustees were responsible for most of the main roads about Malvern and by 1827 there were five turnpike gates including one at Newland. Seven public coaches a day travelled between Malvern and Worcester, calling at the Swan.

From at least 1900 to 1908 the inn was run by Mrs. Eleanor Cross, a rare woman publican in her own right rather than having succeeded her dead husband. Like many another licensee in Malvern, she introduced a token which could be exchanged for a drink, though hers was unusual in being made of copper.

In the 1960s the landlord was Mr. G. Hewer who, at Harvest Festival time, decorated the bar with produce and fruits of the harvest. After a thanks-

*Possible coaches or carriers' carts that travelled between Worcester and Malvern in front of the Swan*

*A Morgan car pictured in front of the Swan*

giving service an auction was held, raising money for the Church of England Children's Society.

The longest serving landlords were John and Barbara L'Huillier who held the lease on the Swan for 33 years from the Madresfield Estate, eventually retiring in 2008 when John was 70 years old. Celebrities served included the comedian Norman Wisdom and Lady Sassoon, wife of race horse owner Sir

*A picture in the inn which makes a play on the current owner, who also owns the St. George's Brewery at Callow End*

*The Swan swathed in vegetation in 2011*

Victor Sassoon. The Morgan Car Club met at the Swan each February, and with up to 40 Morgans lined up on the front, it made for a wonderful spectacle.

The inn was taken over by Duncan Ironmonger, who also owns the Nag's Head at Link Top, the Chase at Upper Colwall, and St. George's Brewery at Callow End. A conservatory was built on the end of the building to extend the dining area and two stables at the rear, now called The Shed, are used as a winter games room. Another stable at the front is used for storage. A large field at the back is the venue for a variety of events, including beer festivals and summer fêtes.

CHAPTER SIX

# North Malvern

Nestling on the northern slopes of the Malvern Hills is North Malvern, an urban extension of Malvern along the foothills of North Hill. The residential development at Link Top in the early 19th century continued along the Cowleigh and North Malvern roads. 'Simple yet dignified' houses were built in the 1840s near the Belvoir Hotel, while a large number of poorer cottages were also built served by beerhouses. From about 1872 until 1970, the Tank and North quarries were in operation, with the hillside blasted with dynamite to release its valuable Malvern stone used mainly in building roads, but also in house-building. They were but two of about a dozen quarries across the Hills and the noise from dynamite detonations and accompanying rock fall could be heard for miles around. The gelignite charges were placed by men on suspended ropes.

Travelling along the Cowleigh Road, on the left-hand side just past Pump Street, one comes to the **Star Inn**, which was constructed about 150 years ago. It is probably named after a religious symbol, either the star of Bethlehem or the Virgin Mary, one of whose titles is the Star of the Sea (*Stella Maris*). Since 1634, a 16 pointed star has also appeared in the arms of the Worshipful Company of Innholders, formerly a guild of innkeepers. There is, disappointingly, no longer a sign depicting this hanging up outside the inn.

From at least 1901 to 1904 the landlord was Josiah Morris, while during the First World War Amelia Baker was in charge until 1919. In 1922 Mr. G.H. Cole was described as the proprietor and in 1928 Arthur Lockett was at the helm.

The Star was a traditional locals pub with a smoke room, a tap room decorated with ornate woodwork, a bar with darts and a back room for pool. Then about eight years ago, the inn was bought by a Chinese businessman who built a separate restaurant serving Chinese cuisine. The back bar was turned into a waiting room for collecting take-aways. The main bar has been decorated in contemporary style with Chinese artefacts, though retaining the Victorian bar back.

In August 2007 the new owner, Michael Choi, was granted permission to build a pair of semi-detached three bedroom houses on land next to the pub, once

*The Star in 2011*

occupied by two houses which were demolished many years ago. However, by the summer of 2011 the plot remained empty with a 'for sale' sign.

To raise awareness of Chinese culture across the district, Malvern Hills District Council organised the first ever Chinese New Year celebration in the town in February 2010 – the Year of the Tiger – with the traditional Chinese Lion Dance being the highlight. The Star Inn played its part a week later by celebrating with a New Year Party at the restaurant, including a buffet lunch and a lion dance. The inn held a similar event the previous year.

Further along Cowleigh Road on the left-hand side is Belvoir Bank at the end of which, at the junction with North Malvern Road, stands North Malvern House, a block of flats, which once was a hotel called firstly the **Belvoir** (French for beautiful view), and later the **North Malvern**. Built sometime before 1848, the hotel may originally have been the **Ark Inn**, according to John Whitmore in his book *Worcestershire Inn Tokens*, but the other possibility that he suggests – that it was the Cowleigh Arms – seems less likely, as the ground to the rear of the inn is steeply sloping.

At any rate the Ark appears in directories for 1851 and 1854 with John Ward Harrop as the occupier, although the earlier entry shows him as a beer retailer without the inn name. However, there definitely was a token produced with J.W. Harrop, Ark Inn, North Malvern on the obverse side and 'Billiard Ground' and 3d on the reverse. This claim for having a billiard ground is again intriguing. As John Whitmore states: 'By the 19th century billiards was invariably played indoors on a table, whereas the word "ground" seems to apply to an outdoor facility of some kind.' However, records show that there was an

*Once the North Malvern, the building has since been converted into flats*

ancient game called ground billiards played on a small outdoor court with a hoop at one end and an upright stick at the other. This croquet type pastime required players to strike balls around the court with maces.

An advert in the *Morning Advertiser*, dated 25 October 1856, reveals that the Tank Brewery was starting business on premises adjoining the Belvoir as the wholesale brewer, Henry Orgee, 'respectfully solicits the Patronage of the Inhabitants of Malvern and Neighbourhood'. From 1864 onwards, the hotel is called the North Malvern.

The *Malvern Gazette* for 1 March 1901 reported that at the Malvern Petty Sessions, Mrs. Mossop, of the North Malvern Hotel, applied for the temporary transfer of the licence to herself from her husband, Mr. A.I. Mossop, who had received a commission in the Imperial Yeomanry and was about to proceed to South Africa. Supt. Harrison said she would make a very suitable landlady, and the application was granted. However, by 1904 Mrs. Alice Franklin was in charge, and from at least 1922 to 1928 Mrs. Frank Harry was the licensee.

Jack and Doris Davies were in charge from 1936 to 1956 before moving to the Fir Tree and then the Cavalry, retiring in 1973 after 43 years as mine hosts. The hotel later came to be owned by Whitbread Flowers. In 1970 the North Malvern Hotel closed and the brewery sold it off to a development company who converted the property into apartments and built other dwellings on the site. Near the front entrance can still be seen a plaque stating 'West Country Ales, Best in the West, 1760', alluding to the time when that brewery must have owned the hotel before it was taken over by Whitbread Flowers.

*This building was once the Moodkee inn*

Back on Cowleigh Road and just on the corner of Old Hollow is an impressive three-storey Gothic building, now a private house called Ashbury, but formerly an inn with the strange name of **Moodkee**, after a 'British Victoree' in India. The property was apparently built and named by a wealthy English army officer returning from the Punjab, where the British, under Major General Sir Hugh Gough, defeated the Sikhs at the battle of Moodkee, or Mudki, in 1845 during the first of two Sikh wars which led to the annexation of the Punjab by the British East India Company.

Before actually becoming a pub, or hotel, though, Moodkee House operated some kind of alternative health project known as Medical Rubbing. According to an advert in the *Malvern News* of 21 August 1869, 'Mr. and Mrs. Cameron practice Medical Rubbing for Sciatica, Paralysis, Headaches, Spinal Diseases and other Disorders. Numerous Testimonials can be seen at their residence, Moodkee House, North Malvern, where they may be consulted.'

It is not clear how long medical rubbing was carried out at Moodkee House but it may well have started operating as a hostelry when work started on the Tank and North quarries on the Malvern Hills in the 1870s. As well as being a hotel, it had a separate bar, known locally as the Spit Bar, used by the quarry workers. Surprisingly it later had a parquet floor with urinals at the rear. There were two doors at the front, one leading to the lounge bar, served through a hatch, and another one leading into the reception area.

In 1900 the licensee was Harry Anson and in 1902 he was replaced by William Hewitt from Droitwich, and in 1922 the proprietor was Thomas Lane. One of the last landlords before the hotel was sold in the 1960s was Peter Woods, who lined the bar's entire walls and ceiling with matchboxes from all over the world.

The Moodkee changed its name to **Ashbury House Hotel** and then became a B & B, a covenant in the sale restricting its use 'as other than licensed premises'. It later became a large family home, then an internet business, before becoming a guest house again in 2011.

Among alterations made since the property ceased functioning as a licensed property are the closure of the lounge bar door, restricting the number of bedrooms to six, and turning the Spit Bar into a garage, although the parquet floor is still there as well as the ladies' loo, complete with sign.

Just a few paces up Cowleigh Road on the right-hand side is a large white house with, on the far facing wall, the just discernible words '**Cowleigh Arms**. Freehouse. Fully Licensed', giving away its former existence as a pub. It was probably built in the late 19th century as a watering hole for thirsty quarry workers.

In 1914 the licence of the Cowleigh Arms was transferred from William Bullock to Edward Reynolds, who was still there in 1922, when he was described as a beer retailer. Among local organisations which met at the pub was the Cowleigh and West Malvern Pig Club who, at their annual meeting in 1953, reported that 12 new members had enrolled and that a profit of £20 had been made. In 1955 the licence was transferred from George Bains to Geoffrey White, and in 1970 it went from Edward Bidwell, who was retiring, to Douglas Crook.

Rose and Peter Davis ran the pub for five years until they decided to retire in 1982 and sold it for £68,000 to Arthur, known as Terry, and Dawn Baldrey, who, according to a report in the *Malvern Gazette*, dated 13 May 1982, had 'big plans' for the place. 'They see it as being one of the best situated pubs in the town' the report added, 'and intend extending the premises to take advantage of the beautiful setting'. Lunchtime and evening meals would be provided.

And when she took over, Dawn had her six sisters and a sister-in-law to give a helping hand.

Unfortunately, things didn't work out as planned. The Cowleigh Arms was then sold in 1987 to Roger and Mary Howes, who turned it into a private dwelling. The present owners have been there since 1999.

Reminders of its previous life as a pub still exist with two cellars made of Malvern stone – the rest of the building is brick – with a water tank and bread oven, thought to have been used for making beer and bread on the premises. As you entered the premises, there used to be a semi-

*The sign on the wall still indicates that this was once the Cowleigh Arms*

glazed partition with a bar on either side, while at the back were two serveries and a long bar with a window looking out on a magnificent view. Two extensions were added including one for the kitchen, the staircase was moved from near the bar counter in the long bar to the front, the outside toilets have been incorporated into the house as an extra bedroom, and the large car park at the rear is now a garden. As a matter of interest, the pavement outside the property was not originally there, while the bay window by the front door was a later addition and is to be removed.

Behind the former Cowleigh Arms is Cowleigh Bank leading into Belmont Road where stands the **Cross Keys** pub, built about 150 years ago, and which may also have been known as the **Albion** or **Albion Vaults**, though the latter may have been a separate establishment that had but a brief existence. Cross Keys is a common sign in Christian heraldry, referring to St. Peter, to whom Jesus said: 'I will give unto thee the keys of the kingdom of heaven'. The Belmont pub's sign has brought forth scorn from Anthony Collis in his *The Inn Signs and Pub Names of Worcestershire*. He writes: 'A new sign has appeared at Malvern during October 2008. The image shows the pub's

*The Cross Keys in 2011*

*The picture on the Cross Keys sign which sets the pub on a palm-fringed beach causes a variety of responses*

not exactly photogenic building set in an exotic location – the result is plain daft! The previous sign showed two "cross" keys fighting in a boxing ring, which until now, I thought won the title of the silliest sign in the county – on a technical knockout.'

In 1901 John Luffman was the landlord and described as beer retailer. The Albion is mentioned in the *Malvern Gazette* dated 16 November 1914 when its licence was transferred to Mr. H.T. Mansell. Frank Holland, also described as a beer retailer, was in charge in 1922.

James and Lucy Bourne were mine hosts in the 1950s when they got into trouble with the police. The *Malvern Gazette*, of 16 September 1955, reported that Malvern magistrates were told the story of how two police officers, one dressed in overalls and the other in a sports coat and flannels, visited the Cross Keys on four occasions and saw betting slips and money passed. Mr. Bourne, the licensee, was charged with using his premises for the purpose of betting, and Mrs. Bourne was charged with assisting her husband. Both pleaded guilty. Mr. Bourne was fined £15 and Mrs. Bourne £20. Mr. Bourne said: 'This is not the only pub it's done in.'

In 1977 the landlord was Joe Taylor, who was also on the committee of the Malvern branch of the Licensed Victuallers Association.

In *Real Ale around the Malvern Hills* of 1996 by the Worcester branch of CAMRA, the Cross Keys was described as a 'community pub tucked away in a back street, with bar leading into games area with darts, pool and large screen TV. Features a model shopping precinct in the yard behind'. It may still be tucked away, but the pub has since then expanded quite considerably. The function room has been increased in size, the introduction of bedrooms allows the pub to do bed and breakfast, and the car park has been enlarged.

For the last 10 years, the Cross Keys has been run by Ann Holden and Reg Reynolds and during that time they have seen it become one of Malvern's top party and entertainment venues. Described as a sports bar/fun pub with live music every week, it has five big screens, two HD projectors, two 50" plasmas and another 50" plasma outdoors, a function room for up to 100 people, and two skittle alleys.

The main bar area has three separate seating areas with raised fixed seating around a large bamboo dance floor and stage area, a settee and seating area, and to the rear a contemporary seated area around dining-style tables. There is a large island servery bar. At the rear is a covered and heated smoking terrace with 40 seats, leading to a beer garden with 24 seats under a giant parasol. The Cross Keys also supports six football teams which play in various local leagues and five skittle teams.

# CHAPTER SEVEN

# West Malvern

The parish of West Malvern was formed in 1844 from parts of Mathon, Colwall and Cradley and was originally called the North Hill District until Richard Winnall, a churchwarden, came up with the present name. It stretches for about two and a half miles along the western slopes of the Malverns from the site where once the **Redan** pub stood on the north to the Wyche Cutting on the south.

Travelling along North Malvern Road near the 90 degree corner into West Malvern Road, on the right-hand side is a steep overgrown plot of land on a wooded hillside, previously numbered 62-64, which was the site of the former Redan pub. Looking at it today, it is almost unbelievable anyone would want to build anything there.

The strange story of the early days of the building was recalled by a former licensee in an article which appeared in the *Malvern Gazette* in the 1970s. Mrs. Gladys Corbett, who held the licence for six years after her husband, Percy, died in 1944 – he had taken it over in 1940 – said that while her husband was there he became very interested in the building's history and collected all the information that he could, putting it together in the following account:

> The road to West Malvern was remade in Victorian times, replacing with higher levels and improved curve and gradients an older and very primitive route still known as the Old Cradley Road. In places these roads run parallel, separated by extremely steep hillside slopes, and in the late fifties of the last century [19th century], a local tradesman more enterprising than prudent selected one of these slopes as a site for a house and business premises to face the new road.
>
> The difference in elevation between front and rear involved a structure so like a fortress that by common consent it was named the Redan, after one of the two great Russian strongholds at Sebastopol, famous in the recent Crimean War. The cost was enormous and impoverished the builder, who later obtained grim compensation. 'An Englishman's home is his castle' and the Redan became that of its owner.

A creditor obtained against him a committal order for non-payment of a judgement debt, but found the Redan impregnable. There the debtor immured himself and 'held the fort', only emerging during hours when arrest for debt was not permissible. After a time it was given out that he had left the country, and later that he was dead; but passers-by reported occasional glimpses of a spectrelike figure stealing furtively through the gloaming and a great story grew up.

As time passed the mystery deepened and it was more than 20 years before it was cleared up by actual death. For that long the stubborn debtor had kept the law at bay by self-incarceration.

The imposing three-storey building, also described as a huge, ugly place, which may have been inhabited by the ghost of its former occupant, did not prevent the Redan from becoming a public house. From at least 1901 to 1925 the landlord was Mr. W. Bowers, described as a beer retailer, who instigated improvements to the inn including an extension to the smoke room, better domestic accommodation, and better sanitary arrangements. In 1910 large numbers of people gathered at the Redan corner to witness Halley's comet in the skies above Malvern.

In 1951, local historian Catherine Moody wrote: 'One of the most curious buildings of the town is the step-like Redan with its two entrances on the middle and lower floors. The slope of the hill is so steep that it forms the wall of the building.' That same year the licence was transferred from Mr. R.A. Steer to Ernest Darke, of Worcester. At some point a stolen lorry, failing to take the bend in the road, crashed through the railings, with its front wheels coming to rest inside the roof of the inn's privy, on which a customer was seated.

*The Redan* c.*1950 (Brian Iles)*

The Redan shut its doors for business in about 1968 when the landlady was Mrs. Colbert, and remained empty for five years before being bought in 1973 by Worcestershire County Council who intended to demolish it, at a cost of £30,000, and hand over the steeply sloping land on which it stood to the Malvern Hills Conservators. However, the derelict building was taken over by squatters as the building became the centre of a 'pull it down/convert it' controversy. Various ideas were put forward in an attempt to save the building, including using it as temporary accommodation for the homeless, turning it into three flats, changing its use from public house to private dwelling, and taking its top storey off to make it more presentable. In the end, in June 1980, the demolition contractors were sent in and the Redan fortress was levelled to the plateau on which it was built below the level of West Malvern Road.

From the Redan site one soon comes across, on the left-hand side, Lamb Bank and the still existing **Lamb Inn**, but in 2011 only just. During the week, it only opens in the evening and there have been several reports of its closing down. The lamb is of great Christian significance thanks to the passage in John 1:29 which reads 'Behold the Lamb of God, which taketh away the sins of the world', thus equating the lamb with Jesus Christ.

On a map of 1839 a beerhouse is shown on this site, owned by Thomas Archer and occupied by William Knott. At first it was called **Happy Jack** and not until the late 1850s was its name changed to the Lamb. Incidentally, Happy Jack probably alluded to a Jack Russell terrier which had recently been bred by a man of the same name and was regarded as a 'happy' dog.

Thomas Trigg, of the well-known Malvern Trigg family, was the proprietor for many years from at least 1901. During the first two decades of the 20th century, the Lamb was the venue for the annual dinner of various clubs and associations. On one notable occasion in 1910, dinner and entertainment were provided for members of the Football, Cricket, Quoits and Air Gun clubs. It also hosted meetings of the Manchester Unity of Oddfellows and also for the Hills Conservators, before they commenced their monthly 'perambulations'.

Later, the Lamb, now described as a hotel, was in the hands of the Macdonnell family with the licence being transferred in 1919 from Mrs. E.B. Macdonnell to Mr. A.Y.C. Macdonnell. Then in 1939 the Lamb was transferred from James Harris to Robert James.

After being repainted and acquiring a new sign, the Lamb hit the headlines, with the *Malvern Gazette* for 7 October 1949 proclaiming: 'Exception taken to Inn Sign. Affront to Christians'. The Rev. L.D. Heppenstall came out with all guns firing:

> Our local Lamb Inn displays a new sign depicting on both its sides the 'Lamb of God' bearing the banner of the cross and with its head backed by the halo combined with a cross (the halo confined to representations of our Lord Jesus Christ), the whole being the emblem of the Risen Lord.

Provided presumably by the brewers whose name it bears, this sign raises three questions:

First, does it call for congratulations from fellow Christians that these brewers and their representatives, the innkeepers, witness to the faith of Christ, and proclaim their allegiance and obedience to Him, so that they brew, distribute and retail their ales to the glory of God, true and just in all their dealings, in every way discourage drunkenness, scandal, gambling, bad language and the like; and generally continue as Christ's faithful soldiers and servants?

If all this is disowned or not acknowledged, perhaps there is an antiquarian motive. This used to be the sign of inns called Lamb and Flag, where the landowners (e.g. St. John's College, Oxford) were by name or heraldically connected with St. John the Baptist, who first addressed Jesus as 'Lamb of God' and consequently is sometimes depicted as carrying a lamb as in the Wilton Diptych. Does this sign then show some connection between the Lamb Inn and some owner whose name or crest recalls the Baptist?

Thirdly, if this inn sign indicates nothing but the brewers' care for artistic signs – a care much appreciated in the Midlands – it is a shocking affront to Christians to appropriate for that purpose one of their most cherished emblems. In that case, will not the brewers make amends by painting out their name from this sign, offering it to the Church of Ascension outside of which, if accepted, it would be an appropriate road sign, and replacing it at the Lamb Inn by a different design?

Mr. F.H. Mason, district manager for Flower and Son Ltd, the owners, was quick to respond:

> The new inn-sign at The Lamb is a copy of one which had been used by many trades in the City of London during the past three or four centuries. The sign is similar to the crest of the Merchant Taylors' Company, which was founded in the 13th century or earlier. The latter is the emblem of St. John the Baptist, the Company being entitled 'Taylors and Linen Armourers of the Fraternity of St. John the Baptist,' and the Chapel of St. John the Baptist in St. Paul's Cathedral was granted to the Company for daily service and prayers. Their hall was in Threadneedle Street, which derives its name from their trade.
>
> The sign has in the past been used by booksellers and confectioners as well as tailors and clothiers. Its connection with inns goes right back to the Middle Ages. It was originally known as the Lamb and Flag, and the Lamb is a much later contraction. Inns used to display this sign to convey sympathy with the Crusades to denote that the innkeeper would be glad to tend to the needs of pilgrims on their way to Holy Shrines, a worthy object which the present innkeeper would, I am sure, be pleased to emulate.

The matter lay fallow for several years until the *Malvern Gazette* came out with a lead story on 16 August 1957 with the heading 'Lamb Hotel sign to be replaced by new sign'. The paper had received a number of letters of complaint, including one from Canon Murray Walton, Vicar of Bromley, who wrote:

> As a visitor to Malvern may I say how shocked I have been to see as a sign of the Lamb Hotel not the conventional figure of a lamb, as one would naturally expect, but the recognised symbol of the Lamb of God. The use of such a symbol of the Christian faith as the sign of a public house is repugnant to all who value their religion; apart from the fact that it is a breach of good taste and liable to create a bad impression in those who visit this lovely spot. I cannot but believe that the landlord, had he been aware of the significance of the present sign, would have had it removed long ago, the more so because I understand it is giving offence to many people locally.

The *Gazette* added that at a recent meeting parishioners of St. James's considered a design for a new processional cross, and this was found to be exactly the same as that incorporated in the inn sign. Commented the vicar (the Rev. N.S.P. Baron): 'It is very unpleasant and distresses us all.' Mr. Baron said he had made no complaint to the inn owners because he felt the sign might have been put up in ignorance.

The Tied Trade Manager for Messrs. Flowers, the owners of the Lamb, responded to the latest discussion: 'This sign is now becoming rather worn, and

*The Lamb Inn in the 1970s (Malvern Museum)*

we will shortly be replacing it, and will select an alternate design when doing so.' In due course a new sign went up bearing the picture of an inoffensive lamb.

In the early 21st century, the Lamb, then owned by Punch Taverns, was run by Colin Robinson who decorated the main bar with flags of the world and inflatable dolls and sheep, and who built up the pub's reputation as a venue for local musicians, including a certain Nigel Kennedy who, at the time, was living in nearby Old Hollow. Colin himself played trombone and trumpet in a brass band. He quit in the summer of 2008 following a review of the Lamb's licence by West Mercia police after they started a clampdown on vandalism and anti-social behaviour in West Malvern.

After a brief spell under another landlord, the Lamb was closed for a while until it was taken over in November 2009 by Mark Stimson, who continued running it as a music-lovers' pub with gigs, open-mike nights and festivals. However, Mark left about a year later and Punch Taverns sold the property to unnamed buyers.

In May 2011, West Malvern Parish Council were told by Worcester-based architects Boughton Butler, acting on behalf of the pub's new owners, that there were three options for the Lamb's future: keeping the pub in its present form, developing the site for housing, or reaching a compromise where a pub is kept in some form while developing part of the site.

As for the current building, the three-storey property is of traditional brick construction under three pitched roofs and has a cavernous main bar with a stage to one side and another, smaller bar by the main entrance. There is spacious living accommodation upstairs and cellars in the basement. Outside is a car park and a beer garden.

*The Lamb Inn in 2011*

*Once the Mount Inn*

Further along West Malvern Road on the right hand side is Mount House, next to Harmony House, which offers B & B, which is one of three flats at 182-186 which used to be the **Mount Inn**, possibly so called because there was a steep climb up to the pub at the rear. In 1866 a conveyance refers to '... those three (formerly two) dwelling houses ... carpenters and butchers shop, school room and other buildings ... called The Mount'. By the following year the northern end of the building had become an inn while the school continued above the butcher's shop next door until the early 1870s.

The Mount is mentioned in *Littlebury's Directory* of 1873, and again in the *Stevens' Annual* of 1901, when John Clifford is recorded as being the proprietor. In a report of the Malvern Licensing Sessions, the *Malvern Gazette* of 15 February 1918 stated that the licence of the Mount was transferred from Edward Freeland (then serving in the Army) to Emily Freeland, presumably his wife. Edward survived the war and was in charge in 1922. Owned by the Worcester brewers Lewis-Clarke & Co, the Mount continued to trade until the 1950s, when it closed down and the property was converted into flats.

Further along West Malvern Road at the left-hand turning into Westminster Bank is Westminster House, a long white building which for many years was a hotel of the same name. It started out life as the **Fox and Hounds**, one of the earliest buildings in West Malvern and probably dating from the 1820s. In 1841 it was the only hostelry in this area advertising in *Bentley's Directory*. The change of name came about soon afterwards at the suggestion of Mr. Winnel, the church-warden, as a compliment to the Dean and Chapter of Westminster, who had been Lords of the Manor of Mathon since 1542, when it was given to Westminster Abbey by Henry VIII out of lands belonging to the Abbey of Pershore.

The church rate book for 1856 mentioned a hotel in St. James's district with Samuel Haywood as the occupier with a rateable value of £27 10s, the rate collected being 6s 10½d.

In August 1860, the following advert appeared in the *Morning Advertiser*:

Mr. and Mrs. Haywood, proprietors of the **Westminster Arms Hotel** respectfully invite public attention to their establishment. It will be their object to secure patronage both by the moderation of their charges and by the strictest attention to the comfort of those who honour them with their support. Families of two members and upwards are accommodated with board and lodging from £2 2s. per week; children under 12 years at half price. A spacious coffee room has been recently added to the hotel, where persons can be provided with breakfasts, dinners, teas, suppers and other refreshment on moderate terms. A convenient smoking room has also been added. A lock-up coach house. Carriages and horses for hire.

In February 1879, the Oddfellows friendly society was founded at the hotel and in May of the same year they held their first fête followed by a ball with a four hour licence extension.

Guests in the 1870s included Dr. Benjamin Jowett, the Master of Balliol, and Dr. Charles Gore, later to become Bishop of Worcester, who worked at the hotel on his *Lux Mundi*, a series of studies in the Religion of the Incarnation. Edward Burrow, in his *Malvern Illustrated*, dated 1895, wrote that the Westminster Arms was 'an excellent hotel, which has a very widespread reputation among visitors'.

Between 1874 and 1904, the proprietress, Miss R. Martin, kept two visitors' books with tributes from hundreds of guests to the very high standard of food and homely comfort. Many stayed for weeks and sometimes, as in the case of Lord Byron, for several months. One man even said, 'the Westminster Arms is an antidote to suicide'. The name of Stanley Baldwin, the future prime minister, can be seen and two other prime ministers stayed there earlier, Sir Henry Campbell-Bannerman in 1907 and A.J. Balfour in 1909. Other visitors included Dr. William Temple (Archbishop of Canterbury from 1942-44), the poet Robert Bridges, Dean Inge (author and dean of St Paul's Cathedral), Sir Jesse Boot (who transformed his father's firm into the national high street store, Boots the Chemists), and Walter de la Mare, the poet and novelist.

At the beginning of the 20th century the proprietor was William Martin, possibly the son, who would often ride about on an ancient pony which eventually died in 1907 at the grand old age of 32.

From at least 1916 to 1922 the proprietor was James Phillips and Charles Longley had taken over by 1928, when the Westminster Arms was described as a 'first class hotel, beautifully situated, officially appointed to the RAC, garage and stabling'. Mr. Longley was still there in 1930 when, in an advert in the *Malvern Gazette*, he described the Westminster as 'a first class, comfortable hotel amidst lovely scenery, sunshine and mountain air'.

William Rellie took over the licence in 1942, but was killed in the Second World War and was replaced by his wife. Dennis Cottrell, another Malvern resident, revealed in *Malvern Voices Wartime – an Oral History* that he followed in his father's footsteps by working at the Westminster Arms. In 1944, at the age of 13, he left school on the Friday and started work there on the Saturday morning:

At 8 o'clock I was taken round the bedroom doors where all the shoes were outside and I had to clean them all. I also had to do all the odd jobs like coal for the fires and polishing the dance floor.

American officers used to come up there nearly every night from Wood Farm Camp to the dances and go in the bar where there were lots of local girls. The lady who kept the hotel lost her husband early in the war and she was very friendly with one of these American officers. I used to clean his car for him and he would give me seven and sixpence, which was quite a lot then. The Cadbury brothers used to stay at the hotel for a holiday every year and they were big tippers too. As soon as their taxi pulled away from the door I had to carry their bags upstairs and they gave me tips.

His wage was £1 5s a week. Mr. Cottrell's older sisters also worked at the hotel.

In the *Malvern Gazette* of 5 May 1945, an advert appeared about the Westminster Hotel stating it 'has pleasure in announcing Summertime Amenities – teas served on the new terraced gardens – also cocktails, aperitifs and iced drinks. Suppers to 11pm. Dinner dances on Fridays and Saturdays to Freddie Waites' Westminster Swing Quartette. Book tables now for VE celebrations. Weddings, banquets, private dances and "Diners" in time'.

The hotel's popularity was probably at its peak during the war and, as Mr. Cottrell mentioned, it was a great favourite with Americans, for whom Mrs. Rellie put on barbecues and other entertainment.

In April 1956, the hotel closed as licensed premises and later that year changed ownership. The property was eventually acquired by St. James's School, a grand building located across the road, and converted into a music school. St. James's later became part of Malvern St. James's School in Great Malvern and the West Malvern premises were purchased by the evangelical Christian mission, the Elim Foursquare Gospel Alliance, and, after a £5 million refurbishment, is now used as its training centre, the Regents Theological College.

Continuing along West Malvern Road one comes to a rough track on the right-hand side leading to the Dingle, and so to **The Brewers Arms**, which dates back to the early 1830s. Apparently Edmund Pitt enclosed church land and built a new house and a shed which he used as a pub. But in 1839 a parish meeting decided he could not use it as a pub any more and that he should pay £1 10s per annum to acknowledge the enclosure. It was not until 1871 that it became a pub again with Henry Turle, beerhouse keeper from Wiltshire, as tenant. In 1873, when Samuel Ruck was the licensee, it was given the name Brewers Arms in recognition of the fact that beer was brewed on the premises.

Not surprisingly with its name emblazoned on the roof, the pub was, and still is, popular with walkers on the Malvern Hills. Originally there were two bars, public and lounge, with the entrance leading to an off sales with window. Bed and Breakfast was also offered. Most of the nearby housing was originally built

*The rear of the Brewers Arms in c.1960s (First Paige)*

*Firemen dealing with the fire at the Brewers in 1992*

for quarry workers. In 1919 the licence was transferred from Thomas Lewis to Alfred Bicheno and by 1922 the licence was held by Mrs. Bicheno.

In the 1970s the landlord was John Perry, whose attractive daughter, Lyn, when not taking part in beauty competitions, sometimes served behind the bar. In April 1977, at the age of 20, she won the Miss ATV competition and in September of that year she was chosen as runner up in the Miss Great Britain competition. The following year she came third in the Miss England contest.

After Ted and Barbara Ekin ran the Brewers Arms in the 1980s, it was taken over by Peter Wood who, in 1992, found the pub's future hanging in the balance following a fire which almost destroyed the property. While repairs were being carried out, Mr. Wood continued to operate the pub from the family room annexe serving beer straight from the barrel. Four months later the Brewers Arms reopened with one open bar instead of the lounge and public bars, but retaining both counters, and featuring traditional-style woodwork of a high quality. International violinist Nigel Kennedy, who used the

*Don and Eileen Long, licensees of the Brewers Arms in the late 1960s (First Paige)*

*The Brewers Arms in 2011, its name emblazoned on the roof to attract walkers up on the Malvern Hills*

pub as his local, helped to raise funds for the restoration by performing in a fund-raising concert in Worcester Cathedral.

George and Vanessa Hillard ran the pub for six years before, in 2005, Trevor Marston and his partner Sue Adamson took over and made it into a community pub. On Sundays the morning papers and breakfast were available, while in the evening the Cheese Club met, and customers were encouraged to bring along exotic cheeses for each other to sample. Fish and chips, at £5, were delivered to pensioners in the village and curry nights were held at £1 an item. The pub also sponsored two cricket teams and two women's hockey teams, had its own quiz team, produced its own newspaper, and arranged live music at least once a week. Trevor also organised other events such as a 'Red Knees Day' crawl to the top of Worcestershire Beacon. He was joined by about 200 people who donned elbow pads for the gruelling crawl, which raised hundreds of pounds for Noah's Ark Trust and St. James' Primary School.

Outside was a small 1920s black and white tea room, which became a Sunday school and is now used as an overspill dining area. And at the end of a raised walkway is a magnificent view across the Herefordshire countryside to the Welsh hills. In fact, the view is so good that in 2005 it was recognised by the *Morning Advertiser* and the brewers Eldridge Pope as the Best Pub View in Britain. And in 2009 the Brewers Arms was named as Worcestershire's top country pub of the year by the county branch of CAMRA.

Then on New Year's Day 2010, tragedy struck – Trevor Marston suddenly died at the age of 48. But later that year, in September, there was reason to celebrate as the Brewers Arms was named Pub of the Year by the Worcestershire branch of CAMRA. Trevor's partner, Sue Adamson, who took over the licence, told the *Malvern Gazette*: 'It is a fitting tribute to Trevor and all the work and effort he put into the pub. He really was the master behind it all, and his personality, drive and hard work are the main reasons why the pub is so popular as it is now.'

Travelling further along West Malvern Road one turns left back into Malvern and the **Wyche Inn** is to be found on the left-hand side. It started life, though, as the **Herefordshire House**, a small inn near the Church of the Good Shepherd at Upper Colwall in Herefordshire at the beginning of the 19th century. The pub must have been well frequented by men working on the construction of the new Wyche Road in 1836, with a cutting blasted through the Malvern Hills, and by quarry workers. Then, in 1860, a railway tunnel was also built through the Hills with even thirstier navvies. The inn, then run by James Bailey, flourished to such an extent that Bailey decided to transfer the business to a better site across the county boundary once the project was completed in 1861. Mr. Bailey duly built a new pub on its present site, retaining the same name, and also built six cottages alongside.

While all the road, railway and quarry work was going on other pubs, or beerhouses, grew up on both sides of the Wyche Cutting including the **Rock Inn**, **Cherry Tree** and **Imperial**, none of which have survived, and the **Rose and Crown**, later to become the home of Arthur Troyte Griffith, immortalised in Elgar's Enigma Variations as the seventh enigma. Small roses and crowns painted on some of the internal doors can still be seen today.

*The Herefordshire Arms in the early 1900s*

*The Herefordshire Arms in the early 1970s (Malvern Museum)*

In 1901, Charles Chapple, described as a beer and spirit retailer, was in charge of the Herefordshire House, while in 1922 the inn was owned by Spreckley Brothers, the Worcester brewers, with Mr. W. Spawton as manager.

Whitbread became the new owners when they took over Spreckley Brothers, but in 1969 they closed the pub as being 'sub-standard'. It was then bought as a freehouse by Derek and Averill Probin, who told the *Malvern Gazette* they were looking for 'a quiet life in a small two-bar pub', after running a pub in Tamworth for nine years. The Probins, who have boxer dogs called Whisky and Brandy, were at a loss to understand why Whitbread failed to exploit the potential of an inn commanding one of the most impressive views in the county. They carried out a modernisation plan and reopened in January 1970 as the **Herefordshire Arms**, with drinks on the house.

Then in 1978 the Probins opened a new 120 seat restaurant, called the Wyche Inn Restaurant, built above a new bar, the Cottage Bar, which was made possible when Mr. Probin bought the six neighbouring cottages when they came on the market. A children's room and garden were also provided. The pub itself was renamed the **Wyche Inn** after the road which, as the name implies, was part of a route taking salt from Droitwich to Wales.

At the beginning of the 21st century, the Probins sold the inn to John Marshall and, since January 2010, it has been run by Stephanie Daly and her partner Tony Kelton. They now offer four letting rooms, with en suite and great views. There is a brass plaque on the bar counter and a stool in honour of customer Chris Barron, who has been coming to the pub on a regular basis since 1968. He also has his own glass with Lord Hobson engraved on it, in recognition of his favourite beer.

# CHAPTER EIGHT

# Malvern Wells

Malvern Wells, previously called East Malvern, was formed in 1894 from parts of Hanley Castle, Welland and Great Malvern, and owes its development to Malvern's 19th-century boom years as a spa town. Lying on the eastern slopes of the Malvern Hills, it takes its name from the local wells, or springs, such as Holy Well and Eye Well. The land was granted to John Hornyold, lord of the manor, by Queen Elizabeth I in 1558 on the understanding that any traveller should be able to draw rest and refreshment from the Holy Well. This still applies today.

Refreshment of another kind is available from the **Railway Inn** near All Saints' Church on the Wells Road, the A449 to Ledbury, at its junction with Peachfield Road. Originally called the **New Inn**, it was built in the mid-19th century at a strategic point close to the Malvern Tollgate and to the forthcoming Malvern Wells railway station. The gate was moved in 1854 to a new site 100 yards south of the inn. Beyond it along the Wells Road, there was still open country as far as the Hornyold Arms.

*The Railway Inn in 2011*

*The sign for the Railway Inn*

The railway station opened in 1861, the time when presumably the inn changed its name, but the station was destroyed by a fire and a new one had to be built, which opened in 1864. A previous sign at the inn showed the famous Rocket engine designed by George Stephenson, who was linked with a tragic accident. William Huskisson, MP, who was brought up at nearby Birtsmorton Court, was the first person to be killed in a railway accident, this occurring at the opening of Stephenson's Liverpool & Manchester Railway in 1830.

The Railway first appears in a trade directory for 1868 and James Griffiths was the occupier in 1888 and 1892. It was during this time that Mr. Griffiths introduced a token which could be exchanged for drinks up to the value of 3d. The token may have been used in connection with the inn's skittle alley, which still existed up to the 1990s. A building next to the pub was used as a railway workshop and two tunnels, since blocked up, probably led to a quarry.

At some point the inn also served as a garage with two petrol pumps on the forecourt with a drive-in on either side. This probably came to an end in the late 1960s.

In about 1995 the pub underwent a major refurbishment with the original two separate bars made into one large open plan bar including a dining area and the skittle alley turned into letting accommodation with three bedrooms.

Owned by Marston's, the Railway Inn has seen several licensees come and go in recent years. Marston's have now taken the pub under their Retail Agreement umbrella with a manager in control and the emphasis on food. It closed during the summer of 2011 before reopening.

Further along the Wells Road heading out of town and close to its junction with Hanley Road stands a large white building converted into flats which was once the **Hornyold Arms Hotel**, originally called the **Admiral Benbow**. Believed to have opened before 1825, it probably received its name from the fine 18th-century house opposite and the latter's connections with relatives of the famous admiral. The house was called Ruby, the name of his last ship, in which Mr. J. Benbow lived in 1820 and Richard Benbow in 1851 as a lodging house keeper.

In 1840, Mr. T.K. Cooke, 'victualler (posting)' was listed in a directory for the Admiral Benbow followed by Jane Sinnick, victualler, in 1845. Thomas Cooke was victualler in 1851 but Jane, who may have been Mr. Cooke's partner, is mentioned in 1860 and again in 1862. By 1876 the landlord was

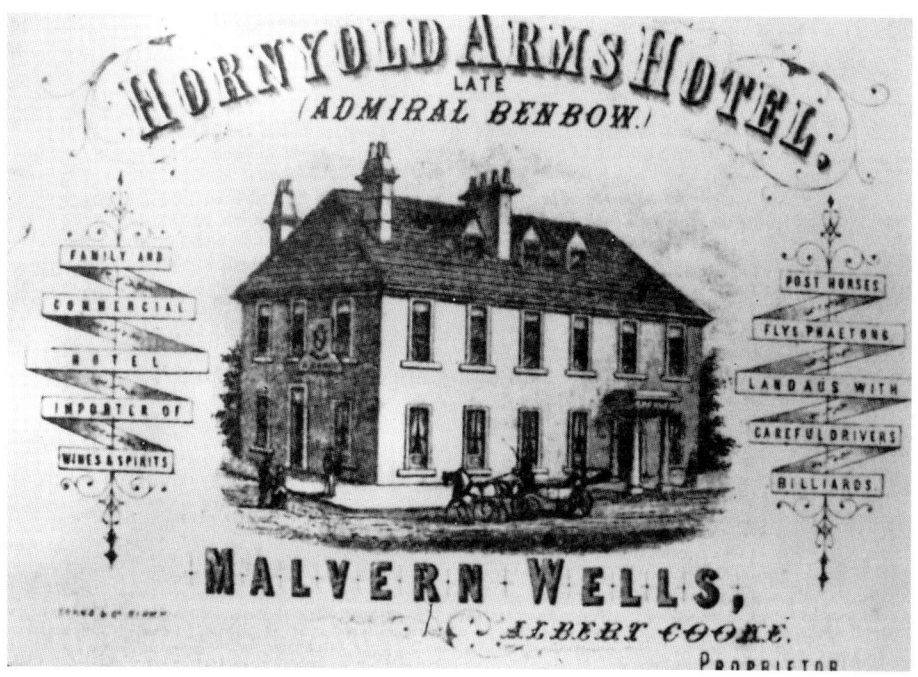

*It was under Albert Cooke that the name was changed from the Admiral Benbow to the Hornyold Arms Hotel*

Albert Cooke, possibly the son, and the hotel had changed its name to the Hornyold Arms, in honour of the Hornyold family who owned a great deal of land in Malvern Wells and had their ancestral hall some three miles away.

An advert in 1876 describes the Hornyold Arms as a family and commercial hotel and importer of wines and spirits. Facilities included post horses, flys, phaetons and landaus with careful drivers, plus billiards.

The *Malvern Gazette* of 11 January 1901 ran the following story:

> A very pleasant gathering was held at the Hornyold Hotel when members of the combined Fire Brigades of Malvern and Malvern Wells met for a dinner and smoking concert. The room had been lavishly decorated with national flags and, in addition, brightly polished helmets and hose nozzles, lengths of hose and life lines, and firemens' axes made most effective and appropriate decoration for the walls. A substantial dinner was provided by the new host and hostess, Mr. and Mrs. Tallboys. Also presentation of long service medals.

A brochure on the hotel, dated about 1910, stated that single rooms were available from £3 3s 6d and doubles from £7 7s a week. For a meal served in bedroom there was an extra charge of 15s 6d, while early morning tea cost 6d. Visitors' servants could be provided with board and residence at a cost of

9s per day, or two and a half guineas per week.

In 1922 Lawrence Hanson was the proprietor and in 1928 Mrs. Walter Smith was in charge. In 1942 the licence was transferred from Walter Hanson to Mrs. Edith Lane, who later carried out alterations to the hotel. Despite the property being expanded in the mid 1950s when Jack George was the resident director, the hotel closed in the 1960s and was converted into flats.

Almost opposite is Holy Well Road and a short distance along this road on the left-hand side is a pillared gateway with a drive leading to a large white building which has been converted into flats, but was once the **Essington Hotel**, named after Samuel Essington who

*The Hornyold Arms with a procession of horse-drawn carriages stopped outside (Brian Iles)*

*The Hornyold Arms was obviously popular with motorists, but as vehicles changed so did the bushes and trees grow (lower image, First Paige)*

*The Hornyold Arms was converted into flats in the 1960s, and is now minus its entrance porch, while the street level seems to have risen*

built the property in 1820. There was some conjecture that it originated as a private house in which Admiral Essington lived. There was indeed an Admiral William Essington, but he died childless in 1816 in London. He was survived by his widow, who moved to Birmingham, and three male cousins.

According to John Chambers in *A General History of Malvern* dated 1823, the hotel had hot and cold baths attached to the building, a wood, a garden and a hermitage. Rates varied from 8 to 14 shillings a week for a room, plus 6 shillings a day for food. These rates included the provision of wine and spirits, but tea and sugar were charged extra. Apparently the hotel became popular with honeymoon couples.

John Chambers quotes a poem written by Mr. Bissett, of Leamington, author of several literary productions, who stayed at the hotel:

> At Malvern Wells, where health bears the belle,
> All visitors notice the famous hotel,
> By Essington kept, where you meet with good cheer
> Good wines and good liquors, good ale and good beer;
> Of damp beds and rough treatment, no person's in danger,
> Whilst civil attention is paid to each stranger;
> Then honour the house if you please, if you call,
> The Essingtons cheerly will wait on you all:
> To serve you with zeal, and obey each behest,
> They'll endeavour to please you by doing their best.

Rules and orders to be observed at the Essington Hotel included the following:

1. Each person to be provided with a lodging room, properly furnished, from eight shillings to fourteen shillings per week; and so in proportion for as many rooms as any lady or gentleman may have occasion for. Each person to pay one shilling and sixpence a week for candles. Five shillings will also be charged for the servants of the house, for each bed room.
2. Each lodger to pay two pounds two shillings per week (or six shillings per day, for a shorter period), for their board, which includes every article except tea and sugar; and twenty-four shillings and sixpence per week, or three shillings and sixpence per day, for each servant's breakfast, dinner and supper; and if a single bed room is required for a servant, then to pay five shillings per week for such room.
3. Each person to be supplied with wine spirits, etc by the master of the house, and to find themselves with tea and sugar; or the master of the house will supply them tea and sugar, charging the same.
4. The company to assemble and dine together, at the public table, in the great room, at three o'clock each day: the first bell will be rung at half past two, and the dinner bell at three o'clock. No lodger to dine privately in the house, unless sickness render it necessary.

Other rules included: 'No petition from travelling beggars suffered to be presented, nor any petition whatever obtruded on the company, or hung up in the long room, without permission of the master of the house. No deductions

*The Essington Hotel*

for children. Fires to be paid for. Dogs will be charged for, but will not be permitted in the parlour or long room.'

By 1830 Mary Essington, presumably Samuel's widow, was in charge. In about the 1870s, the proprietor was Victor Tussaud, who had been part proprietor of Madame Tussaud's Exhibition in London. At such time a brake passed the hotel to and from Great Malvern every few minutes.

In his autobiography, *Fourscore Years*, Mr. G.G. Coulton, who was schoolmaster at Wells House, when it became a preparatory school for boys, wrote that his classroom had a magnificent view and he could see both the Hornyold Arms and the Essington Hotel, 'with an enormous whitehart cherry tree, glorious alike in spring and summer and autumn. In good years, all through June, a gypsy family encamped under the tree with their antique shot-guns, hired to keep off the birds by some fruiterer who had contracted to buy the whole crop ...'.

The hotel was sold at an auction in 1919 when the whole of the Hornyold estate, amounting to 3,266 acres and numerous properties, was sold off. Most of the Essington's grounds, described as pleasure gardens with a number of walks, were later sold on and developed for housing.

For some years the hotel was owned by Walter Hanson who, on his death in 1953, left the property 'together with furniture, effects and goodwill' to four staff members, housekeeper Julia Jones, head waitress Annie Young, junior waitress May Evans and general helper Arthur Herbert. The four were said to have helped to make the hotel into one of the most popular in the district. But by 1959 the Essington was owned by Mr. and Mrs. Peter Emms, who, in just under a year, transformed the hotel into an establishment catering for all tastes. In February 1960, Joe Erskine, ex-British and Empire Heavyweight champion, reopened the hotel at a champagne party given by the owners.

However, in May of the same year, the hotel was sold again, this time to Miss D.M. Smith and Miss E.T. Such, with Mr. D.K. Reeve as manager. In June the new proprietors gave a cocktail party at the hotel, at which Noelle Gordon, star of ATV's Lunch Box programme, was guest of honour. The hotel eventually closed down in the early 1990s, was converted into flats and is now known as Essington House.

Known locally as 'the hotel on the hill', **The Cottage in the Wood** is, as the name suggests, tucked away amongst hillside trees close to the Holy Well high above Malvern village. Dating from the late 1790s, it was originally built as a summer residence of the Hornyold family and comprised three buildings with, at the heart, a former Georgian dower house.

The property was part of the Blackmore Park seat of Thomas Hornyold, the Hornyold and Lygon families being the two largest landowners in the area. When Thomas died in 1859 the estate passed to his nephew John Vincent Gandolphi, Count of the Genoese Republic, a title bestowed on him by the Pope. On the count's death in 1918, his heirs divided up the estate and sold it in 500 lots in 1919. Lot 107 was what now is The Cottage in the Wood, then a private house let to a Mrs. Russell for £125 per annum rent and called simply The Cottage. There was also The Gardener's Cottage, now Beech Cottage, and The Stabling, including a pigsty, later renamed the Coach House, in the loft of which the then owners arranged recitals including, so it is believed, some by Elgar, who lived not far away at Craeg Lea from 1899 to 1904.

Surrounded by seven acres of natural woodland, the three buildings were turned into a hotel later described as having 'a luxurious yet informal air'. The new proprietors in 1966 were Mr. and Mrs. Michael Ross who upgraded the restaurant and made it available to non-residents. The number of bedrooms was increased to 30 with the addition of a separate Coach House comprising eight bedrooms with their own bathrooms.

In 1976, when Michael Ross was listed as the owner, The Cottage in the Wood was designated as being of 'outstanding merit' with the AA award of two red stars instead of the customary black stars. In 1977 it became a member of Prestige Hotels, a select group of 36 hotels, giving it access to better marketing.

For the last 23 years, the hotel has been owned and run by John and Sue Pattin and family. The hotel is now a member of Signpost, which recommends selected hotels. In 2003 the original Coach House was demolished and replaced with a new building called The Pinnacles.

*An early engraving of The Cottage in the Wood (Malvern Museum)*

Just above The Cottage in the Wood is **Wells House**, now apartments, but previously a school and before that a hotel, built in 1741 as Malvern's first water cure hotel having been built near both the Holy Well and the Eye Well. The Holy Well was in fact the earliest recorded water bottling site in England.

*Wells House in the late 19th century (top) and in 2011 (bottom)*

Alterations to the hotel were carried out in 1761 and 1769. In 1781 the weekly charge was 14 shillings, with five shillings extra for the superior Red Rooms.

At the beginning of the 19th century, Wells House was owned by Mr. William Steer, who sometime before 1817 also opened Rock House, right next to the Holy Well, with private apartments. In his *A General History of Malvern – A Guide*, dated 1823, John Chambers wrote: 'This Hotel is the resort of much company, drawn by the contiguity of a charming landscape: here is a table d'hote, with the usual accommodations of houses of this description, billiard table, piano fortes, chess boards, etc.' Mr. Chambers continued: 'This lodging house is seldom visited in the winter, the air here being very sharp during that season, but, in the summer months, this spot is most delightful ...'.

A regular penny post-office was established at the hotel, added Mr. Chambers, from 6 May to 6 November, which went out every day, except Mondays. The remainder of the year, letters were circulated on Tuesdays, Thursdays and Saturdays only and a person was sent to Worcester for letters on those days which the mail did not arrive at Little Malvern. Divine service was performed every Sunday morning, from May to October, at one o'clock, by Mr. Turberville, the rector of Hanley, or his curate, or any visitor of the clerical profession who might be staying at the hotel.

With a dwindling interest in the Holy Well, Wells House closed down as a hotel in the mid 19th century and reopened as a preparatory school for boys. One of the teachers was no less a person than Edward Elgar, who augmented his income by teaching music there. Wells House school closed in 1991. Acquired in 2005, the building has been totally refurbished with a new interior and a huge glass plated front entrance, and converted into 18 apartments and four houses.

Another inn believed to have existed in Malvern Wells was the **Lord Nelson**, mentioned in a guide for 1855 when it was run by John Millner, victualler.

# CHAPTER NINE

# Barnards Green, Poolbrook, Guarlford & The Hanleys

Barnards Green is one of Malvern's main population areas with several large housing developments around a busy shopping centre. An interesting feature is its pear-shaped roundabout where seven roads all meet. It is also the home of QinetiQ, specialists in aerospace, defence and security.

In Clarence Road opposite the Malvern Parish primary school is the old **Cavalry Arms** recently renamed **The Morgan** following the demise of the Link Top pub of the same name. Mentioned as a beer retailer in *Littlebury's Directory* of 1873, the pub used to boast a sign showing the badge of the local regiment, the Queens Own Worcestershire Hussars. Now it shows one of the locally made Morgan sports cars.

In 1901 the proprietor was Charles White, while in 1922, the proprietor was George White, possibly Charles's son. In 1964 the pub's licence was transferred to Mrs. Ivy Noctor, widow of the former licensee, Bernard Noctor. The pub had a large bar with darts and a pool table, and a smaller lounge.

The pub was owned by West Country Breweries – their iconic Best in the West plaque can still be seen by the front entrance – before being taken over by Whitbread in 1963 and then by Punch Taverns. The bar used to be adorned with regimental plaques presented by soldiers serving at the nearby RSRE (Royal Signals and Radar Establishment) before it became QinetiQ.

More recently, the Cavalry had a chequered career, being sold, closed and reopened on more than one occasion with a succession of tenants, and was in a run-

*The sign for the revamped Morgan*

down condition, until in 2009 the owners, Punch Taverns, agreed to sell it to Wye Valley Brewery, based at Stoke Lacy, who already owned the Barrels in Hereford and the Rose and Crown in Bromyard. As Stoke Lacy was the home of Mr. H.F.S. Morgan, founder of the famous car company, the brewery decided to call their new pub The Morgan. After a major refurbishment, later in 2009 with Morgan Motors present with two of their cars, the pub reopened under managers Daniel Grice and Abby Wright.

In nearby Court Road as it merges with St. Andrews Road stands a substantial building which for many years was run as a children's nursery but which at one time was the **Fountain Inn**.

The Fountain is mentioned in *Littlebury's Directory* of 1873, when it was described as a beer retailer. At the turn of the century the pub was rebuilt with the addition of stables and in 1900 the landlord, Harry Smith, successfully applied for a full licence. In 1904 the landlord was still Harry Smith, with Walter, possibly his son, having taken over by 1916. In 1922 the proprietor was Mr. T. Alderman, while in 1928 the inn was run by Mrs. Harriette Gould.

After the Second World War, the Fountain was run by Capt. Jack Lenham, who, in 1952, received the Meritorious Service Medal for which he had been recommended 17 years before in 1935. Capt. Lenham took an active part in the Barnards Green branch of the British Legion.

*The building that was the Fountain Inn*

*Details of the stonework above the ground-floor window on the front bay*

The pub was taken over by Bob and Iris Thomas in 1958, when their beer cost just 11d a pint and was brewed by Spreckley's, a Worcester brewery operating until 1968. Mr. and Mrs. Thomas, who retired from the trade in 1981, told the *Malvern Gazette* they had seen a transformation of the traditional idea of the British pub during their time at the Fountain, and felt that the changes had been for the better.

'Whilst we have been here, darts and cribbage have mainly been replaced by pool tables, space invaders and bandits,' he said. Mr. Thomas, who was secretary of the Malvern branch of the Licensed Victuallers Association for 23 years, saw public houses becoming social centres for the whole family rather than drinking refuges for men.

The pub was then taken over by Martin and Sheila Jones and later by Bob Thomas, who was the last landlord when the Fountain ceased to trade in the late 1980s, early 1990s. It was then run as a nursery for 10 years until in 2008 it was sold and is now rented by Kenneth Gough, who lives with his family upstairs. At the time of going to print, he was planning to open the ground floor of the building as the Fountain Stores and use the upstairs as offices for an internet venture.

On the corner of Barnards Green Road and Wilton Road is the **Foresters Arms**, an unpretentious community pub which has seen a more illustrious past. The name could relate to the fact that the area around Malvern was part of the royal hunting ground of Malvern Chase and it is believed the building may have started life as a shooting lodge for the Beauchamp family. A more mundane origin may be a reference to the Ancient Order of Foresters, a friendly society.

There is, apparently, a photograph taken at least a hundred years ago showing the inn's walls covered in ivy and a dirt road

*The sign for the Foresters Arms*

*The Foresters Arms*

to one side. The landlord in 1901 was Albert Blake and by 1922 Frank Rudd was the proprietor. Frank, who was also licensee of the Nag's Head at Malvern Link, invited Wally Weston, a veteran of the First World War who had his left leg amputated after fighting in the Dardanelles, to become manager of the pub. 'It wasn't long before the Foresters Arms became a centre for anyone interested in sport, but particularly boxing,' wrote Frederick Covins in his book *Malvern Between the Wars*.

'Wally began to train boxers including five who became Lonsdale belt winners,' he added. 'He trained alongside his boxers, running eight miles with them every morning and sparring with them in between running the pub.

'The same enthusiasm Wally brought to living, not unnaturally, affected the clientele of the Foresters Arms; it was in those days, the place to be. Whenever the aristocracy came to Malvern they, sooner or later, found their way to the Foresters and Wally Weston; cards were played regularly for crates of champagne, a case of white port figured daily in the spirits book, whisky and milk was the favourite tipple and even royalty have been known to find their way to the Foresters after a garden party at Madresfield Court.'

Mr. Covins went on: 'Fred Astaire's sister, Adele, once danced on the tables in the Foresters and once, after taking one of his boxers (Ben Foord) to Berlin to fight Schmeling during the Nazi reign before the war, Wally received a very unwelcome visit from Oswald Mosley and a group of blackshirts. During World War II Wally served in the Merchant Navy as a cook.'

After the war, Wally Weston returned to the Foresters Arms and remained there until the early 1960s. Ted Avery was the landlord until 1980 and Brian Cherry until 2002, when the present landlord, David Rudd (not related to Frank Rudd of the Nag's Head) took over. In 2007 Mr. Rudd, who has known the pub since 1979 when he was a boy, and the owners, Marston's Pub Company, jointly funded a major refurbishment including a new bar, new fixtures and fittings, and an outdoor seating area. Originally there were three separate bars including a smoke room and a snug, then it had become two with one wall knocked down, and this renovation created just one open plan room. An alcove in the lounge used to be a kitchen. Part of the pub was sold off and is now a private dwelling. To one side of the pub is a room measuring 11ft by 24ft with a pool table, which once had a boxing ring and was used by many champion boxers, including Jack London, for training purposes.

At the junction of Pickersleigh Road and Madresfield Road is a spanking new Tesco Express shop which was built in 2011 on the site of the former **New Gas Tavern**, also known as the **Langland Arms** and the **Gas Tavern**. Three two-bedroom town houses have also been built on the site.

First mention of the Gas Tavern, no doubt named because of its close proximity to the gas works, also since demolished, was in *Kelly's Directory* of 1860. In the 1890s the landlord was John Lee, described as a beer retailer, who introduced a token, with his name and the name of the pub on it, to the value of 3d which could be exchanged for drinks. Mrs. Lee, presumably his widow, was in charge in 1901.

By 1903, however, the landlady was Miss Dance who was on duty when money was stolen from the pub. The *Malvern Gazette* of 4 July reported: 'A repulsive-looking fellow named Richard Price, of no occupation, and said to be a native of the Wyche, was charged with stealing 3d from the Gas Tavern. The landlady, Miss Dance, said she refused to trust prisoner with a pint of cider, and he left. Whilst she was in a backroom, prisoner returned, and subsequently she missed 3d, which had been placed on a table. The bench sent him to gaol for one month.'

In 1922 Mr. A. Brace was the proprietor and by 1970 the pub had changed its name to the Langland Arms, with no doubt the new licensees hoping that the 14th-century author of the epic poem *Piers Plowman* might give them good fortune. Langland Close is of course just behind the inn, while Langland Avenue is not far away. The original Gas Tavern name was briefly revealed for a time during redecoration in 1986, a preservation order on the building allowing the name to be covered but not removed.

In 1996 the Langland Arms (owned by Punch Taverns), which comprised a lounge bar and another bar with pool table and darts, was described as a community pub in need of 'some modernisation and refurbishment'. The pub was under threat of closure and redevelopment in 1999, but was given a reprieve. Soon afterwards its name was changed back to the Gas Tavern but with the prefix New.

Unfortunately the name change did not seem to make a lot of difference and the tavern suffered troubled times, reopening under different ownership on several occasions. Then in 2009 the New Gas Tavern ceased trading and remained boarded up and empty for several weeks. Admiral Taverns, the last owners, then sold the property and a planning application was submitted to redevelop the site for retail use by Warwick-based developer Hinton Properties Ltd.

*The New Gas Tavern boarded up prior to demolition*

Although two previous applications for the site had been turned down, and despite protests from Malvern Civic Society, CAMRA and a number of local residents, Malvern Hills District Council gave the go-ahead in November 2010 for the New Gas Tavern to be demolished and a Tesco Express shop and three houses to be built on the site.

On the way out of Barnard's Green on the road to Upton-upon-Severn one soon comes across, by the common, the **Bluebell Inn**, which was originally spelt as in **Blue Bell** rather than for the flower. Nationally, the sign probably started out some centuries ago as an actual bell coloured blue, but nobody seems to know why.

The Bluebell is certainly very old, with timbers dating back to the 17th century, possibly even to the 16th century, and it was probably used as a staging post between Malvern and Upton. The landlord was Walter Clarkson in 1860, when the inn was involved in a Malvern court case. The *Malvern Advertiser* of 4 August 1860 reported: 'Isaac Cowles, shoemaker, was charged with stealing 3s 6d and a tobacco box, the property of Thomas Fowler. Prisoner snatched the box out of the hand of the prosecutor as he was handing it to a friend in the Blue Bell public house at Barnard's Green, and immediately made off with it. The landlord afterwards saw him take the money from the box and throw the box away. The prisoner upon being taken into custody denied all knowledge of the box. He was found guilty and sentenced to one month's hard labour.'

*A 1960s advertisement for the Blue Bell (Brian Iles)*

Cowles was then charged by PC Bevan with assault as he arrested him. Bevan said he was kicked severely, with his skin knocked off in several places, and that Cowles became so violent that it became necessary to tie his legs together in order to cart him to the station. For this offence, the Bench fined Cowles £1 and expenses, or one month's imprisonment.

In 1901 William Browning was the proprietor, while Mr. V. Lewis was the proprietor in 1922. In about 1937 Horace and Annie North were in charge,

*The now one-word Bluebell in 2011*

running the place for the next 21 years before Horace died in 1958 with Annie staying on until January 1960, when she retired.

Haydn and Sheila Davies then took over the Blue Bell. An advert taken out sometime in the 1960s exclaimed: 'Modernised but not spoilt. Original exposed ceiling and wall beams in all rooms - set in two acres of lawns, rose arbours and flower beds, with large kitchen gardens producing ample fresh vegetables for our resident guests. Hot and cold - shaving points - Dimple heaters in all bedrooms - Television and writing room - Ample car parking space. The inn is selective but inexpensive.'

Taken over by Marston's, the inn stopped providing accommodation, instead concentrating on providing food and becoming one of their chain of Tavern Table pub/restaurants. A large garden and heated patio area became popular features. In 2009 a large extension was built to one side of the building, providing even more space for dining.

Nearby is the village and Malvern suburb of Poolbrook where, on the Common, can be found the **Three Horseshoes**, built some 200 years ago and originally a row of three cottages. Why three horseshoes and not one or four people may ask, but at least the inn should have treble luck so long as the open end is not pointed downwards. Horseshoes used to be hung inside the house to ward off witches. The sign also refers to the Worshipful Company of Farriers, established in 1673, and to the Ferrers family, earls of Derby.

*A horse-drawn 'omnibus' outside the Three Horseshoes in the late 1800s (Brian Iles)*

*The Three Horseshoes in 2011, showing a ground-floor extension to the front of the building since the photograph opposite was taken. The current inn sign is shown on the right*

In 1901 John Goode was the landlord followed by Edward and Helen Hughes, described as beer retailers, with Mrs. Hughes, presumably on the death of her husband, still there but on her own in 1922. The ales came from the Birmingham based brewery, Showell's. In 1976 Howard Thomas, who had run the Gloucester Hotel for 16 years, became the licensee. Originally there was an off-sale hatch near the front door and two separate bars, but in the 1990s an extension at the back was built to double the size of the property and a wall was knocked down to provide one large bar.

Guarlford has two ancient hostelries, the **Green Dragon** and the **Plough and Harrow**, both of which are still very much in existence. The **Green Dragon**, situated on the Guarlford Straight by the common, was originally a black and white cottage with a thatched roof, which was built before 1820. It is mentioned in a directory for 1855, when Joseph Sheen was listed as a 'beer retailer', and in 1860 William Hall was the landlord. Stanhope Burston was in charge from at least 1901 to 1916 and Mr. Cooper was in charge up until about 1923 when the pub was pulled down.

Apparently the remains of the cottage were buried in the cellar and the present Green Dragon was built on top. While it was under construction trade continued in a hut, to which the licence was transferred, erected alongside the present beer garden. Even a wedding reception was held there, and later it was used as a changing room for the local football team and as a meeting place for village functions.

The new building provided a Jug and Bottle for off-sales in the middle and a bar to either side. At some stage Bill Powell was the landlord, followed by his son-in-law and daughter, Fred and Violet Hyde, then Mrs. Win Howard and later Richard Hargreaves, an ex-police Superintendent, and his wife Connie, before Ron and Betty Hale took over from 1983 to 1987.

*Mr. Cooper, landlord of the Green Dragon, c.1850*

Then in 1987 Mark and Sue Jones arrived and they are still the incumbents, making them the longest serving landlord and landlady in the Malvern area. During their tenure several changes have been effected including the removal of the shed, latterly used for storage, and the building in 2004 of a conservatory to provide a dining area.

One customer, 79-year-old Stan Jackson, has been coming to the Green Dragon since 1949 and his father before that. Stan recalls a smoke room on the left and another bar on the right where darts, quoits and crib were played with a piano-led sing-song on a Saturday night.

Reminding customers of the pub's name is an impressive-looking green dragon near the front entrance. This was acquired some years ago by Mr. Jones from the Royal Shakespeare Company, who had used it at perform-

*The Green Dragon in the pub's garden, and the pub itself, in 2011*

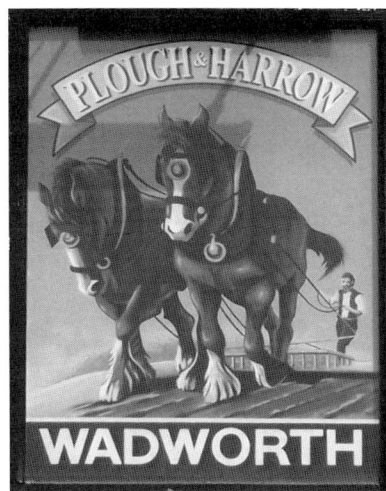

*The sign for the Plough & Harrow*

ances at Stratford, with dry ice emitted from the dragon's nostrils to simulate smoke. Apparently when coloured green, the dragon is considered malevolent. It also appears on the arms of the Earl of Pembroke.

The **Plough & Harrow** appears to be a fusion of different elements over the years including a coal store, a dray house and stable, and a tannery, not forgetting a featured old well. The pub was licensed only as a beer and cider house before the Second World War.

In the book *The Guarlford Story*, villager Sam Beard described the Plough & Harrow as it was in the 1920s and '30s. 'The locals gathered here on a regular basis; work on the farms was discussed. There was no bar as such in the pub, but the landlord positioned himself by the doorway leading into the inner area, kept a watchful eye on the white mugs with the golden band around them and refilled them as required.'

In the same book Derrick Bladder stated that the Rev. Frederick Newson (1913-1965) always maintained that the two most important places in the village were the church and the pub. 'The bishop used to have a walkabout in the summer and the Rector would bring him into the Plough and say, "This is where I meet most of my flock". The Rev. Newson also said at Confirmation classes, "If you want a drink, you should go into the pub and buy a drink, like I do, and not round the back door (off licence) with a black bag."'

After the Second World War, the new licensees Dick and Pam Capstick obtained a full licence and refurbished the pub. In the last two decades of the

*The Plough & Harrow in 2011*

20th century there were various licensees including the jockey Denis Atkins, who had won the Paddy Power Gold Cup at Cheltenham in 1976 and the Scottish Grand National in 1980 with Neville Crump as trainer on both occasions. A major refurbishment was carried out early in the new millennium and once the pub had been taken over by Wadworths, the brewers, Juliet Tyndall and Michael Weir became the licensees. Their emphasis on food paid off; the Plough and Harrow was the only pub in the Malvern area to feature in the 2009 *Michelin Guide to Eating out in Pubs*.

A settlement known as *han leah*, Old English for a high clearing, existed in Saxon times and originated as a clearing in the forest from the Malvern Hills to the River Severn, according to Malcolm Fare in *The Hanleys*. The Saxon chief Brictric built a manor that later formed the basis of Hanley Castle. The forest reverted to the king when William the Conqueror came to power and when these rights were given to a subject the forest became known as a chase, administered by forest laws designed to protect hunting. This is what happened when Henry I gave the hunting rights to his illegitimate son, Robert Fitzroy, Earl of Gloucester with Hanley becoming the administrative centre.

The castle, built for King John between 1207 and 1212, was a huge square building with a turreted tower at each angle and a keep, surrounded by a deep moat. Left to fall into decay at the beginning of the 16th century by Henry VII, it was further wrecked during the Civil War by the Roundheads. Today the site is just a grassy mound.

With the availability of good clay, a plentiful supply of trees for charcoal, and the river for transport, the two Hanley villages developed a thriving pottery industry. In 1296 there were no fewer than 16 potters. Blackmore Park mansion, the manor house owned by the Hornyold family in Hanley Castle, was burnt to the ground in 1926, but Severn End, the home of the other major gentry family, the Lechmeres, still remains in Hanley Swan, although ravaged by fire in 1899.

Part of the parish of Hanley Castle, Hanley Swan was not officially recognised as a separate village until the 1890s, when a post office was opened. Its main features are a traditional village green with duck pond, a village stores and a public house called the **Swan Inn**, after which the village was named, although it once boasted as many as three pubs. Situated on an old drovers' road from the Welsh hills to the ford across the River Severn at Hanley Quay, there has been a hostelry on the site for hundreds of years.

According to Malcolm Fare, the earliest documentary evidence for its existence is from the Land Tax Assessment record of 1781, when Edmund Jones paid a quarterly tax of 6s 8d 'for the Swan'. 'He was still there when the Enclosure Map of 1797 was published and is identified in the first directory of Worcestershire in 1820 as a "vict" (victualler - a purveyor of provisions).'

*The Swan Inn with a butcher's shop annexe in the 1930s (Brian Iles)*

Around 1850 the Tomlinson family began their long association as landlords of the Swan, John Tomlinson handing over in 1876 to his son, Benjamin, described also as a farmer, who was still in residence in 1904. But the following year the third generation Tomlinson, Percy, set up a butcher's shop annexe and the pub passed into the hands of Frederick Flux. In 1908, *Kelly's Directory* identified the Swan Inn for the first time as being in Hanley Swan.

A few years later the Swan was sold to the Cheltenham Original Brewery, which let the premises to the Foord family in 1916. When Nugent Foord died in the late 1930s, his widow Emma took over, keeping the pub open during the war years. Emma's son, Bill, ran it after the war, handing over in the 1950s to a succession of landlords while the owners merged with West Country Brewery in 1958, which five years later was taken over by Whitbread. The Swan was later sold to Inn Business who in 1999 were taken over by Punch Taverns. In

*The Swan in 2011, rendered over and extended since the 1930s*

2004 a major refurbishment was carried out. The large interior is now divided into many small areas, and there are five en-suite bedrooms.

Nearly opposite to the Swan is the Hanley Swan village stores and post office on a site which, according to the Enclosure Map of 1797, used to be a gravel pit. It was owned by the Lechmere family, one of the most redoubtable and wealthy in the area, who during the early part of the 19th century built a coaching inn on the site. The census of 1841 shows that it was occupied by Joseph Pratt, coach proprietor, and his wife, Mary, publican. Nine year's later *Kelly's Directory* listed the building as the **Coach & Horses**, with William, probably Joseph's son, as landlord.

The inn is mentioned in 1860, but in August of that year Sir Edmund Lechmere converted it to the Hanley Castle Working Man's Institute, which he established to provide accommodation for single men and for the improvement and recreation of the labouring classes of the neighbourhood.

'The new institute has, by some skilful alterations and additions, been constructed out of the old Coach and Horses public house,' a local newspaper reported. 'A range of stabling at the back of the public house was unroofed, the walls raised and the interior converted into 12 dormitories, each lofty and well ventilated, and capable of holding two small beds ...'.

The report added: 'A bathroom and a schoolroom were attached to the building and a further four dormitories were fitted within the old pub. The large tap room became a library and reading room, the bar parlour a refreshment room and the bar itself a smoke room where, however, "no stronger libations than tea and coffee will be permitted."' A mixed school was held on

*The Hanley Swan village stores and post office, once the Coach & Horses*

the premises until St. Gabriel's was built in the village in 1862. However, the Institute did not last long, being converted to a grocer's shop in 1867, with the post office coming in the mid-1890s.

More recently closed was the **Ewe & Lamb** inn, Welland Road. It was started by a local butcher, James Jones, and his wife Caroline, selling beer from their black-and-white cottage in the 1850s. Following the closure of the Coach & Horses, they expanded the premises, which was run by two generations of the Jones family until it was taken over in the early 20th century by Fred and Elizabeth Badham. The inn, which had its own cider mill, also offered accommodation for cycling and picnic parties. In 1916 it was sold at auction, ownership passing through various breweries including Spreckley Brothers, the Worcester brewery, which stopped brewing in 1968, and Whitbread. A hatch for off-sales faced the front door with a lounge to the left and a bar area to the right. At the back was an orchard.

The Ewe & Lamb was apparently popular with the Americans during the Second World War and was the scene of a legendary drinking contest 'between an old local known as "Slingum" Bradley and a hard-drinking US serviceman. After 16 pints, the American gave up and Bradley asked for the remaining beer to be put in a bottle for him to take home for his supper.'

The landlord in the 1950s was Bert Hawtin and in the 1970s it was Mr. A. Marshall. Closed in 1985, the pub resumed trading but eventually closed for good, was bought by a development company and demolished almost overnight without warning, according to neighbours. A number of large oak beams, considered too heavy to transport elsewhere, were burnt in a colossal bonfire. The developers then built a small housing estate, The Walnuts, on the site and adjoining land. The only remnant of the inn is a wall of the former cider house and the original cider mill. The inn sign was also saved and in 2002 was sold at auction for £200.

Today Hanley Castle is centred around a barn-like church of Norman origin but of 14th century design and a 17th-century public house on a tiny green with a massive cedar tree.

Although the roughly painted inn sign shows the Magi or three wise men, the **Three Kings Inn** was in fact named after three Kings brothers who owned the inn in the late 17th century. One of them, Richard Kings, sold the property to Anthony Lechmere in 1710 for £4 15s and it has been owned by the Lechmere estate ever since, but not always in the same location. At the time of the Enclosure Award in 1797, the Three Kings alehouse, with outbuildings, yard and garden, was established in the cottage now known as Hobbits opposite the school. It was not until the early 19th century that it moved to its present location, being built on the site of a medieval church house. Behind the Georgian brick façade the building's timber beams were fashioned from 15th- and 16th-century ships' timbers. The inn retained its church connections

*An advert for the Three Kings in the 1960s*

with various parish events being held there, and an upstairs room, approached by an outside staircase, was used for tithe audits and club meetings.

In the early 1850s, the innkeepers Joseph and Sarah Hughes renamed the pub the **Hare & Hounds**, although it is also thought that there was a separate pub by that name. Only when they left some 20 years later did the name revert back to the Three Kings. The landlords changed regularly until 1911, when Fred and Ethel Roberts took over, passing the licence on to their son George in 1960. Fred was also a bricklayer, while George worked on the railway and also served as school caretaker and local postman. It was during George's tenure that the house next door was assimilated into the pub, and as it had been occupied by Old Nell, a former schoolmistress, the lounge is now known as Nell's Room.

According to Anne Bradford in her book *Haunted Pubs & Hotels of Worcestershire*, the pub is haunted by Old Nell, though this is disputed by the present landlady. Anne Bradford wrote that a lady saw Old Nell's ghostly form in front of the fireplace in 1981 and described her as dressed in a red bodice and skirt, black overskirt looped up at the sides, white shawl and Welsh-style black leather hat. 'The only way I knew it was a ghost', the lady later wrote,

*The Three Kings c.1920*

*The Three Kings in 2011, showing remarkably little change from almost a hundred years earlier*

'was because the back of her skirt went through the wall and parts of her were missing.'

George's widow, Sheila, took over the Three Kings in 1990 and on her death about three years ago, their daughter Sue became mine hostess, helped by brother Dave. With the year 2011 having been reached, a centenary of stewardship of the Three Kings by three generations of the Roberts family was celebrated. In 1993 the pub received CAMRA's highest accolade, being voted National Pub of the Year, and was runner-up in 1998. It is also on CAMRA's National Inventory of Historic Pub interiors and in 2003 was top of a list of six of the best historic pubs selected by Victorian Society chairman Geoff Brandwood. Another interesting fact is that since records were started in 1992, the pub has served more than 3,500 different real ales. It is still owned by the Lechmere estate.

Visiting the Three Kings today is like venturing into a time warp, especially the front bar. A sliding door opens into a tiny tiled-floor tap room furnished with a giant settle facing an equally vast inglenook fireplace, and a serving hatch. Another room has darts, dominoes and cribbage. A separate entrance leads to Nell's Room with another inglenook fireplace, kitchen range and antique furniture including another high-backed settle. A sole double bedroom provides the pub's accommodation, the pub also serving meals of the simple kind.

Close to where the former ferry crossed the River Severn at **Hanley Quay** used to be an inn of the same name. According to A.W. Gwilliam, in his *Old Worcestershire Inns*, it was much used by watermen from the barges landing coal and bricks for Malvern, and in the summer its tea garden was crowded with folk from Upton. An old lady who used to live in a cottage in the lane leading to the inn told of the days when 'frequent balls and parties were held during the winter, in the long room upstairs. The inn had so much to do with the business and pleasures of the village.' She recalled the many dances in which she had participated in her younger days, the fêtes that were held on 29 May, the space the crinolines took up, and how fights were settled at the inn by drink or fisticuffs. As Mr. Gwilliam notes, perhaps things became too rowdy, for the Hanley Quay Inn was closed by Sir Edmund Lechmere when the village institute was opened in 1860.

On the way out of Hanley Swan on the B4208 to Welland one soon comes to Tyre Hill with, on the right, Tyre Hill Cottage, which used to be the **Tyre Hill Inn**, built by John Vivian, a local lime and coal dealer, in about 1840. His brother, Andrew, ran the pub for a year and then it passed into the hands of Mr. Romney, a solicitor. It was leased for a time to William Hadrin, who left it to take over the Black Bear in Tewkesbury. Mr. Albert Sherwood then took it on and was succeeded in March 1936 by William Smith. He supplied lunches, teas and cold snacks as well as ale from Lewis Clarke's Worcester Brewery. The inn closed in the late 1930s since when it has been a private dwelling. To the left of the front door where there is now a window, there used to be a door leading out to the back where three stables were located, which still exist. On the right is the kitchen which was the public bar where sing-songs were held round a piano.

*The Tyre Hill Inn with William Smith in the doorway (Brian Iles)*

# CHAPTER TEN

# Welland, Castlemorton, Birtsmorton, Longdon & Rye Street

Together with Little Malvern, which rather surprisingly does not ever seem to have possessed an inn or pub, Welland is a parish in the District of Malvern Hills, surrounded by farms and common land. There is also Upper Welland, which seems like a separate village. At the centre of Welland by the crossroads is the **Pheasant Inn** situated between the church and village green, with title deeds dating back to the mid-1700s and believed to have been an old coaching house. The original building was connected to an apple barn and pig sty, now a private dwelling, allowing carriages to drive through to the stables behind (since demolished). The circuit judge held his court here. It was listed as an

*The Pheasant Inn c.1920s (Brian Iles)*

inn in 1841, and in 1904, when described as a hotel with Frederick Wigginton in charge, it offered 'excellent accommodation' for cyclists, travellers and visitors with 'good stabling'. Henry Pudge was the landlord in 1916, when it was still described as a hotel.

In 1929 the Pheasant Inn was taken over by Mr. and Mrs. Francis Elms. During the First World War, Mr. Elms served in France in the Monmouthshire Regiment and in 1917 he was awarded the Military Medal with Bar for bravery. He was wounded four times. The couple stayed at the Pheasant until 1954 when their son, Mr. Southwell Elms, became licensee.

The owners, Ansell's, put the pub on the market and in 1983 it was bought by Mike and Helen Yorke and Mike's sister, Sally Griffin, and her husband, Neil, who together had been running the Berkeley Arms at Spetchley for the past year. After an extensive re-vamp the Pheasant reopened in July of that year with Mike and Helen, aided by Mike's mother, Enid, behind the bars. The functions room, into which a car had crashed earlier in the year, was completely renovated, while outside, the local council had put up a crash barrier to prevent a recurrence of the incident. One of the walls in the bar was lined with old deeds of the inn which Ansells handed over to the new owners.

Unfortunately the inn's future later became unpredictable, culminating in its sudden closure in 2010 after being called an 'unviable proposition' by its new owner, Peter Bailey. The pub then had a multi-level lounge bar, an eating area and upstairs letting accommodation. To one side was a large functions room used for conferences and dinner parties which was originally a skittle alley, while to the rear lies a spacious car park. With rumours circulating that the premises would be turned into an old people's home or into housing, a number of neighbouring residents kept a vigil every night for 13 weeks to maintain a community presence and safeguard it against vandalism.

Mr. Bailey told Welland Parish Council that the Pheasant had seen no fewer than five tenants come and go since 1998. 'They have all complained to me about lack of patronage by the local community and turnover had gradually dropped to just over £100,000 per year,' he added. But Mrs. Carolyn Stewart, the landlady who had vacated the premises in July 2010, painted a different picture. 'I wish it to be known that under no circumstances should the Pheasant Inn be considered an unviable business,' she said. 'The business at the Pheasant has shown steady growth in the last few years and under the right management should continue to develop and be more of an asset to the village.' In 2011 David Jenkins, of Tewkesbury, twice sought to buy the lease, but pulled out. At the time of going to print the inn is still closed.

A story is told by local inhabitants of a gypsy family who some years ago stayed for several days in Welland and often frequented the Pheasant. One gypsy liked the village so much that before he left, he threw a stone over the church wall and said that was where he wanted to be buried. And he was.

*The Marlbank Inn in 2011*

To be named after a fertilizer is rather strange, but that is what happened to a pub to the west of Welland. The **Marlbank Inn** is called after the old clay or marl pits that used to be prevalent in the area. The clay was used for 'puddling' – the waterproofing of ponds – and possibly also for the manufacture of bricks and tiles. For many years the Marlbank Inn was a two-room pub surrounded by countryside.

In the 1980s the pub also boasted a rather unusual customer, a young owl no less, who was taken in by the landlord, Gordon Owen, and his wife Jacqueline, after being injured by a car. Once released again, the owl, named Solomon, became a regular customer, and was soon making friends with their cat, Thomas.

The Marlbank was owned by the brewers Banks, Wolverhampton & Dudley and then Marston's, before being taken over by Avebury Taverns and later by Admiral Taverns. Now a freehouse, for the past six years it has been run by Debra and Tony Pugh.

During the winter of 2008 and 2009, the Marlbank was extensively refurbished and improvements made including a larger bar-lounge area, a terrace and three en suite bedrooms to complement its adjacent camping and caravan site.

To the east of Welland at Hook Common is **The Inn at Welland**, in Drake Street, which used to be the **Anchor**, first appearing in a local directory dated 1855, and is believed before that to have been a 17th-century farmhouse. According to the 1842 tithe map this area was called The Lake, a large pool of water giving rise to the name of the pub. The far end of the building, where

*The Inn at Welland in 2012*

the main entrance used to be, is the oldest part with a small room attached that apparently acted as a toll house to collect money from fishermen using the nearby pool. Over the years, numerous extensions have been made to the property, which has also been used for different purposes including that of a garage with petrol pump and service area for commercial vehicles.

From being a watering hole for the locals, the emphasis later centred on food served in the separate restaurant. It was awarded the accolade of the Dining Pub of the Year in Worcestershire in 2002 by the *Good Pub Guide*. The pub also provided bed and breakfast, camping and caravan facilities and a beer garden.

In August 2010, the Anchor was bought by David and Gillian Pinchbeck, who from 2004 to 2007 had run the Verzon Hotel, near Ledbury, and who began a major refurbishment programme to upgrade the establishment, given the new name of The Inn at Welland. Work included replacing the roof and fitting dormer windows, building a porch for a new entrance, moving the cloakrooms to the back to provide extra dining space, an area which opens onto the gardens, retaining the toll house although it has space for one table only, and lining the floors with flagstones. The grounds cover two and a half acres, with pride of place going to an apple tree reputed to be one of the oldest in Worcestershire. The Inn was reopened in June 2011 and is now operating as a bar, eating house, coffee shop and delicatessen from 9.30 in the morning until late. Is this the latest *modus operandi* for pubs?

In Upper Welland, not far from the Spar shop but on the opposite side of the road, a private house, No. 175, used to be the **Hawthorn Inn** which closed down six years ago. James Stuart, the owner, and his family still live on the premises. The name is derived from the bush which was used in the coat of arms of Henry VII, who stayed with his son Arthur, the Prince of Wales, at Great Malvern Priory. The Magnificat window in the priory's north transept is dedicated to him. Bunches of hawthorn were tied around the end of an ale stake (a stick used to stir beer) which was hung above the door. The Romans considered that a hawthorn bush would act as protection against sorcery, and placed hawthorn leaves in the cradles of their newly-born babies. In medieval times hanging a piece of bush at the door of a building would signify that it was an inn.

The building is at least 250 years old and may have been frequented by drovers following a nearby trail to by-pass the Malvern Hills on their way to Worcester or Gloucester. Originally there were two cottages down the side of the building. These may have been used as accommodation when it was described as a hotel at the beginning of the 20th century, a time when its frontage was extended.

Owned by Flowers Whitbread in the 1960s and 1970s, it was closed for two years before the freehold was bought by Charlie Rawlins who set it up as a pub restaurant, with an outbuilding at the back being converted into a dining area.

In 1983 the Hawthorn was taken over by John and Margaret Bird, who re-developed the back room as a restaurant with food prepared by their daughter, Ann together with a cocktail bar was provided for the diners. The pub had a single main bar but with various nooks and crannies. Then at the beginning of 1990 the Hawthorn closed, and six months later an application was made by Mr. D. Price, of Worcester, to build a nursing home on the site, about twice the size of the current building. The application was turned down as local people were concerned that the village would permanently lose a valuable focal point if the pub was converted.

*The Hawthorn (Brian Iles)*

The pub reopened a year later having been bought by Mr. Stuart, but closed again in 2005.

Malvern pub landlord Duncan Ironmonger offered to buy the Hawthorn and save it from closure as villagers met to save their pub. But in a letter to the villagers, Mr. Stuart said: 'Not only was this a business, but it has been our home for over 14 years and will continue to be so. You are behaving as though the pub was a public amenity which the locals are entitled to, but it was a business that was haemorrhaging at a disturbing rate and it had to close.' CAMRA representative Mark Haslam said that whilst it was unreasonable to expect the Stuarts to run a non-viable business, they should not preclude others from making a go of it.

*The Hawthorne as a private residence in 2012*

Today, the Hawthorn name is no longer to be seen, although the post on which the sign hung is still *in situ*. Inside, the bar is being used as a store room while work is being carried out at the back by the owner with the counter still in its original position.

An unsourced article about the village states that at the turn of the 20th century, Upper Welland was a thriving community with several shops. 'Dating from 1730, the oldest surviving house was originally the **Black Horse Inn** whose one time landlord, Joe Potter, had the doubtful reputation of being able to swear so loudly he could be heard at the top of the Malvern Hills.' The inn was probably located near Assarts Lane, which saw the beginnings of the village.

Travelling south one comes to Castlemorton, which has an ancient church and the earthwork remains of a medieval castle belonging to the De Montes family. Nearby is commonland usually the scene of quiet grazing and a walker or two, but in 1992 the peace was shattered by the arrival of between 20,000 and 40,000 ravers who enjoyed a week-long free festival with nonstop dance music relayed over large sound systems. The police were powerless and for a while Castlemorton made national headlines. The revellers eventually dispersed, and to ensure there would be no repetition new national legislation was introduced to control specific genres of popular music (raves) in public and the use of public spaces.

On the edge of Castlemorton Common lies the **Plume of Feathers**, one of two pubs in the village, which derives its name from the plume of three ostrich feathers displayed in the crest of the Prince of Wales. It also refers to the everyday expression 'a feather in your cap' which in turn refers to the custom amongst primitive people of adding a feather to their head-dress when they had killed an enemy. Dating from the 16th century, the inn, also known simply as **The Feathers**, was part of the Eastnor Estate and supplied rum to the riders, including nobility, when they were out hunting in Malvern Chase. The inn was sold off by the estate in 1917.

In 1931 the landlord was T.H. Lawrence, licensed to sell beer, wines, spirits and tobacco, and in 1959 it was taken over by Peter Wilkes, who was the landlord until the late 1960s and then leased it out till the present day.

At the beginning of the 1980s the pub kept irregular hours for a couple of years but in 1984 new tenants Gordon and Ann Simmons returned to traditional opening times and retained the pub's simple character. Running a pub was a new venture for Gordon, who had previously been regional manager for a large motoring company for 20 years. In the last 15 years there have been numerous tenants and the present incumbent has been there since the spring of 2012 after the pub had been closed for about four months.

The small beam-bedecked bar is the oldest part of the pub, which also has a small side room with darts and television and a separate dining area. The long outbuilding to the front, now a private dwelling, was once run as a café by Peter Wilkes' mother when the M50 motorway was being built in the 1950s.

*The Plume of Feathers in 2012*

On the Gloucester Road is an authentic black and white country pub, the **Robin Hood**, with the original part having been built in 1562 and once used as the king's hunting lodge when Castlemorton Common was part of Malvern Chase. Today, the pub is open plan but the old part is a square room by the bar counter. Although miles away from Sherwood Forest, the Robin Hood name for inns became popular in the 19th century when the Ancient Order of the Foresters, a Friendly Society, opened new lodges or meeting places, often in inns.

*The Robin Hood showing marginal changes down the years*

*The hunt gathering outside the Robin Hood*

Before the Second World War it was known as **Ye Old Robin Hood** and sold Royal Well Brewery ales. In the *Malvern Gazette* of 1958, the Editor's Notebook column was full of praise for the Robin Hood, saying it had been transformed in the previous seven years from a 'rather ordinary little place into a showplace'. The editor went on: 'Probably the oldest inn anywhere around – it was once a woodman's hut mentioned in *Malvern Chase* [published in 1880] – the house is full of fine old black timber beams, a magnificent collection of old brass and copper assembled by the hostess and even, to add period charm of another kind, a King Charles spaniel, Nelson. Parties of Danes make it a regular place of call; other visitors this summer included Americans, South Africans and French.'

Pat and Barry Smith were licensees for at least 15 years until 2005 when the present landlords, Rob and Mary Biddle, took over. The owners are Punch Taverns. The pub is also well known for its food, has a large garden with views of the hills, and provides camping and caravanning facilities.

Almost opposite the Robin Hood is New Road, down which the first turning on the right is a lane known as Eight Oakes leading to the common and Hangman's Hill. On the left is Plough Farm with a white cottage which used to be the **Plough Inn**, set in six acres of land.

According to local historian Heather Hurley a cottage inhabited by the Lewis family stood on the site of the present Plough Farm from the early 1700s as part of a squatter settlement. By 1752 Richard Bullock of Castlemorton had acquired the cottage which, on his death in 1795, passed to his son William. Now described as a smallholding, the property was transferred to William's brother Thomas, then to John Bullock, a maltster from Stafford. It was during his occupation that a beerhouse was established.

In 1865 John Bullock sold the property to Francis Davis, a farmer and dealer from Castlemorton, for £640, and by 1879 the house was called the Plough Inn. With Davis finding himself in debt, the inn came into the possession of the trustees of the Severns Pride Lodge of Oddfellows, a Friendly Society based at Upton-upon-Severn, with William Hooper as tenant beer retailer.

In 1897 the trustees sold 'All that messuage tenement or Beerhouse known as The Plough Inn ... with the outbuildings, garden, orchard and pieces of parcels of land' to Arnold Perrett & Co Ltd for £800. This Gloucestershire brewery was later taken over by a Cheltenham company in 1924, when the Plough Inn was sold to George and Susannah Prosser. They continued to run it as an inn until 1927 when it was de-licensed. The Prossers are the ancestors of the present owners. Although damage was caused by a fire in the 1930s and the cottage is presently being refurbished, traces of how the building was as an inn can still be seen. The bar counter faced the main entrance with a door behind, now sealed up, leading to the cellar, which is now entered from near the kitchen. A snug was to the right of the front door.

It is thought that trade would have come from two nearby quarries, where workers quarried for Malvern stone. The perry pear and cider apple trees, still part of the Plough's orchard, may well have provided home-made perry and cider.

Further along the Gloucester Road is a turning on the right marked Golden Valley, at the very end of which is a private dwelling which used to be the **Lodge Inn**, a 15th-century, possibly even 14th-century, building which started life as a lodge used by hunters of game in the Malvern Chase area. Over the years it continued providing refreshment and hospitality for, first drovers, and then travellers by horse and cart on their way via the common and Hollybush to Ledbury. At one end of the premises was a cider mill producing cider for sale, while later on beer was served straight from a barrel at the back. In fine weather customers sat supping their beverages under an ancient yew in the garden. The Lodge was also frequented by fishermen using the nearby millpond. The original black and white building was bricked over by the owners, Mitchells and Butlers brewery.

For many years the pub was run by the Biddle family, then by the Andrews before Fred and Doris Reynolds became landlords in the mid 20th century. In 1963 a big fire broke out, burning down a barn and badly damaging the property.

The *Malvern Gazette* of 13 March 1964 reported that the Upton-upon-Severn Licensing Justices provisionally renewed the pub's beer and cider licence, but that it would be referred to the Worcestershire Compensation Committee as a possible case for closure. Mr. E. Hill, for the owners, Mitchells and Butlers, contended that as the premises were a 'pre 1869 beerhouse', a licence could not be refused without reference to this committee, but that the brewers had no objection to the premises and licence being declared redundant. At the hearing before the licensing justices, Mr. E.H. Eeles, for the brewers, produced a lease for the property dated 23 November 1898, together with an earlier conveyance. The police opposed the renewal of the licence, setting out a number of reasons including that the general comfort for customers was well below the standard of other licensed houses in the area; that within a mile radius there were 200 people, including children and teetotallers, yet within a mile and a half there were three other pubs – and so considered that there would be no hardship to the local population if the premises were closed. It was confirmed that trade in winter months was slack, but that it built up in the summer. In the 19 June 1964 edition of the *Malvern Gazette* it was reported that the Worcestershire Compensation Committee had indeed refused the renewal of a licence held by Mr. Frederick Reynolds. Mr. and Mrs. Reynolds bought the property from the brewery and lived there until their deaths about 20 years ago. Since then it has been the home of their grandson, Roy Shailes.

*The one time Lodge Inn*

Not far away, by the old Hollybush Quarry owned by the Eastnor Estates, is a dwelling called Vault House on the main A438 to Ledbury, which in the 19th century was a tavern, **The Vaults**, serving the Hollybush villagers and surrounding area. Before the building of the A438, it may also have been used by drovers making their way to the Golden Valley road and beyond. It still retains a brick tunnel-like structure going back 30 yards into the hill, after which it was named, and still has the original well which supplied water to the tavern and to the nearby Manor House and cottages. Beer, cider and ice would have been stored in the vault, which was entered through a smaller cellar on the ground floor. From records dating back to the 1820s, the tavern accommodated about 10 people, some living in the attic. Travellers may have hitched their horses at the timber yard across the road.

The property later became the house of the quarryman in charge of Hollybush Quarry until it closed in the mid 1970s. It then lay derelict for some years until it was put up for auction by the Eastnor Estate in the 1980s and bought by a local builder who gutted the building, put on a new roof and carried out a 10-year renovation programme. Many of the original features such as oak beams, inglenook fireplaces and timbered walls remain. The present owners, Dan and Tracey Marsh, who bought Vault House four years ago, have unearthed several old glass bottles and flagons in the garden, consistent with its once having been a tavern.

*The one-time Vaults*

*The Duke of York in 2011*

Travelling along the A438 towards Tewkesbury one comes to Rye Street, where the **Duke of York Inn** has been operating since the 15th century. The pub's sign depicts Frederick, the second son of George III, who commanded the English army in Flanders 1794-95, and is better known as the Grand Old Duke of York of nursery rhyme fame. Presumably it originally traded under another name.

Despite a fire in the late 1970s, the inn has managed to retain much of its original character with lounge and bar areas together with a separate dining area. At the rear is a large field for touring caravans and where caravan rallies can be held. In 1983 the landlords were John and Vivienne Hodson. It was then run for about six years by Sheila and David Flack, but after their departure about three years ago the owners, Enterprise Inns, put in managers. Then on Boxing Day 2010, the pub suddenly closed after flooding caused by burst pipes due to the big freeze. It reopened at the beginning of 2012.

Adjacent is the Duke of York meadow which the pub sold to the Worcestershire Wildlife Trust. It is famous for its wild daffodils and has over 120 species of flora and several butterflies.

In Birtsmorton, there is a black and white country pub off the beaten track called the **Farmers Arms**, which was built in 1480 and was originally a drovers' pub selling porter and cider. It has a small, low-beamed lounge plus

*The Farmers Arms, Birtsmorton*

larger bar with darts, and a dining area. It is the only present-day example of the name throughout agricultural Worcestershire. The crest's motto reads 'Give us our Daily Bread'. The sign shows that it is a freehouse but also that it sells Hook Norton Ales, which are the house beers. In 1978 the landlord John Parker held a harvest festival service in the pub followed by a produce auction for three local charities. Today, the pub is run by Julie Moore and her mother Jill, who have been in charge for the last 26 years.

*The Plough at Longdon boarded up in 1992*

*The Plough in 2012 in its much refurbished form as a guest house*

One of the pub's regular customers, Vinny, aged 72, is remembered with a plaque on a stool at the bar counter 'from his friends at the Farmers Arms' followed by the words 'I'm Happy'.

The Old Plough B & B at Longdon was formerly the **Plough Inn**, which traded as a pub from the early 18th century up until 1997. Originally there was a courtyard with a well between the stone-built pub and the village post office. In the 1970s the main building was extended to join up with the post office, the top floor of which was used as a skittle alley. The pub itself was divided into several areas including a stone-flagged bar and an area for darts and pool. In the late 1970s, when there was a lot more parking space, landlord Frank Higgins, who himself owned a Honda CBX, held a motorcycle night every Friday, with bikers coming from far and wide.

Owned at various times by Ind Coope and also by Mitchells and Butlers, the pub had several landlords and was closed in about 1992 before the by now derelict property was bought just before Christmas 1993 by Haydn Lamb, who ran it with his wife, Susan, (mainly by her) until they decided to close it as a pub in 1997. Since then the premises have been completely refurbished, resulting in a large family home with guest accommodation in three en suite rooms. The skittle alley is now a billiard room and the well has been covered over.

On the way into the village on the right hand side is a white building known as Longdon Cottage, which used to be another **Farmer's Arms**, owned and run by Beattie Hughes, who also owned the Plough. She sold the Farmer's in the early 1950s on the understanding that whoever bought it would not reopen it as a pub while the Plough was still open. It later became a petrol filling station and then a village shop, but in more recent times it has been used as a private dwelling.

CHAPTER ELEVEN

# Colwall, Chances Pitch & British Camp

On the western side of the Malvern Hills lies Colwall, an elongated village comprising Upper Colwall, Colwall Stone and Colwall Green. Formerly known as *Collius Vallum* and Cold Well, Colwall was referred to in the Domesday Book. The name Colwall (*Colewelle* in Domesday Book) may mean cold spring, or it may come from the Latin *collum vallum* – the pass by the fort.

The village has moved three times. The first known settlement was the British Camp on the Herefordshire Beacon, built between 400 and 100 BC. Then it moved down the hill to Primeswell and Evendine. Colwall's population increased over the years but was devastated by the Black Death in 1349, dropping from 1750 to 150.

A new village grew up centred on Evendine and the Green, castles were replaced by farms and extensive changes occurred following the building of the railway in 1860. Various projects were introduced including a water bottling plant, brickworks, bottled fruit and vinegar production, while outdoor pursuits included cricket, football, tennis, two golf courses, a racecourse and a number of outdoor swimming pools.

From the 1920s, the settlement around the station known as Colwall Stone grew rapidly and took over from Colwall Green as the main settlement. Two men, Stephen Ballard and Roland Cave-Brown-Cave, were mainly instrumental in turning Colwall from a sleepy agricultural village into a more vibrant community. Ballard, who built the Temperance Hotel and Lecture Hall opposite Colwall Stone, the remains of an ancient cross, was the civil engineer in the building of the railway tunnel through the Malvern Hills, laid on supply of well water to the village, and was mainly responsible for Jubilee Drive. Cave-Brown-Cave planned the Colwall Park racecourse, the golfcourse and rebuilt the Horse and Groom, and was also responsible for the Park Hotel. There were nearly 20 shops then.

From 1900 to the start of the Second World War, crowds flocked to the village for regular National Hunt meetings at the racecourse, which became quite famous. Attendances were usually over 3,000 with over 4,000 on one occasion. Elsie Godsell, in *Colwall Village Past and Present*, recalled: 'It was exciting to see the horse boxes arriving bringing the horses, people streaming from trains at Colwall Station, and the Bookmakers arriving with their stands and boards piled on top of their cars. There was a sea of cars with several light aircraft.'

Schweppes opened their Colwall Springs factory to produce carbonated waters in 1892. Since 1928 the Malvern water has been piped from Pewtress Well on the lower side of the main road below the Herefordshire Beacon. Schweppes has been associated with Malvern Water since 1851, when they supplied the Great Exhibition at the Crystal Palace. Queen Elizabeth II has taken Malvern water while travelling abroad and thus the bottling plant had her royal warrant. It later became Coca Cola Schweppes before ending production of Malvern water in 2010 and 150 years of local history. Interest has been expressed by several parties in purchasing the site and re-starting water bottling, but at the time of going to print the factory is still closed.

In addition to William Langland (see Wellington Hotel) and Dame Laura Knight (see Colwall Park Hotel), other well-known people connected with Colwall include Mazo de la Roche, the Canadian novelist, and Elizabeth Barrett Browning, who lived at Hope End in the early 19th century.

And then there is Upper Colwall, on the western slopes of the Malvern Hills, where the **Chase Inn** can be found, named no doubt after the Royal

*The Chase Inn in 2012*

Forest of Malvern Chase. The first landlord was Charles Bowers, a baker by trade, who converted part of his shop into a beerhouse around 1865. Although small and cramped, it received official recognition four years later. It provided basic accommodation, simple meals, home brewed ale and stabling. Originally, the inn brewed its own beers, the popular Colwall drink being a form of malty mild that varied considerably from brew to brew, but with a high specific gravity of about 1060.

Harriet Oatridge ran the business from 1887 to 1899, with James Cooper then taking over at around the time when the inn was acquired by Worcester brewers Spreckley Brothers, with Cooper remaining as tenant until 1928. It had a seven day licence with one bar, a tap room and five living rooms. Thomas Bridges was landlord from 1928 until 1945 with William Phillips taking over until 1958.

The pub was sold to Cheltenham and Hereford Brewers who, after merging with the Stroud Brewery, became in 1958 the West Country Breweries with nearly 1,300 houses. They in turn were taken over by Whitbread in 1963. Later the Chase Inn became run down until it was purchased in 1972 by Dennis and Dorothy Smith who modernised and extended the premises with the inclusion of adjoining cottages. A new lounge bar was created and two patios and, being a racing man, Dennis couldn't resist calling the bar Puckham – after a chaser he part-owned which was stabled by Michael Scudamore at Hoarwithy. The bar was opened by Mr. Scudamore in 1975; a mammoth cake was made for the occasion covered in icing with pictures of the pub, the horse and other views. It raised some £20 in a raffle for the Injured Jockeys Fund. The main bar had darts and crib facilities.

From 1993 Peter and Eunice Bailey were in charge and in 2004 the Chase Inn was bought by Duncan Ironmonger as the second of three Malvern pubs he now runs together with the St. George's Brewery in Callow End.

Opposite the remains of an ancient cross in Colwall Stone, and adjoining the station entrance, is the imposing **Colwall Park Hotel** which was built around 1906 to accommodate race-goers attending the National Hunt meetings at the newly built racecourse on the other side of the railway track. Both hotel and racecourse were built by Mr. Cave-Brown-Cave. Designed by architect H. Percy Smith, the hotel was built on land belonging to Stone Holt Farm, with the black and white farmhouse still standing next door, and opened in 1906 or 1907. An advert in the *Malvern Gazette* in 1909 stated: 'Colwall Park Hotel. Recently built. Every modern improvement and comfort for visitors. Heated throughout. Suites of apartments. Smoke room and billiard room. Loose boxes for Hunters. Excellent stabling. Motor pit.'

The original leather-bound spirits book reveals that large quantities of champagne were consumed by the race-goer guests together with Holland Gin and Negus (a spiced port drink). The licence, incidentally, had been transferred from the 'small Oak Inn lower down the village'. Having later been bought by Col. Scott-Bowden, additional work was carried out on the hotel after the First World War. There was a total of 40 bedrooms.

In 1926, Mrs. Scott-Bowden, the owner's wife, organised a festival of women's cricket which was so successful that the National Women's Cricket Association was formed, with the hotel continuing for many years to be a base for the festival.

During the Second World War, Dame Laura Knight, the Impressionist artist, lived and worked in Colwall, usually staying with her husband at the Park

*Two views of the Colwall Park Hotel in the early 1900s*

*An advertisement for the Colwall Park Hotel (Brian Iles)*

Hotel. From 1947 until 1961 she actually had a studio in the hotel, commemorated by a plaque at the hotel's front entrance.

Having become uneconomic, the public bar was in 1977 turned into the Old Racecourse Grill, as a reminder of the former National Hunt racecourse and the hotel's connection as a centre of social activities for the racing fraternity.

In 1982, new owners Basil and Elizabeth Frost embarked on a five-year plan of extensive renovations, including opening up the ground floor to create a feeling of spaciousness, bringing the bar, restaurant and ballroom back into use, and providing conference facilities for up to 100 people. The bar was enlarged to include a former reception office and passage, whilst half the hotel was reroofed, the kitchens were retiled, and a new heating system was installed. Thirty bedrooms were fitted with new baths and showers.

Today, the Park Hotel is owned by Ian Nesbitt, who has been there since 2000. Actors appearing at the Malvern Theatre have often stayed at the hotel, including Penelope Keith, Joan Collins, Patricia Routledge and the late Edward Woodward.

Moving down through the village one soon comes to the **Crown Inn**, which started life as a beerhouse in the latter part of the 19th century and had George Paton as a beer retailer around the turn of the century. At the beginning of the 20th century John Pullen owned it for many years, with Emily Horton as tenant. The original bar was quite small with just the two windows, a cellar underneath the bar counter and a large orchard at the rear. Extensions at the side and back of the building provided space for a public bar.

*An advert for the Crown Inn in the late 1960s (Brian Iles)*

In 1975 the licence was transferred from John Hughes to Idris and Margaret Elton who were soon advertising special Sunday roasts with half a chicken at £1.75 and steaks from £2.50. When Ansell's Brewery began shedding its network of tenanted and managed pubs in 1982, the Crown was included on the list. It was bought by Keith and Elizabeth Scott who refurbished the two bars, turning the public bar into a games room, the dining room and residen-

*The Crown Inn in 2012*

tial accommodation. The exterior was redecorated and a substantial car park created in what used to be the old orchard. Today, the Crown is owned by Enterprise Inns and run by a manager.

Just further down the road past the public library with its clock tower – known as Aunt Alice in memory of the wife of Tom Pedlingham, a local dignitary – one comes to a little cluster of cottages and shops including a dwelling called The Oaks, which used to be the **Royal Oak** inn. Originally it was a cottage built on a piece of land which formed part of the Court Estate (later becoming Old Court). The building might date back to the 18th century, when it had a thatched roof, and might have been called Bucks House after a meadow called Bucks Close (now named Walwyn Meadow).

As the Royal Oak it was mentioned in the 1881 census with William Rogers, who also acted as local butcher, as innkeeper. There is mention of the inn in *Kelly's Directory* in 1902 with Thomas Smith as landlord.

Thomas Collis was another beerseller from a beerhouse, perhaps called Aston Cottage, where he was living in 1881. He was then described as a 'rope-maker employing one man and two boys'. However, in an 1891 directory he had become a 'beer retailer' as a well as a 'rope and twine manufacturer'. Apparently there was a rope walk, a passage where the twine was twisted in long lengths, between The Oaks and the nearby **Mount,** which may also have been a pub, and down to what is now Crescent Road.

By 1895 the property is believed to have included a butcher's shop, coach house, stables, slaughter house and farm buildings, with Jack Bishop building the butcher's shop. At the beginning of the 20th century it is possible that the poet laureate John Masefield (1878-1967) and friends bought the Royal Oak and also the Box Bush, a grade II listed former inn, in nearby Ashperton. But with the licence being transferred to the Colwall Park Hotel, the Royal Oak must have stopped trading in about 1905. In the 1990s the owners built a new kitchen and conservatory and also a fourth bedroom.

*The one-time Hop Pole*

Other cottages which were in use for a while as either an inn or beerhouse were **Bucks House**, a cottage on Court Estate, later Old Court, which was an inn from 1887 to 1905; the **Dog and Pheasant**, one of four cottages in Stone Drive which were all demolished in 1880; and the **Hop Pole** in Stowe Lane in a building part of which was the old village school.

Between Colwall Stone and Colwall Green is a large former inn on the right-hand side which is now the Thai Legend Restaurant. It was originally called the **Horse & Jockey**, then the **Horse & Groom**, after which it fluctuated between the two names, later becoming the **Oddfellows Arms** for a short while before reverting to the Horse and Jockey. The building started as a small black and white cottage with a thatched roof, with the *Hereford Journal* for 12 February 1784 advertising a messuage to be sold 'at the dwelling house of Thomas Gilding, known by the sign of the Horse and Jockey, in the parish of Colwall'.

By the 1820s it had become the Horse and Groom and in the 1850s and '60s Henry King was landlord, although he also had many other interests, being a farmer and landowner at Colwall Park and Sly House Farm as well as being a shopkeeper. By 1881 Edmund Nash had taken over the inn, but some ten years later he was listed as a 'shopkeeper and miller (water)'.

# HORSE AND JOCKEY HOTEL

**COLWALL, MALVERN**

Telephone:
COL 247

Proprietors:
Mr. and Mrs.
E. RICHARDS

•

FULLY
LICENSED

This hotel stands 500 feet above sea level, on the sunny side of the Malvern Hills. Charmingly situated and surrounded by beautiful country. Excellent Cuisine and Personal Attention. Ballroom for Private Parties and Dances. "Weddings a speciality"

*Two images of the Horse and Jockey in the mid 1900s when it was operating as a hotel (Brian Iles)*

At the time of the building of Colwall Park Hotel and the racecourse at the beginning of the 20th century, the Horse and Groom also came in for some rebuilding work, with Mr. H. Percy Smith again being the architect, from which it emerged better equipped to deal with the new century. It was now also a hotel and put up the grooms and jockeys taking part in the National Hunt meetings, while the trainers and owners stayed at the Park Hotel.

Having gone back to its original name, the Horse and Jockey, the inn closed in 1993 but reopened a year later under the name of Oddfellows, after the friendly society which held meetings in a separate building at the back. The curate of Colwall, the Rev. Ellen Clark-King blessed the pub with holy water, a first for her and for new landlady Mrs. Fiona Evans. It was the first pub Fiona and husband Keith had run as licensees. The interior was refurbished with new features including a children's room.

Then it was taken over by the rock band AC/DC, who made the bar open plan with the lounge being incorporated into the bar area. Terry Lee, who now lives in Spain, then became owner but towards the end of 2001 the inn closed its doors and all the ground-floor windows were boarded up. When it reopened it was as a Thai restaurant with the interior furnished in Far Eastern style with plenty of exotic oriental statues. The main entrance is now from the car park with the roadside front door and porch only used in an emergency. The bar counter remains in the same place.

*The Horse and Jockey in 2012 after its conversion into a Thai restaurant*

On the way out of Callow Green on the left-hand side is the **Yew Tree**, the oldest inn in the village, believed to date from the 17th century. It is named after a yew tree which blew down in 1915 taking the thatched roof with it. In 1881 Charles Pedlingham, who had seven children, was the innkeeper. He was probably the same Charles Pedlingham who was recorded as a 'corn and flour dealer and beer retailer' at the Terrace in Colwall Green in 1867. The Yew Tree was probably a beerhouse in the 19th century, as Thomas Orgee is listed as beerseller rather than an innkeeper in an 1891 directory. It was evidently owned by the Pedlingham family as in 1910, when Mrs. Kate Jones was the tenant, Mrs. C. Pedlingham lived on the premises.

Another Orgee – Harvey – had taken over in the 1950s, as recalled by local inhabitant Richard Fleetwood, who first visited the Yew Tree 54 years ago at the age of 14. 'It was a cider house then owned by West Country Ales,' he said, 'and there were spittoons and sawdust on the floor and a separate smoke room on the left which is now the cellar. Out the back was a shooting alley which was demolished when the Greens came.' (West Country Ales was taken over by the Cheltenham and Hereford Brewery which in turn became part of the Whitbread empire.)

Joan and Rowland Green took over the Yew Tree in 1957 and today it is still in the Green family although Rowland died in 1999 and Joan in February 2011. Soon after they came, they converted the cellar at the rear into a lounge.

In 1983, the *Malvern Gazette* reported that Whitbread were criticised for the second year running at Ledbury Brewster Sessions for failing to maintain one of their public houses, the Yew Tree, at Colwall. The chairman of the licensing justices, Col. Michael Singleton, said the licensees, Mr. and Mrs. Green, were not to be blamed in any way and, indeed, ran an excellent house in an attractive corner of the village. 'But I think the Dept. of the Environment might agree that it is becoming an eye-sore,' he said. 'As I said last year it is astonishing that a company of the size and reputation of Whitbread should have its name in large letters on the side of a pub which is such a poor adver-tisement for it.' He said Mr. and Mrs. Green, who had managed the pub for over 25 years by then, did all they could to make their customers comfortable. Whitbread declined to comment on the criticism, which the justices asked should be forwarded as an official complaint.

A year later the licensing justices told Whitbread again to put the Yew Tree in order if it wanted to have the licence renewed. Whitbread responded by saying that work costing £25,000 to improve the pub was due to start shortly.

A few years later the pub was bought by Mr. and Mrs. Green, who came to some arrangement to sell Banks' beer. Remnants of the old days include an off-sales counter at the front entrance into the bar, and a large pipe from the fireplace alongside the bar counter to provide heating. Adorning the walls are lots of photographs of the local football team, which still meets up at the pub.

*The Yew Tree in 2012*

Following the death of Mrs. Green, who had been ill for several weeks, the pub was taken over by her son, Dennis, with help from her daughter, Wendy.

Standing out on a limb from Colwall Stone is the church of St. James on the eastern side of which is the **Church Ale House**, a rare survivor of this type of building. Dating back to 1530, by 1600 its main use was for Church Ales – fund-raising activities rather like today's village fêtes – held several times a year. Specially brewed ale was sold and money was collected for church purposes. A fair amount of merriment and carousing took place, causing Jervis Markham in 1600 to include a description in his poem 'New Metamorphosis' (or a 'Feast of Fancie', the original of which is now housed in the British Museum), as follows:

> Church Ale at Colwall
> Oh, howe they doe profane the Saboth here!
> I doe protest it made me quake for feare.
> For popish superstition they doe still imbrace,
> Whereby Religion they doe quit deface.
> They have their Church-ale and old popish guise,
> Mother of errors and of monstrous lyes.
> The neighboure townes, they on the Saboth faste,
> A Master of Misrule enterteynes the guest
> With drums and Bagpipes and with warlike gunnes.
> Thus as to May-games all the people runns ...
> About Mid-service, they go in a Rowe
> After the Priest, into the Church-ale house
> (Which in the churchyard standeth) to carouse.

*Colwall's Church Ale House*

Puritan disapproval in the 17th century led to the closure of the Colwall ale house, but it survived as an almshouse until the early 1930s. About that time it had a thatched roof and was used as a simple cottage. In 1989 it was restored to become the church hall.

Leaving the Malvern Hills and travelling towards Ledbury on the A449, one soon comes across the **Wellington Inn** at Chances Pitch on the edge of the hills. The area is apparently named after a carrier who hired out extra horses to help pull waggons up the hill to Little Malvern.

*The Wellington Inn in the 1950s (Brian Iles)*

*How the bar once looked at the Wellington Inn*

Originally a cottage, the premises must soon have started supplying refreshment for passing travellers and was later much extended. The original front door is now behind a modern extension. A skittle alley was converted

*A landlord's family and staff and outside the Wellington Inn in the 1950s*

*The sign for the Wellington Inn*

into a restaurant with on the floor a wooden hatch to the cellar. Charles Green became manager in 1977. More recently, the inn has been owned by Mr. and Mrs. Sanger, of the Chocolate Box, Ledbury for about 10 years, while a recent landlord was Giles Goodhew, brother of Duncan, the Olympic gold medal swimmer, who took over in 2005. The grandfather of Giles, who was in the wholesale wine trade previously, was a director of Watneys, the London brewers, before in 1929 setting up a chain of Goodhew pubs.

Near the Wellington is the Pewtress Well from which Schweppes piped the Malvern water to their Colwall Springs factory. And it is believed that by the stream which bubbles out of this well, William Langland had his dream of wandering 'in a May morning on Malvern Hills' which became his famous work, *The Vision of Piers Plowman*. Son of a peasant woman, the 14th-century poet may have lived by Langland, the long field adjacent to the south west boundary of the parish. He was educated at the Malvern priories.

Continuing along the A449 back towards the Malvern Hills, one comes to Wynds Point where in a prime position at the junction with Jubilee Road stands the **Malvern Hills Hotel**, previously known as **British Camp** and before that as **Peter Pocket's**. Although the present building dates from the early 19th century, there has been a hostelry on the site for over 500 years.

During the Civil War the inn was used as a place of refreshment and billeting by Royalists, especially during the campaign which ended with the Battle of Worcester. From being a small building, two wings were added about 1848

*This page and opposite: three views of the British Camp showing, opposite, the effect of quarrying on the area, and overall the gradual accumulation of tree cover at this pass in the Malvern Hills (lower photo, Brian Iles)*

when it was owned by the Myddleton Biddulph family, of Chirk Castle. Peter Pocket was the licensed victualler in 1881 when he was 62 years old and still bringing up children, the youngest, Lucy, being only four years old. In 1878 the hotel was leased by the Biddulph family to Charles Hall at a yearly rent of £38 3s. In 1891 Richard Myddleton Biddulph, as tenant for life under the Settled Land Act, sold the hotel, now called British Camp after the Iron Age hillfort overlooking the premises, to Arnold Perrett, the Wickwar brewers. The landlady was Mrs. Annie Ingram, whose advertisement stated that 'picnic parties, tourists etc accommodated'. In 1894 the hotel was bought for £3,350 by Fred and Fanny Jones from Arnold Perrett.

In *Kelly's Directory* of 1916, an advert states that British Camp Hotel, with Mrs. F. Jones as proprietress, was the highest situated hotel in the Malverns, at 900 feet above sea level. 'This hotel has been greatly enlarged under the present management and Visitors, Tourists and Sportsmen will find here the comforts of a quiet home at Moderate Charges. Large Dining Room with Separate Tables for Visitors. Ladies' Drawing Room, Smoke rooms. Garage and Stabling.'

One of the hotel's most flamboyant owners was Billy Parrish, who bought the hotel in 1936 for £9,750 from Edward Berry. While living in Dudley, Mr. Parrish had become the owner of several collieries and brickworks in Dudley, and he also owned a number of racehorses, including Golden Fleece, the winner of 39 races. He also won a £100 bet by drinking a bottle of champagne in a lion's den. He died in 1946.

According to a letter to Mr. Parrish from a firm of estate agents in 1935, the hotel then consisted of 15 guest bedrooms, seven staff bedrooms, two sitting

*The British Camp in the 1930s*

*The swimming pool at the British Camp built in the 1930s*

rooms, a dining room and a tea room seating 80 people. A separate cottage on the main road had been converted into a shop with tea room attached and tea garden. The whole site extended to over five acres, and the annual turnover was £6,482.

'Recent extensions, redecorations and re-furnishing, have equipped the hotel with every detail of modern hotel comfort, convenience and service,' a brochure proclaimed, 'the magnificent panelled lounges and pleasant roof garden being especially attractive.' The tariff for a weekly stay was 3½ to 5½ guineas, with a double room costing 19/- a night, with a private sitting room at 10/6 and an all-day fire 3/-. Breakfast cost 3/-, luncheon 2/6 to 3/6 and dinner (table d'hote) 5/-. Dogs were not allowed in the public rooms, but accommodation was found for them in suitable quarters at 1/- per day.

A big attraction for guests and the general public alike was a large open-air swimming pool, built at the beginning of the 1930s, and located on the opposite side of Jubilee Drive, below what are now the public toilets. The pool was closed in the 1960s. In 1967 Mitchells & Butlers bought the hotel (as part of nearly £1½ million deal involving 119 pubs) from Atkinson's Brewery, Smethwick, Staffs, who had purchased it in 1959 for £34,159 16s 3d.

In 1975 the hotel changed its name to the Malvern Hills Hotel. A year later, a new lounge called the Jenny Lind lounge was opened by show jumper Alison Dawes following completion of £15,000 of alterations. Jenny Lind was the famous Swedish soprano who captivated the hearts of Victorian England and lived at Wynd's Point, the grounds of which adjoin the hotel, from 1877 until her death ten years later. An article of 1884 said: 'The house is built in this rocky quarry. From the house can be heard at times the innocent revelry at Peter Pocket's humble hostelry, so well known to tourists.'

The new lounge utilised space from the old snug and dining room and sported an extended bar. The oak panelling, which reputedly came from Ludlow Castle, remained intact. Improvements were also made to the Romulus restaurant with new decor, and the bar was re-named the Trappers. The proprietor then was David Elliston.

In 1988 Bass Mitchells & Butlers sold the business to David and Carole Fryer. The cottage was sold off two years later for £100,000 with the proviso that it only be used as a dwelling house, although a kiosk fronting the road for ice creams, beverages and snacks was allowed. Most of the land was also sold off. In 1996 Carole Fryer made a net profit of £115,556 on gross income of £297,395, as compared to a profit of £72,054 on £255,021 in 1994.

The Cooke family, from Birmingham, took over the hotel seven years ago with Mr. Matthew Cooke as manager, and from its neglected state have turned it into an upmarket hotel with a conservatory-style restaurant at the rear and a modern dining room, as well as the lounge bar with its 18th-century oak panels, newly refurbished conference facilities and 14 *en suite* bedrooms.

# CHAPTER TWELVE

# Powick, Bransford & Callow End

The parish of Powick includes the villages of Callow End, and the hamlets of Bastonford, Clevelode, Colletts Green and Deblins Green. Powick village was established in the early 8th century just above the flood level, and the manor of Powick was owned by Pershore Abbey but later given to Westminster Abbey by Edward the Confessor. At one stage Malvern lay within the Powick manor.

During the Civil War, Powick saw two battles take place. The first, really a skirmish, happened at Powick Bridge in 1642 with the Royalist Prince Rupert seeing off the Parliamentarians. The second, in 1651, the last battle of the War, saw Prince Charles' army of 16,000 defeated by Cromwell's New Model Army of twice the size.

Just outside the village is a large housing estate which for many years used to be an asylum, known first as the Worcester County Pauper and Lunatic Asylum when it was founded in 1847, and then later as the Powick Mental Hospital. It originally accommodated 200 patients, but the number increased to over 1,000 in the 1950s. The hospital closed in 1989 and all the workshops were bulldozed to be replaced by about 200 new houses. The main building was converted into flats. Interestingly, Edward Elgar was bandmaster at the asylum from 1879 until 1884.

Hop-picking was the big annual farming event with thousands of women and children being taken on as temporary workers at local farms. Saturday nights were usually spent at nearby pubs. Until fairly recently the Guinness company owned the hopyards at Braces Leigh farm, which is between Malvern and Powick.

The **Red Lion** on the A449, just off Powick's 'one way system', bears one of the most popular pub names, derived from the badge of John of Gaunt, Duke of Lancaster, the fourth son of Edward III, the most powerful man in England for much of the 14th century. The sign became even more widespread when James I (James VI of Scotland) came to the throne and ordered that a heraldic red lion should be displayed in public places.

A row of timber-framed cottages by the Red Lion were supposed to have been used by Cromwell as a hospital during the Battle of Worcester in 1651.

Sometime in the 18th century the end house, No. 45, which is now the Red Lion had a fire which also destroyed part of No. 44. The two fronts were rebuilt in brick, the cellar was used to dump the rubble and its entrance at the rear was bricked up. In the 1980s, the pub owners bought No. 44 to extend the property and also built an extension at the rear as a restaurant.

The Red Lion was first mentioned in a directory in 1840, with William and Mary Kerby the licensees in 1841. In 1884 the landlord was Alfred Knot. The pub would have been very busy during the hop-picking season as extensive hopyards existed nearby. A traffic island used to be in front of the pub but this disappeared in the 1960s when the road became one way.

For 66 years the licence was held by the Rodgman family, initially by Alfred who was there from 1897 until the late 1940s. Besides being a publican he also had a carrier business and hired out horses and carriages up until the First World War. Dinners and teas were also provided. He later became a butcher/farmer and, according to his grandson, Wally, during the Second World War killed sheep at the back of the pub for sale to the villagers. For many years a feature on the inn's terrace were two handsome stone lions, which he acquired from Hopton Court. The licence was taken over by his son Harry who stayed there until 1963, about which time the lions also left. Les Davis took over until the late 1970s, followed by Jack Oliver until the late 1980s.

The Red Lion was owned for many years by Whitbread, who sold it in 1995 for about £70,000 to Enterprise Inns as part of a chain of about 300 pubs. In the 1990s, the pub was described as having a comfy lounge area and a bar area with pool table; these areas have since been transformed into an open plan space. From 1998 to 2005 the landlord was Charles Ellis, a member of the parish council who in 2003 sent questionnaires to residents asking for

*The Red Lion at Powick in 2012*

comments on the prospect of incorporating a new village shop in the pub. There was no interest, however, and the shop never materialised.

In 2011 the pub closed for about 13 weeks before reopening in August with Mark Daniels as the new landlord. A local man, he also runs a pub in Worcester.

The **Crown** at Bowling Green, on the main Malvern Road, was a half-timbered inn built in the mid-19th century, which was much frequented by the local gentry when the area had one of the most popular bowling greens in the country, second only to Hadley, Droitwich, which boasted one of the oldest crown bowling greens (ones that use the whole green and can be undulating rather than flat).

Mentioned in a local directory of 1855, the Crown continued as a black and white cottage-style roadhouse with a main bar, an L-shaped cellar and a small wood-panelled snug at the back. A large garden was much used during the summer. The property backed onto the Powick Mental Hospital, some of whose inmates, accompanied by carers, used to frequent the pub, going into the back snug. Some used to wander down the road in carpet slippers.

But the writing was on the wall for this congenial but old-fashioned pub. The owners, Marston's, decided that the future lay in providing family-type food, especially after 200 houses were built on part of the Powick Hospital site. Thus at the beginning of the 21st century it underwent a rather radical refurbishment: it was simply demolished, the site cleared, and a new timber-framed building erected in its place. Much larger than its predecessor, it has

*The completely rebuilt Crown at Bowling Green in 2012*

one dining area after another, but a wealth of layered oak beams and open fires does help to give it something of the feel of a traditional pub, although barn-like. Meals are available all day, every day, with a 'two for one' meal offer.

There was also another pub in the area called the **Bowling Green**, which has probably been long since demolished. In *Kelly's Directory* of 1884 Geoffrey Oliver is described as beer retailer at the Bowling Green, while in 1904 David Slade was the beer retailer.

At No. 6 The Village is an Indian restaurant called Cromwells which used to be the **Vernon Arms** and before that the **Yellow Lion**. The new name is an obvious reference to Powick's connection with the Civil War, whilst Vernon is not a reference to the famous 18th-century Admiral Vernon or Sir George Vernon, of Hanbury Hall, but to Vernon Smith, from Malvern, who after buying the pub decided to name it after himself. The earlier use of 'Yellow' to describe a lion may have been to differentiate it from the nearby Red Lion; Yellow Lion pubs are certainly rare.

A faded picture in the restaurant shows the Spring floods of May 1886 when the area surrounding the pub was under water. In 1904 the landlord was George Hodges.

In 1951, Worcester County Licensing Sessions were told that although alterations to the Yellow Lion, entailing the provision of a servery and modern sanitation, had been approved, they had not been carried out. Supt. E.T. Jackson said: 'In particular lavatory accommodation is very badly needed indeed. This house lacks proper car parking facilities. I am somewhat perturbed that nothing has been said.' The Superintendent was to report back in three months.

The pub was called the Vernon Arms in 1985. In 1996 it was described as having a plush lounge and lively bar, but presumably not lively enough, as at the beginning of the 21st century it closed its doors as a hostelry and reopened as an Indian restaurant, now specialising in both Bangladeshi and Indian cuisine. While the whole interior has been gutted and transformed into an Asian area, the front door and windows are unchanged.

In what remains of Powick village after the road redevelopment is a lane on the left side of which are four cottages which used to form the **Coventry Arms**, named after the Earls of Coventry who resided at Croome Court and owned much of the land in the area.

The main bar was in what is now the lounge of No. 1 and there was also a snug. There was a cellar which is now the kitchen of No. 2 while at Nos. 3 and 4 was a brewery. On the opposite side of what until the 1950s was an unmade road, was a butcher's shop and slaughterhouse. In 1884 the landlord was Henry Finch.

The last landlord was Trevor Thackeray, and the inn closed down in the late 1960s. In 1971 the owners, Flower and Sons, already absorbed into the

Whitbread empire, sold it to Robert Ines Macadie Development Company, which converted it into four cottages.

The **Halfway House**, on the A449 at Bastonford, was so named because of its location between Worcester and Malvern. The back part of the pub and also part of the next door house used to be an ancient coaching inn, while the garage was the old stables. The front half of Halfway House is Georgian.

Until the A449 was built the main road to Malvern passed the pub's front door after crossing an ancient ford from which the village took its name. The road now stops in front of the pub. In 1904 Mrs. W. Sudds was in charge. For many years it was owned by Marston's, who sold off the freehold about 20 years ago. The present owner and chef, Steve Croft, took it over in 2005 from Brian and Pamela Burke, who had been in charge for

*Four views of the Coventry Arms down the years, that at the bottom showing how the pub has been converted into cottages with No.2 being refurbished in 2012*

several years. The layout remains the same with a bar in the middle and two dining areas on either side, one side technically in Worcester and the other in Malvern. Steve added accommodation with two letting rooms.

When in 2005 Steve decided to hold a lobster festival he never expected the kind of reaction it received. He hadn't heard of the Lobster Liberation Front! After word got around, the front wall of Halfway House was daubed with the words 'Scum', 'Free the Lobsters', 'Lobster Liberation' and 'ALF' (Animal Liberation Front) in red and black paint. Pickets were stationed outside and protests made inside the pub for about five days. A spokeswoman for People for the Ethical Treatment of Animals said that cooking an animal alive was 'inherently cruel and violent'. But the protests had the opposite effect to that intended; the profile of the festival was raised and over 500 lobster portions sold in a month following lots of local support.

Undeterred by all the fuss, Steve held another lobster festival the following year, again incurring the wrath of the animal rights activists, who this time slashed the festival sign and picketed the pub with loudspeakers and klaxons. He decided against holding a third festival, but still serves lobsters.

A traditional 19th-century ale-house, the **Three Nuns** at Colletts Green is so called on account of three nuns from Stanbrook Abbey in Callow End who were given dispensation to live close to the area of the present-day pub. The Benedictine nuns came to Stanbrook in the 19th century, with the abbey church

*The Halfway House in 2012*

completed in 1871. Owned by Marston's, the pub has just the one bar with darts one end, lounge area the other end, with dining tables in the corner, in an area which was originally a private living room. The staircase has been moved from the front round to the back, and there is traditional wall and window seating.

*Passengers for coach tours waiting at the Three Nuns over the years*

Coach outings from the pub were a popular feature in the 1920s and just after the Second World War.

Gerald and Mal Robinson were in charge for nearly 30 years before retiring in 2004. They organised many different events including an ill-fated attempt to form a Powick and District Sumo wrestling league in 1996, which foundered when only Gerald could make the weight! David Redfern and his wife Lesley took over around 2007. In 2010, they were forced to remove an advertising sign which had been drawing in passing trade for 20 odd years. The hand-painted sign, measuring about four feet by two feet, was located on the A449 to attract custom to this tucked away pub. It featured an arrow pointing towards the Three Nuns and advertised 'pub grub'. However, Worcestershire County Council decided the sign caused a legal obstruction of the highway and was to be removed. Ann Morgan, known as Nanny Ann, the

*The Three Nuns and its inn sign in 2012*

captain for 28 years of the Avengers womens darts team, based at the Three Nuns, died in May 2011.

**The Fox** is located on the A4103 at Bransford Bridge and is a large roadside Chef and Brewer pub with the emphasis on food. Before that it was a Miller's Kitchen pub. The pub was first listed in 1841 and there is a reference to the Fox in the *Malvern Advertiser* of 25 August 1860 in a case of assault and robbery being heard at Malvern Petty Sessions. A labourer aged about 18, named George Anthony, was charged by William Griffiths, a carter, with assaulting him in the high road near the Fox Inn and robbing him of his watch. Anthony was committed for trial at the assizes.

Flooding by the Teme River occurs on a regular basis with one of the worst recorded in *Berrows Journal* of 9 September 1852. The paper stated:

> The Teme rose considerably in this locality [Bransford] about 12 o'clock, and the roads were to a large extent inundated. Great fears were entertained for the safety of the Bridge (a wooden structure) but we are glad to state it has been ascertained to have escaped uninjured. The Fox Inn, situated in its close proximity, was deluged with water, which filled the cellars, kitchen, bar and parlour, covering the floors to a depth of nearly five feet. In the retreat of the unwelcome visitor the floor of the parlour was found to be covered with a layer of mud some six inches in depth.
>
> We must mention that some poor Irish people, consisting of two women and six or seven children, were sleeping in a stable adjoining the Fox Inn, when the flood reached them, about one o'clock. The poor creatures alarmed for their lives rushed through the rapidly rising water and craved admission to the inn in piteous accents. Their request was at once granted, although the interior, from its flooded state, was scarcely more comfortable than the exterior, and they huddled together in the vicinity of the fireplace until morning. It affords us much satisfaction

*The Fox at Bransford in 2012*

to state that no loss of life, either of man or beast, took place here. The lightning and thunder were described as having been most terrific.

Soon after this, in 1860, a brick bridge was built across the Teme to take the Worcester to Bromyard railway line. It collapsed in 1890 after floods undermined its foundations.

A building at the back of the Fox, which doubled as a hop-pickers' bar usually on a Saturday night, was the venue for the Bransford Oddfellows' Fete in 1909. One landlord, John Turner, founded the Fox Cricket Club in 1946, which continued into the 1970s, and is also remembered for giving free drinks at New Year rather than Christmas, lining up bowls of punch for everyone to help themselves. After the Second World War, horticultural shows were also held in the back building, later called the Oddfellows' Room. There were also ladies' and men's darts teams.

Until about 15 years ago, the Fox was a typical country pub with a west-facing verandah along the front, and until the building of the A4103, the main road to Malvern passed along the front of the building. But all this changed. A large restaurant extension was added at the back and a children's playground built at the side with an enclosed play barn. Sports and pub games teams faded. However, the original tiled flooring in the main bar remains and the old layout before walls were knocked down can still be discerned. During a refurbishment in 2010, the wooden model of a fox and squirrel was taken down and put up over the fireplace in the bar, and a new sign with just a fox was installed on the roadside post.

On the side of the **Bear and Ragged Staff**, in Station Road, Bransford is a sandstone block with the date 1861 and the capital letter B, presumably meaning it was built in 1861 by the Beauchamp family, owners of much land in the area. It was originally erected as a base for collecting rent from local tenanted estates and only later became a pub, first appearing as the Bear and Ragged Staff in a local directory of 1873. The sign depicts the county crest of Warwickshire. The Bear and Ragged Staff were first used by the Beauchamp family, who became Earls of Warwick in 1268, as a mark of identity and also used on their great seal. Another Earl of Warwick to use the two devices was Richard Neville, (1428-1471), known as The Kingmaker, who married Richard Beauchamp's daughter and heir. According to legend, the first earl killed a bear by strangling it, while the second earl killed a giant with a ragged staff.

The inn stands on what used to be the main road to Worcester and the side lane went down to the railway station. It was part of the Croome Estate with the land owned by the Earl of Warwickshire. Over the years it has evolved considerably. There used to be two side entrances on the side of the building facing the lane, while a stable at the front has been incorporated into the pub. Next to the front door is a separate entrance leading to an upstairs flat called Windyridge. A nearby window was at one time the stable door leading to a small courtyard with a urinal to the rear. Further along still remains the door used by the carriages, with a hay loft above. The original oak window frames are still *in situ* on the upper floor. An extension was built at the back to accommodate the toilets.

Mr. G. Grainger was landlord from at least 1884 to 1904. Up until the early 1960s, the Bear and Ragged Staff was one of the most popular watering holes for the hundreds of temporary workers brought into the area during the hop-picking season. In about 1966, the landlord Arch Maund bought a steamroller but never had it restored. However, a village group got it into workable condition and gave Mr. Maund the inaugural ride in 1967 to the Fox – a distance of about two miles.

For between 10 and 15 years, the inn was called the Cobblers Restaurant at the Bear, until in 1997 the property was bought by Gary Whitby and Lynda Williams, who brought back its original name and carried out renovations to make it a food-orientated upmarket pub. In 2006 it was the Worcestershire Dining Pub of the Year. Margaret Elgar, great niece of the composer, who was the last member of the family to bear his name and who could remember him, was a regular diner at the inn until her death in 2010.

*Two views of the Bear and Ragged Staff at Bransford,
in the late 19th century and 2012*

Callow End is perhaps best known for Stanbrook Abbey, the Benedictine monastery. The nuns were in residence from 1838 but the dominating tower with its unique clock was only built in 1871, by Pugin the Younger, son of the Pugin who designed the Houses of Parliament. But in 2009 the nuns relocated to Yorkshire and the abbey has since been extensively refurbished and is now used for weddings and other functions. Another building of interest is Prior's Court, an early manor house, renowned for its ghost, the Grey Lady, and there is also a pound, though this no longer retains lost animals.

A sign with a Roman soldier carrying a bowl of evergreens on the main road leads down a lane to **The Old Bush**, formerly the **Ewe and Lamb** and first listed in 1840. The sign harks back to Roman times when evergreens were displayed outside taverns to indicate that wine was available. Later poles were decorated with ivy as signs (known as ale stakes) to identify alehouses. The sign at Callow End reinforces the Roman connection.

Built about 250 years ago, the pub has undergone significant changes over the

*Above: The sign for the Old Bush, harking back to Roman inn signs*
*Right: The Old Bush in the 1960s. The lower photograph taken in 1969 shows that the topiary in front of the inn has been cut down and a new entrance doorway created*

*Above: The hunt meets at the Old Bush in the 1970s, after the front had been rendered and given mock beams*
*Left: The inn in 2012*

years. Originally a small brick building, the front was given a black and white facelift in the 1970s with the brick rendered over and wooden beams added. Two extensions with flat roofs have been added at the back – the first one to provide a dining area and the second to create even more space and to build a new kitchen. It is basically one bar, although there is a small separate area which used to be the old kitchen, while the bar counter has been moved.

In the 1950s, it was run for seven years by Jack and Sylvia Bennett, members of the Bennett family who have lived in the village for 150 years. In those days, the pub was packed out at weekends and it ran successful darts and crib teams and a football club. The pub was flooded out once after torrential downpours had sent water cascading down from the hills behind the building. Mr. and Mrs. Davis ran the Old Bush in the 1960s, Fred Weston was there from 1969 for about 10 years, while Mal Williams was landlord in the 1980s. Dene Williams and Joanne Letties were licensees from 2001 until mid 2012.

For many years the pub was owned by the Lewis Clarke brewery of Worcester. They stopped brewing in 1970, since when it has been a Marston's pub.

The **Blue Bell** was listed in 1855 and is still open today. The bell is one of the commonest pub names in England, but when the name is coloured the bell is always blue for some unexplained reason. In 1884 the landlord was Alfred Copson and in 1904 it was James Copson, presumably a son. The pub was badly damaged after a fire broke out one winter when Wallace E. George was the publican, at a time when the pub was a free house. In the 1990s it was described as a large pub in a small village with a spacious lounge given over to the food trade, and a basic bar. It was a venue for auctions.

In August 2002, plans were submitted by landlords Bill Price and Ann Curnock to open a post office in an existing office and private lounge on the pub's ground floor, following the closure earlier that year of the village post office. The public areas would be unaffected by the alterations. These plans took a step closer after the owners of the pub, The Union Pub Company, run by Marston's, agreed terms on a new lease on the premises. In March 2003,

*The Blue Bell around the end of the 18th or early 19th century after it had been badly damaged by a fire (Brian Iles)*

the post office at the Blue Bell was given the go-ahead and it was opened that summer. In August 2008 it was announced that the post office would move from the Blue Bell to the village shop, instead of being closed.

The pub was flooded during the big floods of 2007 soon after Sue Donohue became the licensee. The same thing happened again on 27 December 2010 when pipes burst, flooding the kitchen and office, and ruining fridges, freezers, food stock and office equipment. It stayed shut for six weeks while repair work was carried out.

There is also a reference in 1855 of a pub called the **Square & Compasses**, later known as the **Magpie**, which apparently burnt down in the 1970s, and at Stanbrook End the **Swan** was listed in 1841.

In Pixham is a long white building, Pixham House, which used to be an inn called **The Boat**, also known as the **Pixham Ferry Inn**, and attached to Pixham Ferry, both part of the Madresfield Estate, which operated a ferry service across the River Severn to Kempsey on the east bank. The inn provided refreshment and entertainment for over 300 years, closing on 10 October 1903. It is now a private residence.

Twice a year Lord Beauchamp's agent held audit dinners at the inn at which each tenant was given a ticket in exchange for his rent. According to local historian Mr. H.W. Gwilliam, the landlords Mr. and Mrs. Edwards told of the 'huge pieces of boiled beef, four or five roasted pigs and six chickens with great cauldrons of vegetables, and dozens of plum puddings' which were available, and they also said that the ale flowed freely.

During the summer, steamers called at Pixham Ferry on a Sunday and unloaded hordes of day trippers, the men spending most of their time bowling at the fine bowling alley and drinking ale, while the women and children picknicked on the Old Hills. On the other side of the Severn, the Ham was used for military reviews which brought huge crowds from both sides of the river.

The ferry continued to operate regularly – in 1930 charges were: foot passengers 2d, bicycle 3d, motor car 1s – and it was capable of taking several horses, cattle and cars at one time. In both 1934 and 1939 it was in need of repair and Lord Beauchamp wanted to hand it over to Worcester County Council. However, the council would not accept it and the ferry eventually became derelict. A smaller boat occasionally operated until 1947.

During the floods of 2007 Pixham House was badly affected, with water rising half way up its walls. The owner gutted the building and completely refurbished it. An extension on the side nearest the river had been built earlier to provide a modern kitchen and utility room.

In the village of Rushwick, now circumvented by the western by-pass, is the **Whitehall Inn**, a traditional country pub, which is about 200 years old but first appeared in a local directory in 1851. In recent years the pub has had at least three signs, according to Anthony Collis, all bearing the same name, but

*The Whitehall Inn in Rushwick in 2012*

each with a separate theme. The present sign depicts a horse being groomed in a stable. This replaced a sign that showed a guardsman on ceremonial duty in London. The earlier sign referred to a scene from one of the Whitehall farces. According to Fiona Goldsby, who runs the pub with her husband Ron, this sign was of a Negro jester in his jester outfit astride a horse. 'The story goes,' she adds, 'that the sign was inspired by a travelling theatre group from the Whitehall theatre'.

Around the Whitehall are numerous small pools and ponds which makes it an ideal place for anglers, so much so that for many years there has been an Angling Club based at the pub.

CHAPTER THIRTEEN

# Leigh Sinton, Storridge, Stiffords Bridge, Cradley, Mathon, Alfrick, Longley Green & Suckley

Half way along Hereford Road in the village of Leigh Sinton is an imposing building with signs proclaiming a Chinese Takeaway which used to be a well-established inn called the **Somers Arms**, probably named after Baron or Earl Somers who was also Viscount Eastnor of Eastnor Castle. In 1794 the Worcester to Hereford stagecoach, known as the Hereford Mail, used to stop at the Somers Arms, which could provide both stabling for the horses and accommodation for the passengers. It cost 10s to travel inside the coach and 5s on the outside. The first listing of the inn was in 1841, and a photograph taken in 1895 shows a notice on the wall saying, 'Somers Arms. Good Stabling', and an illuminated sign with the words: 'Salt & Co Ltd, Burton Ale and Stout'.

It appears that the inn was closed for a while during the Second World War as the *Malvern Gazette*, dated 25 March 1944, reported that the 'former pub, the Somers Arms, may be turned into a nursing home with 30 residents and staff'. However, it was reprieved. When taken over by Dennis and Sybil Clewer in 1952, the bedrooms had jugs of washing water and a slop basin, with chamber pots under the beds, and an outside toilet. Large club-rooms were used by several local organisations – the Darby and Joan Club and

*The Somers Arms in 1895*

Leigh United Football Club amongst others – and it was the base for crib, quoits, men's and women's darts teams, table tennis and skittle teams. When it started doing catering, the Leigh farmers held dinners there. It was also a venue where the Croome Hunt would meet.

The Somers Arms was at its busiest during the hop-picking season, with pickers coming from Wales and the Black Country. As many as a dozen coaches might park in the village with many of the passengers finding their way to the hostelry. Its lawn, running from the road to the back of the building, would be packed with children. The Clewers also organised a number of fund-raising events including a party attended by 160 children, and a country and western evening which raised £650 for the Worcester Royal Infirmary. After 21 years as mine hosts, Dennis and Sybil retired in 1973, having to leave the business prematurely because of ill health.

The inn closed around 1995 and, now known as the Old Somers Arms, houses a multitude of businesses: a Chinese takeaway, the Malvern Martial Arts Centre, Burton Printworks, Bromyard Tae Kwon Do, Burton Properties and AS Consultancy, as well as the Barn Nursery in part of the old bottle store at the rear. The Martial Arts Centre also boasts a multi-purpose gymnasium, open for private bookings.

*The Somers Arms in 2012, with a close up of the sign that is above the window to the right of the door*

Just off the A4103 in Malvern Road, Leigh Sinton, is the **Royal Oak**, an 18th-century building which first appeared as an inn in a local directory of 1841 and to which originally two cottages were attached. At the back of the Oak, which it was usually called, was a skittle alley where a former landlord, Bill Costello, managed to build an early hop-picking machine in collaboration with another villager. He moved the machine to a local farm and later produced a portable machine which could be taken to the hop-yards.

In 1937 the pub was taken over by Henry Davies, who was born in the village and was a male nurse at Powick Hospital for 21 years before trying his hand in the licensed trade. He ran the pub with his wife, Frances, who was also a nurse at the hospital, for the next 38 years, not retiring until January 1975 at the age of 73. He was the oldest member of the Worcester and District Licensed Victuallers Association. It was during his tenure that the cottages and skittle alley were demolished.

When Bernard Atkinson became the next landlord, the Royal Oak was fairly run down, but the brewery made improvements and Mr. Atkinson built up the trade, reputedly sleeping with a gun under his bed so as to be able to protect the night's takings. Two men's darts teams met there on Monday and two women's darts teams on Tuesday, with darts and cribbage on Wednesday, while the Savings Club met on Friday. Customers saved the whole year for Christmas, and one year the pub paid out £30,000. A clay-pigeon club was also formed.

In the early 1990s, the inn was taken over by Irishman Brian Lynch, known for his outrageous behaviour. Before going into the pub trade he had been an engineer officer in the Merchant Navy, serving on the liner *Queen Elizabeth*. In 1998, Martin and Caroline Roberts took over as tenants. A former butcher in the Channel Islands, Martin turned the public bar into a restaurant and helped the Royal Oak win several awards for best pub garden. 'Gardening is the way I relax,' said Martin, who was also the chef.

In February 2010, Mark Lennard, a builder by trade, took over the pub, by then owned by Marston's Pub Company, with his partner Pauline Goodman. They have enhanced the pub's sporting tradition with the installation of a shooting range for air rifles and air pistols, with the Worcester Air Ambulance as beneficiaries from range fees. The clay-pigeon club is still going strong, a

*The Royal Oak in 2012*

*The inside of the Royal Oak in 2012*

boules team utilise an outdoor pitch, a dog club meets monthly, and there is also a golf society and darts team. Although much modified over the years, the Royal Oak retains its oak beams and brass work, and there is an excellent smoking area in the rear beer garden which also features a flat-screen TV for the viewing of mainly sports events.

No inn has existed within living memory in the separate village of Leigh although apparently there was a beerhouse called the **Bridge Inn** mentioned in documents relating to the Old Rectory in the early and mid 1800s. There was once the **Half Moon** in Dingle Road and **The Bluebell** in Top Cottages, on the Alfrick Road, but no records of either have been found.

On the A4103 at Storridge is the **New Inn**, adjacent to the Worcester Way, a 40-mile walk from Bewdley to Great Malvern. First listed in 1841, the pub was run by John South, described as a horse dealer and beer retailer, from 1876 until 1891, while Mrs. Elizabeth Ody was in charge from 1902 to 1917. William Edmunds took over in 1922 and was still there in the 1930s when it was owned by Lewis Clarkes Ltd, the Worcester brewery, which was taken over by Marston's Brewery, of Burton, in 1937.

In the 1950s Les Cridland was landlord, with Fred Artopp taking over in the 1970s. Then, in the late 1980s, following the death of his wife, Mr. Artopp committed suicide by shooting himself in the head in what used to be the private lounge behind the bar but is now the kitchen. For the last seven years

Alan and Jean Jethcott have been the licensees, with Admiral Taverns the owners for the last five years.

Four years ago a major refurbishment was carried out during which a restaurant extension was built on what used to be the beer garden. A new bar counter was installed, but the window seating was retained. An open-air shooting range is available in a field at the back of the pub, which hosts the Hilltop Mini Club, together with crib, darts and quiz teams.

Alfrick has the reputation of being the most haunted village in Worcestershire. Lewis Carroll, author of the *Alice in Wonderland* books, visited the village when his brother was curate. It also had a certain reputation for tippling as far back as 1625 when the Worcester Quarter Sessions reported that 'Richard Child of Alfrick presents that Walter Phillips selleth

*The New Inn at Storridge*
*Top left: in the 1930s when a Lewis Clarke's pub*
*Top right: in 2001*
*Bottom: in 2012, after a major refurbishment and extension*

ale by unlawful measure and keepeth a disorderly house namely suffering disordered persons to drink and swill the whole night together in his house.'

Ghosts, however, do not seem to have appeared in the history of the **Swan** public house, which is now a private dwelling called the Old Swan on the right-hand side of the main road from Leigh Sinton into the village. The smaller of the two buildings, a timber-framed cottage with lath and plaster, was the first to be built some two to three hundred years ago, followed later by the main building. The Swan was originally a farm, certainly in Victorian times, with a butcher's shop and slaughterhouse on the other side of the main building, whilst at the rear was housing for the cattle awaiting slaughter. It then began selling cider and was soon making beer, the brewing equipment being kept in the cottage, before being granted a full licence. It was first listed in 1873.

For many years at the turn of the century, the Swan was owned by James Coles, who described himself as both butcher and landlord. In 1905 the *Malvern Gazette* reported the theft of ferrets in an unusual court case. The two animals, worth 10 shillings, were the property of Mr. Coles, and stolen from a shed behind the Swan. A Leigh man, who pleaded guilty to the theft, was sent to prison for 28 days with hard labour. It was reported that he was a member of the Coldstream Guards, who had deserted whilst serving in South Africa in order to come home.

Five years later the landlord was in the news again, this time for reckless driving of a horse and trap on the Worcester-Alfrick highway. Rather surprisingly, a photograph was taken of Mr. Coles being handed the summons by Police Sergeant Griffin. Mr. Coles later sold the pub to Flower's Brewery of Stratford-on-Avon.

In 1948 a young couple, John and Joan Barker, took over the licence and remained there until he retired in 1997 after 49 years as landlord, the then longest serving landlord in the West Midlands. Their daughter, Diane, who was born in the pub, remembers as a child the autumn days in the 1950s when hop-pickers from the Black Country descended on the village, staying in

*John Barker behind the bar at the Swan, not long after taking over at the pub in 1948*

*An older John Barker behind the bar at the Swan*

barrack-type tin buildings at a nearby farm. Her father turned the garage into a bar for the thirsty pickers and levied a deposit for a glass. It was not until hop-picking machines were introduced that the annual influx of hired workers dried up. She also recalls that the regular customers, with names like Shady and Rosie, came to the pub on foot or by cycle, and across the fields.

In the late 1950s, the brewery remodelled the pub, flattening the front of the building by removing the original two bay windows, together with the one on the adjoining cottage, transferring the staircase from the front to the back of the building, and providing a flat roof to a lean-to building between the main building and the cottage. This area was also used as a bar and became known as The Passage. The main bar was adorned with various collections including horn cups, beer jugs, bottles with marble stoppers, and beer mats.

The Barkers introduced annual events such as the Harvest Festival auction, first held in the 1960s, and a Bonfire Night, both in aid of Cancer Research. Also the North Ledbury Hunt, led by the indomitable Lady Waechter, would meet there.

*The pub sometime after its 1950s remodelling*

*Harvest Festival at the Swan*

The Swan became the centre for village activities including rifle shooting, a cricket team, and the Alfrick tug-of-war team, which pulled against the Welsh champions, whom they beat in a competition at the Royal Oak Inn, Malvern Link around 1980. When Whitbread's, who had taken over Flower's in 1961, decided to sell off their pubs in 1990, the Barkers decided to take advantage of the situation and bought the Swan with help with the mortgage from another brewery, Marston's, provided they sold their beer. Then in 1997, after 49 years at the helm, John Barker called it a day. After trying unsuccessfully to sell the pub, he obtained planning permission to convert it into a private dwelling. With her parents now both dead, Diane Barker lives in the cottage while the main building is rented out. What used to be the butcher's shop was sold and has since been enlarged and converted into a private residence.

At one time Alfrick Pound, so named because it was once an area where stray livestock were held in a pound until the owner was traced, boasted two pubs, a village school, a sweet shop, bakery, blacksmith and even a police house. The tide of time has seen their closures, but many of the original buildings remain such as the **Wobbly Wheel,** a timber-framed, brick-panelled construction dating from 1640. Known first as the **New Inn**, it may have been built as a coaching inn. A record of 1745 mentions a court being held at the house of William Hall, a victualler in Alfrick Pound, though whether his house was also the inn or another building is not known.

*The current house sign on the building that was once the Wobbly Wheel inn*

Barrels were lined up in a room which is now the kitchen, and the beer served through a hatch, while in a 40ft-long out-building to the rear of the property, skittles was a popular pastime. In about 1951 the name was changed to Wobbly Wheel, so named because buckled wheels came in useful as inn signs. A wobble-shop in the low slang of the 19th century was a shop where liquor, called Wobble and the last 'shut' of the brew, was sold though the proprietor had no licence. During this period, one landlord, Mr. Brown, kept a pet parrot much to the amusement of customers.

The Wobbly Wheel was owned for many years by Spreckley Brothers, the Worcester brewers which closed in 1968, and then by Marston's. A Marston's price list of 1971, shortly after the introduction of decimalisation, shows that a pint of beer ranged from 11p for PXX IPA to 21p for Owd Rodger, whilst Guinness cost 17p, a small cider 8p, and Babycham was priced at 90p.

In about 1972 or '73, a few years after the introduction of the drink/driving laws, the Wobbly Wheel ground to a final halt and was converted into a private house, but retained the name.

The other pub in the village was the **Pound House**, listed in 1855, which became redundant in 1906 and closed. It was named, of course, after the enclosure in which stray animals were impounded.

Since 1850 the sprawling parish of Suckley (meaning 'wood where the birds are found') has been well known for cherry orchards and hop gardens and has boasted no fewer than eight public houses, probably even more during the hop-picking season. One of the earliest records of drinking was recorded in the Worcestershire Quarter Sessions of 1625: 'William Pryse selleth ale without a licence and saith he will do the same again despite of him that speaketh against him.' William Pryse, a weaver, clearly had something of a reputation, for it is recorded that he 'entered the house of Roland Walker and put them in great fear and did assault Roland Walker'. Another record notes that Widow Gale of Suckley 'is one of many ale sellers selling without a licence'.

*The Nelson in 2012*

Only two of these pubs now remain open and one of them, **The Nelson**, is in the village of Longley Green and apparently has always been a freehouse. Some years ago an extension was added to the front of the building to form a restaurant in which the old well, which used to be outside, is now a feature. To one side is a long building which serves as a multi-function room including a skittles alley, behind which is a large field owned by the pub. There is also a beer garden and children's area.

Nine years ago the pub was bought by Rod and Belinda Barlow and for the last three years it has been run by Mrs. Barlow and her son Maxwell, while Mr. Barlow works for an oil company based in Malvern. Twenty-year-old Maxwell is one of the youngest landlords in the West Midlands.

Past the post office/shop is a minor road on the right and at the top of the hill is a white building called Old Byeways, now divided into two private properties, which was once an inn called **Byeways**. Built in the early 19th century with wattle and daub panels, it was originally a farmhouse called Mars, with a bakery to one side and stables, occupied by a family of Mormons who would have attended local revivalist meetings in the 1840s. However, they could not make a go of the farm and they decided to emigrate to America, ending up in Salt Lake City.

Later the property became an inn, with the front door opening into the public bar and a trap door leading down to the cellar. A team of horses would have been provided to help haul waggons up the neighbouring hill, and the surrounding fields were covered in daffodils, cherry and cider apple trees. About

*Still called Byeways, this building was once an inn*

50 years ago it closed as a pub and became two separate properties, with the stables on one side of the building being converted into a dining room.

Not far from the Nelson are two old houses which were formerly public houses – **Seville House** and **Rough Leasow**. Originally built in the 16th century as two dwellings, Seville House later became an inn. A hundred or more years ago Polly Beard was the landlady; she was apparently well off, owning a cottage and land at the back of the pub. A well-worn windowsill near the front door used to be a serving hatch through which drinks were passed. Some time ago there was a fire in the storeroom, which has since been converted into a dining room. Seville House closed as a pub in about the 1970s. The nearby Rough Leasow, meaning rough pasture land, is a grade II 17th-century building, which operated as a cider- or beerhouse in the 19th century and early 20th century. It was restored in the late 20th century and is now two cottages under one continuous tiled roof. One cottage is timber-framed, the other built of brick, but both have two storeys with an attic.

On the road to Acton Green are two private dwellings which used to be cider houses, probably again in the 19th century, and still retaining their pub names. The **Plough** is a 300- to 400-year-old building with a Victorian addition to one side, and next door is the **Crown**.

*Three buildings in Suckley that were once pubs. From top to bottom: Seville House, The Plough and The Crown*

On the very edge of Suckley is the popular drinkers' haunt called the **Cross Keys**, a name referring to the keys entrusted by Jesus to St. Peter with the words: 'I give unto thee the keys to the kingdom of heaven'. The inn was originally known as the **Saracen's Head**, which often appeared in the coat of arms of noble families whose members had taken part in the Crusades and waged battle against the Saracens, or Turks. According to the 1841 census, Lucy Pressdee, aged 30, was the publican followed in 1851 by another woman, Elizabeth Redding, aged 34, whose husband, Thomas, was described as a carpenter. Ten years later, and now called the Cross Keys, the innkeeper was Theophilus Eberal, aged 70, who ran it with his wife, Sarah, aged 69.

In 1863, 'Samuel Stinton sold the Cross Keys inn with barn, stable, cider house, mill, cart and horse and other buildings, gardens, orchard and land to Thomas Rowley Hill and Thomas William Hill, esquires of the City of Worcester, selling at £330'. On the death of Thomas Rowley Hill's son, Edward Henry, part of the estate passed to his nephew, Richard Willis Kane, including the Cross Keys. In 1871, Thomas Wood, aged 64, was described as publican/grocer/carpenter, while ten years later William Watkins, 38, was the beerhouse keeper living with his 76-year-old mother, Hannah. Percy Burgess, described as both publican and butcher, took over but was soon in trouble with the law. Worcester's *Berrow Journal* reported in 1901 that Percy Burgess 'was fined £2 by the County Magistrates for permitting drunkenness on his premises and also allowing drinkers to remain there for a nine-hour period. Police officers reported finding two women and several men sprawled drunk at the beerhouse.' By 1911 William Griffin, who was also a blacksmith, was in charge.

In 1916, the freehold inn and premises together with the butcher's shop, garden and pasture orchard were put up for sale. At the time it was let to Messrs. Lewis Clarke & Co., Brewers, Worcester, on a yearly tenancy determinable on six months notice at £46 *per annum*. The description added that the Cross Keys, 'which is well-built, contains an entrance hall, tap room with fireplace and bay window, bar parlour with bay window and fireplace, kitchen with range, back kitchen with furnace and sink, beer store cellar, pantry and four bedrooms. Shop is newly built and [with] tiled roof. Other buildings comprise slaughter house with furnace, fasting pen, two-stall stable with loft over, pig sty, tank house, WC and urinal.'

The pub was sold to John Gutzmer Hossack of Bond Street, London in 1918. Hossack shortly afterwards sold it to Lewis Clarke & Co for £835. William Griffin, who was also a blacksmith, ran the pub from 1911 to 1923, when he was succeeded by his son, also called William, who remained there until 1961. Albert and Ada Gardner were the landlords in the 1960s with Marston's buying the property in the 1970s. A price list of that time shows Pedigree pale ale costing 13p a pint, Mild 11p, and Guinness 17p. Ken and

*Albert and Ada Gardner, landlords of the Cross Keys in the 1960s*

*The Cross Keys in 2012*

Maureen Clarke were at the helm in the early 1980s. Among the many events that took place during this period were sponsored wheelchair races, quiz nights, crib matches, harvest suppers and auctions for charity, and darts matches between the pub and staff at Worcester hospital to raise funds for an ultrasound machine. Also the North Ledbury Hunt met regularly in the car park to fortify themselves before hunting.

Postman Jim Cairns and his wife Michelle took over the Cross Keys in 1985, bought the property from Marston's in 1992, and in 1998 carried out some major building and renovation work which revealed a 106-feet deep well with running water at the bottom. Originally outside the back door, the well now makes an interesting feature in the extended bar area. A conservatory lounge was added three years ago. Rifle shooting, crib, darts and musical evenings are catered for.

Jim, who was postman for Suckley and Acton Green for 15 years, kept a variety of livestock in out-buildings at the back of the pub including pigs (hence the collection of pottery pigs in the bar), cows, chickens and ducks. After nearly 30 years as landlord of the Cross Keys, Jim died in July 2011, leaving Michelle to continue running the pub. He had been married five times and was described as 'a BIG character – loud, funny, rude, flirtatious, kind'.

Further along the road on the opposite side is an old and attractive cottage which used to be a public house with the unusual name **The Gate Hangs Well**, usually a reference to a church or toll gate and traditionally accompanied by a verse such as: 'This gate hangs well and hinders none,/Refresh and

*Once The Gate Hangs Well*

pay, and travel on'. The inn is mentioned in a directory of 1873, and in the census of 1881 Louisa Walter, aged 47, was the innkeeper. Her son, John, a gardener/domestic servant, also lived there together with two boarders, both agricultural workers. The pub was listed again in 1900, but then it disappears, so presumably around this time it would have closed down.

Along the Bromyard Road leading down to the Worcester/Hereford road on the left hand side is Ridgeway House, which used to be the **New Inn**, a pub and farmhouse. In 1834 it was owned by John Yapp and occupied by William Edwards, who was presumably the landlord. But by 1855 it had acquired its present name and Mr. Yapp was farming there.

At the bottom of the road on the right-hand side is a private dwelling which was formerly a pub called the **Quiet Woman**. Originally a small farm called Mockhall, it was occupied by Timothy Hill, a master shoemaker employing four men and two journeymen cordwainers. In 1851 this was also a beerhouse, with the

*The Quiet Woman in the 1930s*

owner paying a fee of two guineas to be allowed to sell beer from his premises in compliance with the Beerhouse Act of 1830. The Quiet Woman was still open as a beerhouse in the 1920s and probably closed in the 1930s.

At Stiffords Bridge there used to be a hostelry on either side of the bridge over Cradley Brook, but today only the **Red Lion** still remains an inn, and that only after being closed for two years following serious flooding. It was briefly reopened but at the time of going to print was closed again and up for auction. It was originally built as a small farmhouse, the core of which was the room which is now the cellar behind the bar. There were barns on one side, including a blacksmith's, butcher's and baker's, and stables at the rear. First reference to the property as the Red Lion was in 1793 when a Cradley general parish meeting was held there, after which manorial courts and parish meetings continued to be held at the inn. In the 1860s the landlord was Henry Orgee, who was also a cooper. In 1862 'the first General Court Baron and Customary Court of James Cuddon, Esq, Lord of the Manor of Cradley, [was held] at the dwelling house of Henry Orgee, called Red Lion Inn, situate at Stiffords Bridge.'

In Victorian and Edwardian times the Oddfellows (the Royal Hope of Cradley Lodge) of the Manchester Union Friendly Society used to meet at the pub. Annual fairs, with swings and roundabouts, were held in the meadows behind and also church parades, headed by the West Malvern Silver Band. Cherry wakes were also held when the cherry-picking season ended, with roundabouts in the meadow.

James Woodbridge, also described as farmer, was the landlord from 1867 to 1891, succeeded in 1895 by his widow, Anne Maria, who stayed there until 1905. For some of the time during the Woodbridge tenure, the pub was simply called The Lion. Thomas Page was there in 1909 when the inn advertised stabling and accommodation for cyclists, motorists and visitors, with good private fishing. Mrs. Sarah Jane Lawrence was

*Two views of the Red Lion in the early 1900s, when what is now the A4103 was a quieter road, pleasant for pedestrians and cyclists*

the landlady from at least 1913 to 1926, with Geoffrey Lawrence taking over from 1929 to the Second World War. About three years ago, a woman visited the Red Lion on holiday from Australia and introduced herself as the great granddaughter of Mrs. Lawrence. At some point an extension was added to the front of the property, similar in style to a house on the other side of the A4103. The bar was divided into several small rooms.

The pub was badly flooded in the 1950s. In 1976 the new tenant was Murray Smith, aged 52, and his wife Christine, who had been in the licensed trade for many years. In the 1980s it was run by Sue and Mark, who bought the freehold from Punch Taverns, and who later sold it to Andy Williams, a retired police officer. The pub was sold on to Ron and Leslie who, after running the business for about eight years including a time when the pub was flooded again, sold it in 2003 to the present licensees, Sally Cooke and Clive Dudley. They in turn suffered even worse flooding in 2007 when Cradley Brook burst its banks and water came 5ft up the walls, completely wrecking the ground floor.

For two years the pub was closed while a major refurbishment was carried out. This included digging out the old floor and replacing it with new slate slabs, replastering the walls, upgrading the electricity supply, removing damaged stud walls, and installing a new bar counter made of brick and Cradley stone. Where possible original beams were kept. The pub is now once again closed.

*The Red Lion inundated with floodwater*

*The Red Lion when up for auction in 2012*

On the other side of the bridge is a private house, formerly the **Prancing Pony** and before that the **Seven Stars**, named after the constellation of stars known as Ursa Major, or the Plough. It is believed a skirmish may have taken place at Stiffords Bridge during the Civil War; a musket ball from that period was found at the Seven Stars.

Built about 300 years ago, the pub is mentioned in the Cradley parish records of 1790 when a parish meeting was held there and the landlord was George Nott. *Lascelles' Directory* of 1851 lists Matthew Boucher, who was also a cooper, as victualler of the pub, staying there until 1867 when Mrs. Boucher, presumably his widow, took charge, followed later by Thomas Boucher, presumably their son, until 1879. Charles Allen was the next landlord – from 1879 to 1895 – when the pub offered stabling and accom-

*Two views of The Seven Stars in the 1900s*

*The Suckley brass band outside The Seven Stars in the early 1900s*

modation for cyclists and visitors, and also good private fishing – followed by Mrs. Lilla Allen, probably his widow.

The Friendly Society, the Pure Order of United Britons, met at the pub in the 19th and early 20th century. Also meeting up at the pub, when it was run by Walter Banner and his wife Harriet in the early 1900s, were the Ancient Order of the Foresters and the Suckley brass band. The band accompanied the Foresters on their church parades, walks through the parishes and on club fête days. In an article about the band, a local newspaper reported: 'When returning from a function at Broadwas Court they had to cross the River Teme – and when the whole band stepped into the ferry boat it sank. The bandsmen grabbed the cords on the side of the big drum and sailed across under their own efforts.' The band continued until the First World War, with Walter Banner remaining the landlord until 1917.

*The sign of The Prancing Pony, the renamed Seven Stars*

About 20 years ago Ray and Queenie White, from Kidderminster, bought the pub from Marston's with their son, Glen, and his

*The Prancing Pony in 2001*

wife, Anna, running the business. They carried out major alterations including the building of a conservatory at the front, two porches, a restaurant, a new kitchen and an extra bedroom. In about 2004 the name was changed to the Prancing Pony. Ray explained that the name change was due to his son, Glen, a great fan of Tolkien's *The Lord of the Rings*, who took the name from the inn in the village of Bree. In the case of the Bree pub, the landlord was Barliman Butterbur and the inn was frequented by men, hobbits and dwarves – and noted for its fine beer. Glen's signboard depicted a fat white pony reared up on its hind legs.

In 2009 the White family decided to close the pub – Ray and Queenie wanted to live there but were too old to run it, while Glen wanted to give up being landlord. The following year an application to turn the pub into a private dwelling was approved. The property now consists of an entrance porch, games room, conservatory, dining room, kitchen, sitting room, cellar and four bedrooms. There is an enclosed courtyard garden at the rear.

Cradley, the largest village in Herefordshire, was probably a Saxon settlement as the name derives from Creoda or Crida, the name of the first king of the Hwicce tribe of Mercia. The Normans built a church there and it was an important village at the time of the Domesday Book. A 16th-century timbered building served as a court house, an ale house, and possibly a poor house, before becoming a boys' school in 1667. As an ale house, it would have provided ale to the villagers on special religious dates rather like at a garden fete. It is now the village hall. Hops were an important crop with, in 1834, 61 fields covering 250 acres.

In 1775 the post office building was described as a dwelling house and farm with stables, cider mill, kiln and brewhouses. It also had a hop-ground, meadows and orchards. It later became a butcher's shop, and in the 1830s it was bought by the rector, the Very Reverend Charles Luxmoore; then it was

*The village stores in Cradley in 2002, once the Bull's Head*

described as a 'small farm and beer-house'. At some point it acquired the title **Bull's Head,** but the occupant in 1881 was John Hughes, described as a 'grocer and farmer'. In 1901 it became Cradley Stores. It is still a splendid example of a 17th-century property.

*Bull's Head Cottage in 2002*

Another 17th-century property, **Bull's Head** Cottage, just over the road from the stores, was also a beerhouse and had a thatched roof at the time. It was still open in the 1920s, when Archie Grubb was the occupant.

From 1829 to 1833, three people from Cradley – Stephen Beasly, Mary Rock and William Roper – were each fined £2 for offences against the Beer Act at Worcestershire Court of Quarter Sessions.

On the road to King's Bridge is an impressive modern house called **The Stable** which used to be a pub of the same name, and before that the **New Inn**. Originally it was a cottage with the fascinating name Mobbledeplecks. According to Wynnell M. Hunt in her book *Cradley – a village history*, 'pleck' is an old English word for a piece of common land, while 'mobble' indicates a clearing where assemblies or 'moots' were held in Saxon times. A document of 1775 records the handing over of the cottage, with its garden and two acres of land, to Richard Yapp. It is not clear when the cottage became a beerhouse, but after 1855 it is referred to, with a number of other properties, as Westfields. By 1876 it is listed in a local directory as the New Inn with John Woodhouse, also described as farmer, in charge. He was succeeded by Alexander Woodhouse, possibly his son, who was still there in the 1920s. At one time the pub was closed on Sundays because the landlord was religious.

Alex Hawkes, who also worked as an agricultural engineer in Malvern, took over as landlord in 1950 when the inn was still without electricity. For many

*The since demolished New Inn, and its long serving landlord Alex Hawkes*

years Flower's owned the New Inn, which had been granted a full licence, but were taken over by Whitbread's in 1961. In 1966 the name was changed to The Stable in dramatic fashion. Apparently conversation in the pub over the weekend often centred around horses as Mrs. Hawkes came from a farming family who were into point-to-points and hunting. The pub also had a stable-door leading to the Jug and Bottle, and, not surprisingly, it was nicknamed The Stable. But some customers decided that the name should be of a more permanent nature. So one night they came on a tractor and trailer loaded with bales of hay, up which they climbed and took the New Inn sign down. A new sign was made with a horse head painted on one side and a horse posterior on the other and the words The Stable. With Whitbread's agreeable to the change in name, the new sign was put up, although the name New Inn could still be seen on the wall.

The pub closed in 1973 or '74, and when Mr. Hawkes died his daughters, Helen and Joanna, inherited the building. It was demolished in 1999 and replaced by a new house, still called The Stable.

At the crossroads in the village is a plot of land containing an assemblage of stone buildings including a large barn and an ancient timber-framed property which collectively were known as the **Crown Inn**. The timber-framed building dates back to the 17th century, although it later was heightened and extended to the west. It was not until the late 19th century, however, that it became connected to the licensing trade when it was a farm called Little Westfields, with John Griffiths listed as a farmer, beer retailer and horse dealer. By 1876 its name had changed to the Crown Inn and Mr. Griffiths remained the landlord until 1891. William Lawrence took over as beer retailer, staying there until 1909, and was succeeded by James Lawrence, described as beer retailer, farmer and fruit grower. A local inhabitant recalls that during the Second World War, beer was drawn straight from the barrel, spittoons were in evidence and quoits was a popular game. Miss Elsie Williams was the licensee at that time, helped by her sister, and stayed as such into the 1950s. Bert and Maude Williamson then ran it for about 30 years until their deaths, and it closed in

*The Crown Inn in the early 1900s*

*The derelict Crown in 2002*

*Bert Williamson, landlord of the Crown between the 1950s and '80s*

1988. In the 1970s the Crown was a popular venue for the rock band Black Sabbath, one member of which – Ozzie Osbourne – owned a house on the B4220 to Bromyard.

Unfortunately this Grade II listed building was allowed to deteriorate until in 1991 it was bought by David Woodward, an independent financial advisor, whose intention was to reopen it as a pub. Before this was possible, however, it had to be extensively refurbished, as the main buildings were almost falling down. With a glut of pubs on the market following brewery sell-offs, Mr. Woodward had difficulty in funding the project and by the turn of the century decided to turn it into houses. This caused a local outcry and the formation of a pressure group, the Cradley Crown Crusaders. Mr. Woodward dropped this plan but submitted an application to convert the barn into bed and breakfast accommodation and build four houses in the grounds. This was opposed by the Crusaders on the grounds that the houses would occupy space needed for a car park and beer

*The Crown being converted into a private residence in 2012*

garden. However, Mr. Woodward successfully applied in 2010 for planning permission to convert the pub into a private residence.

During the 17th to 19th centuries Mathon was a thriving community with acres of hop fields, often growing the famous Mathon White, and many fruit trees, together with two shops, four inns and a variety of different trades ranging from blacksmiths and bakers to shoemakers and glovers. The timber-framed houses in the village street were originally thatched. Drink seems to have been readily available, with Luke Staunton, victualler, appearing at Worcester Quarter Sessions in 1634 for 'suffering the parishioners of Mathon to be continually drinking at all seasons, whole nights and days together'. And in the early 18th century, James Parker, a butcher, was fined the sum of 4d for selling ale without a licence.

Today Mathon is a quiet backwater with not even one pub. The last remaining one was the **Cliffe Arms**, a long established hostelry, which closed in 2004 and is now looking forlorn and abandoned surrounded by a jungle of weeds. Named after the family which flourished in Mathon from the end of the 17th to the middle of the 19th century, commemorated in the parish church by some eight memorial tablets, the inn was probably built in the 17th century with cruck end frames, formed from curved oaks halved along their length and set against each other to make an 'A' frame for the gable end.

According to local historian Ralph Spencer, it was here that the bell ringers came on 5 November each year, after ringing a special peal, for their ale, provided by the parish and costing six shillings. It was here, also, in 1826, at the end of their period of office, that the 12 'paymasters' of the village ordered their luncheon on Easter Monday, 'the expenses not to exceed £3'.

In the early 19th century the Cliffe Arms was run by John Ravenhill and then, as mentioned in *Bentley's Directory* of c.1841, by Thomas Ravenhill, victualler, who was also a tailor and owned 22 acres of land. A cottage next door still bears the name of Ravenhill. After a succession of landlords, the licence was taken over in 1937 by Leslie Hatch, who ran it until his death in 1959 at the age of

*A memorial to one of the Cliffe family in Mathon church*

51. He brewed his own beer, and during the Second World War served for a time as a special constable. Mrs. Hatch took over until the 1960s.

In 1976, Ted Dawe, originally a bricklayer who built up a successful construction company, became landlord, succeeded by Brian and Melissa Carr, who not only wanted the pub to have a new look but also a new name. After refurbishing the lounge bar, they changed the name to the **Trundle Inn,** as a play on the word trundle, a type of wheel, or a reference to trundling in for a drink.

The following year retired farmer Martin Hankins of Bank Farm celebrated his 85th birthday and his 50th year at the inn with a Christmas party at the pub. The *Malvern Gazette* reported that he had been a regular at the inn since 1932 – when a pint of beer cost five old pennies. Martin reckoned his longevity was largely due to his life-time habits before he retired at 67. 'I got up at 4am and started the day with the best breakfast you can get – toast and cider,' Martin said. 'Every evening after work I'd go down to the pub and drink about 14 pints of beer.' These days, the paper continued, Martin has curtailed his boozy evenings on his doctor's advice. He limits his visits to the Trundle to twice a week – and usually drinks a dozen brandies! 'It does me good and keeps the winter cold out,' he said. Landlord Brian Carr said: 'He's amazing – I've never yet seen him the worse for drink.'

Peter and Eunice Bailey then ran the pub, now called the Cliffe Arms again, until 1993 when Dilwyn and Christine Jenkins took over and refurbished the premises, including converting the barn to the rear into a restaurant. Their son, Philip, and wife Caroline, then ran the pub for the next 16 years, leaving in 2003. The pub stayed closed for many months before it was bought by Tom Hayes, from Hallow, in August that year. He made his nephew, Antony Lofting, a former insurance broker with no experience of running a pub, the new landlord. After an extensive refurbishment, the pub reopened for a few

*The Cliffe Arms in 2011*

months in the spring of 2004, but has been closed since. In 2006, 200 people signed a petition calling for the pub to be reopened.

Continuing along the village street one comes to a sharp bend on the right-hand corner of which is an ancient house called The Elms, which used to be a pub with the unusual name of **The Case is Altered**, sometimes abbreviated to Case Alter or just Case. In his book *The Old Community – a short history of Mathon,* Ralph Spencer explained: 'The name came from a title used by Ben Jonson for a 16th-century comedy, and refers to a story about an eminent lawyer, Edmund Plowden, who was once asked what grounds there were against the owner of pigs which had invaded the complainant's garden. 'Very good grounds,' he replied, but when told the pigs were his own, he said 'Then the case is altered.' The phrase became almost proverbial. As a pub name, it would come about after the landlord's situation altered for some reason, perhaps in some dispute with the licensing authorities.

In 1840 The Elms was owned by William Spurrier and occupied by Thomas Ravenhill, who probably at that time turned it into a beerhouse and gave it its new name. When he died, his widow took over. *Billings' Directory* of 1855 lists William Thomas, the grandson of Thomas Ravenhill, beer retailer at The Case is Altered. In 1902 Thomas Lloyd was described as a farmer at The Elms, so by then it had stopped trading.

*The private house that was once The Case is Altered pub*

The property was originally built as two cottages in the 18th century. On the roadside there used to be a cellar which was blocked up, while an extension was built on the other side. After being a pub and a farmhouse, it later became a post office and is now a private dwelling.

In Harcourt Road on the way to West Malvern is a prominent house called the Old Bell, which was formerly the **Bell Inn** and originally the **Fox and Hounds**. It is believed to have been built in the 19th century to provide refreshment for the thirsty workers at the brickworks in a field at the back, and was constructed from the bricks that they discarded as being too misshapen or under- or over-fired. In those days the men worked ankle deep in cold, wet slurry and were then roasted as they unloaded the kilns. Most of their deaths throughout the industry were related to consumption of alcohol or accidents caused by alcohol. It was also right on the edge of the estate belonging to Lady de Walden, who lived in Mathon Court. Mr. J. Yapp, also described as victualler, was the landlord of the Fox and Hounds, as listed in *Bentley's Directory* of 1841. The name was later changed to The Bell and was probably owned by the Royal Well Brewery. By 1872, however, it was owned by Robert Wall who sold it to Joseph Rushton for £405. James Parsons, aged 35, was the beerhouse keeper, who retained the lease until 1880 when Mr. Rushton sold the pub to Thomas Allen and George Allen, of Allen Brothers, the brewers, for £420.

In 1933, Jonathan Bowden, of the Park Hotel, Colwall was the owner, but sold it to Henry Mellings, the then occupier of the Bell, for £1,000. Mellings, in turn, sold it to Flower & Sons in 1943. The brickworks stopped operating by the end of the Second World War. For some years the Bell was run by Miss Nancy Lawrence, a local farmer, and her sister Freda, but it closed as a pub in 1967. The Lawrence sisters bought it from Flower's in 1969 and they let it out. The property was in a derelict state when it was bought in 1986 by the present owner, Tim Rowe, who, with his son, Simon, runs Harcourt Design Associates. The building also had a public health notice on it and the adjoining field was filled with a whole array of rusting farm implements. For 18 months Tim, partner Anni, and Simon lived in a caravan on site while

*The Bell Inn in the 1960s, and landlady Nancy Lawrence*

carrying out work on the building, originally a two-up, two-down with a lean-to, increasing the space by over 100 per cent.

After moving in they soon found that the Old Bell was frequented by a few ghostly visitors from the past, one manifesting itself at first by trying to enter the front door at about opening time and then revealing itself to Anni. It was an unkempt looking old lady. The story goes that while the Lawrence sisters were running the pub, a female farm-worker employed by them on the farm, came to the pub for her evening drinks. She was so unkempt they made her sit outside. Another ghostly appearance was when a neighbour having dinner with the Rowes distinctly heard the sound of a horse and rider coming down the lane, but when the front door was opened there was nothing there. Anni saw yet another ghost, this time a figure wearing a sack over its head, as people in the past did in bad weather, who just walked through the porch wall.

Just past Mathon parish church is a turning on the left which leads to **Moor End Cross**, which in the 19th century was a small community with a pub of the same name. It is listed in 1841 but does not appear afterwards. Yet another short-lived pub in Mathon was the **Oak**, recorded in the 1871 census as being run by William Hobbs.

## CHAPTER FOURTEEN

# Upton-upon-Severn

For many years a thriving inland port, Upton-upon-Severn is a small, historic town with a mix of half-timbered and Georgian buildings now better known for its small, independent businesses and as a centre for the popular arts.

First recorded in 897, Upton grew to be a busy town based on its river and quay activities and associated services such as distribution of merchandise. Single and twin-masted trows were the favoured vessel and along many stretches of the Severn they had to be hauled by gangs of men until horses took over the arduous work. Later the railways replaced the river as the transport network. Hauling a boat of up to 120 tons was thirsty work and as a result a series of pubs sprang up on or close to the river. At these, the hauliers sealed verbal contracts by accepting a mug of beer or cider, hence the name mug houses. Between 8 and 20 men were needed to tow a barge for about 15 miles. Their day's work earned them 2s 6d, two meals, and the ritual mug of drink.

By the Middle Ages there was a ferry across the river at Upton, followed by the building of a wooden bridge towards the end of the 15th century. A bridge of red sandstone was built in 1605 which, having survived damage during the Civil War, 'concluded its own history by falling down during a high flood which occurred in February, 1852'. It was replaced by another structure which in turn was replaced by the present steel bridge built some distance up the river at the start of the Second World War.

A feature of the town is the old church tower with a copper-clad cupola, nicknamed the Pepperpot, the only remnant of a 14th-century church that was replaced by the present church opened in 1879. John Dee, astrological and scientific advisor to Queen Elizabeth I, was rector of Upton in the 16th century, although it is unlikely he ever visited his parish.

Upton has always had its fair share of inns and drinking places which in the main were, according to Pamela Hurle in her book *Upton*, law abiding and caused the parish constables little trouble. There were some instances of bad behaviour, however, such as that by John Browne in 1634 who sold ale at all times and 'keepeth odious and sinful drunkenness in his house so that his neighbours cannot rest in their houses'. He also shot a man one night. In 1660

Thomas Browne, perhaps his son, sold ale by unlawful measure and brought a diseased horse into the town. The curate, Richard Turberville, wrote in 1737 'What a number of Publick Houses are set up in this little town and what Vile Doings are in some of them'. One reason for so many pubs in Upton was that the town was at the highest reach of the tidal river until the building of the locks at Gloucester and Upper Lode. This meant that boats coming downstream were forced to stop at Upton before proceeding on the next tide, and the waiting crew needed somewhere to have a drink. At any one time there were between 200 and 300 vessels moored at Upton.

Emily Lawson suggests in her book *The Nation in the Parish, Records of Upton-on-Severn*, published in 1884, that Upton had an evil reputation for drunkenness, aggravated by the habit of 'treating', or giving drink as part of wages. 'For instance, when a boat is unloaded, the employer gave a certain amount of money to each man, and also sent him to the nearest pub for so much beer or cider. If a man declined the drink, he got no extra cash.' And the custom of 'treating' was prevalent on every occasion of public or private life. Men were given drink for ringing the bells, or oiling them, for taking relief to the sick or for carrying a corpse to the grave. Women were also given drink for services rendered. Parish meetings were great times for drinking, and club

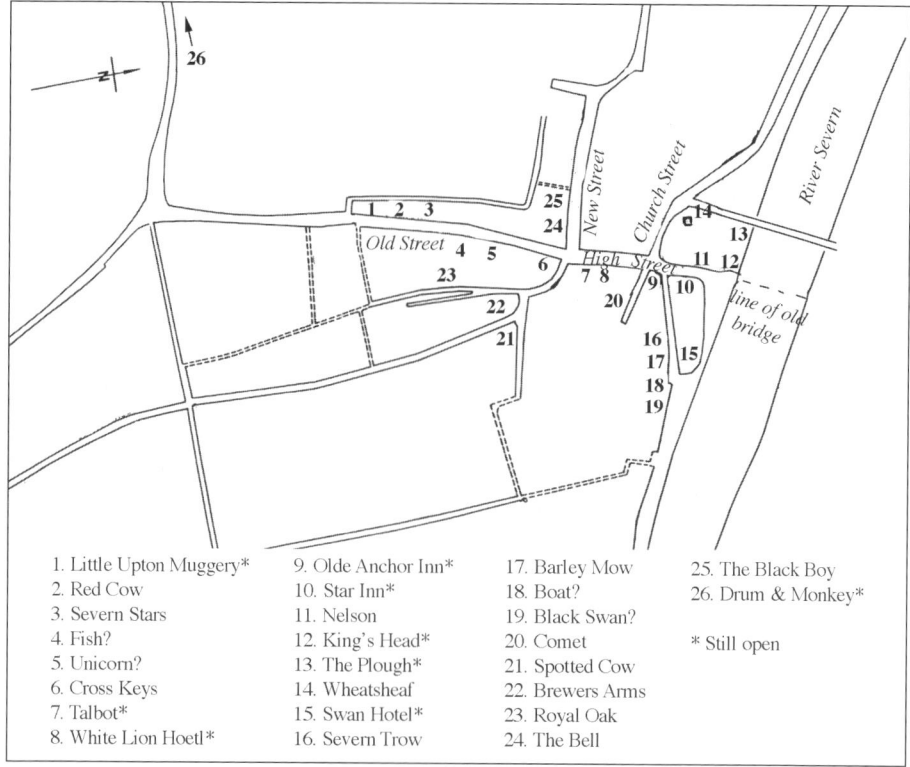

*Map of Upton showing the location of the inns mentioned*

feasts. Then there was the practice of 'wetting the bargain' with an adjournment to a pub. Alcohol was also given in every kind of illness.

According to *Pigot's Directory* of 1822, there were 17 inns and taverns in Upton serving a population of 2,319. Today that number has reduced to eight and in 2005 the town had a population of about 3,000.

On the other side of the river is a modern marina, home to numerous privately owned boats, built near a rubbish tip and close to the former brickworks. This has helped revitalise the river and attract tourists alongside three major music festivals, folk, jazz and blues.

The town has sometimes been dubbed Upton-under-Severn so often is it flooded, as witnessed recently in 2000 and 2007, when the town was cut off for several days. The *Malvern Gazette* reported that in the flooding of January 1960 the river was 18ft above normal level. This flood approached the 1924 level, but was about 3ft below the level recorded in 1947. However, a new flood defence scheme has been installed, at a cost of £4 million, which it is hoped will prevent flooding in the future.

The first pub one encounters driving into Upton on the A4104 is **Little Upton Muggery** in Old Street, and originally known as the **Crown** and the **Old Crown**. It was first recorded as the Old Crown in 1820 when Mr. W. Page was the landlord, and then in 1835 when it was called the Crown with Mr. G. Page in charge. *Robson's Commercial Directory* of 1838 showed that Ann Page was the landlady, as she was in 1841. A succession of landlords followed until 1904 when the pub, now called the Old Crown again, was run by Harry Bache, and in 1916 James Cooper was the landlord. At some point it became a hotel incorporating the house next door, today called Old Crown Cottage. From the main entrance there used to be a passage with doors leading off to an off-licence and bar on one side and the lounge, or smoke room, on the other.

Charlie Bridges was in charge in the 1940s and early 1950s, so was there when the pub was badly flooded during the floods of 1947. It was then run by Lesley, known as the Black Widow, who left in the 1960s to take over the Jockey Inn in Baughton, where she died in the 1970s. In the 1980s the pub changed its name to the Little Upton Muggery when it was taken over by Colm 'Mad' O'Rourke, who founded the Little Pub Company which had a small chain of distinctive pubs. Nick and Hannah ran the pub, which during a refurbishment became open plan. Mugs began to be collected in 1989 and today the ceiling and walls are covered in nearly 4,000 of them. There are special novelty mugs as well, such as the Mug Scone, the Nangking Mug, Miss Muggery, and Wolfgang Amadeus Mugzart. The Nangking Mug was one of a number of mugs found in the Nangking Congo, so the spoof caption states. 'Many Upton mugs were of course exported to China and those in the Congo were thought to be seconds being returned. Legend holds that drinking from the Nangking Mug makes one go blind.'

In 1991 Muriel Ovenden, the present landlady, took over. In 1998 Ushers Brewers acquired the Little Pub Company for £6.5 million, and four years ago Little Upton Muggery was bought by Brandstar. Mrs Ovenden still runs the pub very much as it was and is rightly proud of the astonishing collection of mugs of all shapes and sizes. The famous Desperate Dan cow pies are still on the menu, while a pool table and darts are provided.

*The Little Upton Muggery in 2012*

*Some of the range of mugs on display at the Little Upton Muggery*

Near the Muggery, on the same side of the street, is a white painted residential building which used to be a pub called the **Red Cow**. It was listed in *Pigot's Directory* of 1822 with Mr. M. Dalby in charge, and *Robson's Commercial Directory* of 1838 when the landlord was William Thomas. First Mr. G. Bruorton and then Mr. H. Bruorton took over in the 1870s and 1880s before John Cooke, also described as a butcher, ran it from 1901 to at least 1922. Reputed to have possessed good stabling, the Red Cow became redundant in 1927. Above what used to be the main entrance is an ancient licence

*The building that was the Red Cow*

*The Red Cow is on the right in this picture of about 1900*

notice, which reads: 'John Laughton, licensed brewer and retailer of Beer, Cider, Spirits and trading in Tobacco'. Mr. Laughton was licensee in 1862. Above a new front façade to what is now a shop is a wrought-iron bracket from which the pub's inn sign would have hung.

Further down is the Highway Gallery, formerly the **Severn Stars**, which was operating as a pub in 1820 when the landlord was Thomas Hancock, who continued there until 1841. John Laughton was licensee in the 1850s before moving to the Red Cow, followed by Mr. E. Hancock, but by 1873 it had ceased trading. It is a timber-framed building with a brick façade. A rear room used to be the main bar, while an off-licence on the side had a separate entrance. In the early 20th century it was again run as an off-licence called Dobell's, then remained empty for a while before being bought in 1970 by its present owners, Michael and Joanna Danniell, who converted it into an art gallery.

*The Highway Gallery (on the right) used to be the Seven Stars with what was an off-licence in the white-painted building*

*The Cross Keys is the second building from the right in the above photograph taken in the early 1900s, and in the photograph of 2012 on the left is shown in its present guise as the Little Gift Box*

On the other side of the road at the junction with Court Street stands the timber-framed building trading as the Little Gift Box. This used to be the **Cross Keys**, first recorded in 1820 when Mr. T. Brotheridge was landlord. The next landlord was Luke Day, who left in 1840 to take over the new King's Head. In 1841, with the pub shown as being in the Pig Market, Mr. Edwin Charlwood was licensee and also described as an ironmonger. Mr. W. Gurney, who was there in 1851 and in 1862, was also a baker, while Mr. J. Cook, listed in the 1880s, was shown as being a butcher. Mr. R.J. Keyes was apparently the last landlord, with the pub closing at the end of the century. For many years it was a grocery before becoming a shoe shop and then, in 2012, a gift shop.

Two other pubs operated in Old Street in the 19th century – the **Fish** and the **Unicorn**, both of which have long since closed. The Fish was only open a short while, from about 1870 to 1884, with Mr. H. Hill described as beerseller, baker and grocer. By 1884 it had ceased trading. The Unicorn, where meetings were held about the Ripple Enclosure in the 1860s, closed shortly afterwards.

*The Talbot c.1910 (top) and with subsequent rendering*

The first of several hostelries in the High Street is the grade II listed **Talbot Head Hotel**, named after an extinct breed of hunting dog, stocky in build with long, pendulous ears, white with black spots, which was adopted by the Earls of Shrewsbury as their family crest. Although the present building is of mid-18th century origin, it was built on an older core which may also have been an inn of the same name as it was mentioned in 1645 during the Civil War when the Constable of Little Malvern was ordered to deliver four quarters of oats to Captain Brewerton at the Talbot.

Mr. J.T. Reece, who was also a cooper, was the first recorded landlord, in 1820, followed by William Hill until about 1851, who was married to Elizabeth and had six children. A number of landlords followed. In 1904 Charles Bradshaw was in charge and was still there in 1916, while Edward Oakley was licensed victualler in 1922 and in 1928 described as the proprietor.

Originally the building had a plain front, as the top picture alongside shows, but later a new frontage was put on with stained glass windows and retaining the Venetian window with parapet over the entrance porch. A skittle alley to one side was a popular feature, but in the 1970s it was converted into a restaurant. In 2007 the owners, Punch Taverns, created a new smoking and drinking area on the patio, adjacent to a large car park. The building was refurbished in 2011 and reopened under a new owner. It now has two bars and a snug, while the restaurant is more a games room, doubling up as a functions room.

There used to be an inn variously called the **Crowne**, **King's Arms** and **Queen's Arms** in the High Street. It first appears in a legal case of 1560 involving control of wine sellers, when it was known as the Crowne Inn owned by John Hall. The Halls also traded in wine which they brought up the Severn from Bristol. John's father had a servant called Gabon, his name suggesting that he came from west Africa; he had presumably been 'acquired' on one of the Halls' trading journeys to Bristol. John Hall died in 1591, after which the inn was run by his wife Anne for some 30 years. In the 1630s and '40s the inn was in the hands of John Best, then of his wife Katherine at the time of the Battle of Worcester. On her death in 1692 it passed to her daughter Mary, and was subsequently sold to Samuel Gatfield. By this time it had become the King's Arms, but on the death of William III and coronation of Queen Anne, the name was changed to the Queen's Arms. Later it was acquired by Samuel Sanderlands, a barber, who seems to have built a malt house at the rear of the property. In the late 1700s Sanderlands changed his line of business to that of a linen draper.

The historic **White Lion Hotel**, also in the High Street, was built in 1510 and, known simply as The Inn at Upton, consisted originally of four buildings, judging by the roof configuration. The sign takes the form of a life-size lion with golden mane standing guard above the distinctive portico, and is probably a heraldic reference to Edward IV. In between the timbers were walls of wattle and daub. An open passage from the front door allowed coaches to pass through to stables and barns at the rear, and also sheep and other animals on their way to a market which was later established at the back. There also used to be a bowling green, a walled garden and an area for bull-baiting. It is believed there was once a smugglers' passage from the hotel's cellars to the back of nearby Georgian houses and down to the river.

During the Civil War, Prince Rupert visited the town in 1642 to summon support and 'ordered refreshment for his troopers at the tavern known as the White Lion'. Towards the end of the war, on the eve of the Battle of Worcester in 1651, the lure of refreshments at the White Lion nearly led to disaster. A small party of soldiers were told to guard the bridge across the Severn which had been partially destroyed, but they could not resist the 'propinquity of the Lion Tavern and drinking Sack mingled with strong waters. Then heavy sleep came upon the sentinels' so that a group of Parliamentarians were able to cross the bridge, capture the church and fire on the Royalists. Gradually Parliamentarian reinforcements arrived, fierce fighting ensued and the Royalists were forced to retreat to Worcester, where a week later their final fate awaited them.

According to R.C. Gaut in his *History of Worcestershire Agriculture*, in the 18th century the White Lion was one of the venues for cock-fighting in Worcestershire. It was also the venue, in 1743, for a meeting of the county's parish constables who were to bring with them reports on 'ye state and condition of the roads, highways, hedges, watercourses and bridges within several parishes'.

The White Lion also witnessed some of the climactic scenes in Henry Fielding's classic novel, *Tom Jones*, first published in 1749 and later made into a film starring Albert Finney. Tom occupied the room called the Wild Goose, while the love of his life, Sophia, occupied that called the Rose. Fielding actually stayed at the hotel and wrote to his friends and colleagues describing it as 'a house of exceeding good repute and the fairest appearance in the street'. *Lascelles Directory* of 1851 stated that the 'celebrated Tom Jones stopped (at the White Lion) and the room is now shewn in which it is asserted he slept'. Both rooms are still available to this day and a cross-stitching by Joy Foulston in 1998, displayed near reception, depicts the seductress Mrs. Fitzpatrick with, in the background, Tom fighting her Irish husband.

In his book *Rides Round Britain*, Colonel John Byng describes leaving Little Malvern to ride to Upton in August 1787:

> Being now on an excellent gravelly road, I soon came to Upton-upon-Severn, so well made known by Fielding in his delightful *History of Tom Jones*. But why he fixed upon this town I know not, as in my opinion it is most untopographically chosen.
> 
> The people who kept the inn in Fielding's time were named Hust; but I do not suppose that he meant to describe the hostess now living or the inn but only made it a fancied station for his wit and description.

The great tragic actress Sarah Siddons (1755-1831) may have acted in one of the rooms of the White Lion, or in a barn at the back.

There was once a tombstone, or so it is said, in the old churchyard commemorating one of the landlords in the following verse:

> Here lies the landlord of the Lion,
> Who died in lively hopes of Zion;
> His son keeps on the business still,
> Resigned unto the heavenly will.

In *Pigot's Directory* of 1822, the White Lion was listed as a posting house, with the Malvern and Cheltenham coaches stopping there on alternate days. A bill of a later date advertised: 'The Great Western will leave the Unicorn Inn, Malvern every morning (Sunday excepted) at quarter past 9, and the White Lion, Upton-upon-Severn at quarter past 10 o'clock through Malvern Wells, Hanley, Longdon, and the Railway Station, Gloucester, in time for trains to London, Bristol, Bath, Taunton, Exeter, Plymouth. Van goods will be conveyed by light cart.'

It is probable that a black-and-white market house on stilts once stood in the High Street near the White Lion, only to be demolished in the 18th century when the new turnpike roads into town brought increased traffic. This same period saw the hotel being given a classical Georgian front, while in the 19th century a new cattle market was set up behind the hotel, which by the turn of the century also boasted tennis courts and quoits grounds. A cobbled yard led to stables at the back. Housing now covers the cattle market, although the auctioneer's office and tethering rings for cattle remain.

In 1838 the landlord was William Symonds, with later landlords including Mr. J. Turberville and Mr. E. Baldwin, while Mr. J.R. Budden was in charge in 1904, and William Tovey from 1916 until at least 1928. During the Second World War the hotel advertised in the *Malvern Gazette:*

> Worcestershire people who comply with the request not to travel far this autumn [of 1942], may like to consider the White Lion Hotel, Upton-on-Severn. American bar, good food. Comfort and Healthy surroundings.

The hotel fell on hard times in the 1960s and was empty for a couple of years before John Hall, a local builder, bought it and carried out a major renovation including covering over the old cobbled way leading from the front porch to

*The White Lion in the 1930s*

*The White Lion in 2012*

the rear of the premises and enclosing that area. After the work was completed Mr. Hall put the hotel on the market and sold it.

The *Malvern Gazette* of 22 May 1975 reported that Mr. David Deamer, manager of the White Lion Hotel, had been declared bankrupt. His wife Barbara was joint general manager. They formed a company in 1973 to purchase the hotel, but it transpired that Mr. Deamer had assumed liabilities in his own name instead of the company's. Robert and Bridget Withey ran the hotel for about 14 years in the 1980s and '90s.

John and Chris Lear, who bought the White Lion in 1997, celebrated its 500th anniversary in 2010, starting on New Year's Eve with a huge party, helped by two enormous bottles of champagne – a Nebuchadnezzar (15.1 litres) and a Salmanazar (9.1 litres). They also arranged for their own special beer called Owd Lion and Pepperpot Ale to be available on tap and in a limited run of 500 bottles. Today, the hotel has 13 bedrooms, all *en suite*, a restaurant, part of which used to be a skittle alley, a lounge and a bar.

Further along the High Street one comes to another historic drinking place, the **Olde Anchor Inn** which, judging by the year 1601 marked on the gable end, is over 400 years old. It has a number of small, wood-panelled rooms, complete with low beams and open fires, ranging over several different levels, all arranged around one central bar area. During the Civil War, the inn was mentioned in Cromwell's despatches and, like the White Lion, also lays claim to being the hostelry where the Royalist troops caroused while the Parliamentarians made their perilous bridge crossing.

The Anchor, as it was then known, featured in an unsavoury incident in 1831. Two bodies, recently buried in Hanley Castle churchyard, were dug up and sent in packing cases to the pub for onward transmission to London. The body snatchers enjoyed a lucrative trade, providing corpses for dissection at medical schools, where there was a shortage of bodies for training doctors. These particular bodies were discovered in time and restored to their resting places, but the culprits were not discovered. *Berrow's Worcester Journal* of 1 January 1831 reported: 'Graves were opened at Hanley Castle churchyard and two recently interred bodies taken away. They had been sent in packing cases from the Anchor Inn to London, but parties following them, found them and returned them to the church. The resurrectionists were not caught.'

The landlord then might well have been John Masters, also described as a farmer, who is listed in 1835 and was there until 1851. There is an earlier reference to the Anchor in *Pigot's Directory* of 1822, when Mr. T. Kale was in charge. The inn continued being run by members of the Masters family until 1873. Towards the end of the century members of the Edwards family were in charge, while in 1904 Edwards & Company were running the business, and in 1916 Miss Alice Edwards was at the helm. In *Stevens Annual* for 1922, Mr. G. Edwards is listed as licensed victualler as well as being a brewer. Six years later Mrs. Emily Edwards was the landlady.

In 1954 Mrs. Kay Clarkson took over and soon started a collection of key rings on the ceiling of the lounge bar. In 1977 she was named 'the most warmly welcoming landlady in Britain', and in 1979 she handed over to a new owner, taking with her the key ring collection, then totalling nearly 1,000.

The new owner was George Soden whose son, Paul, a 24-year-old medical student, later became interested in brewing and, after six months of secret preparations, in 1983 opened the Jolly Roger Brewery at the rear of the premises. Aided by his brother, Martin, he produced four barrels a week of three different strengths named Jolly Roger Best Bitter, Severn Bore Special and Old Anchor

*The Olde Anchor Inn in the 1940s*

*The Olde Anchor Inn in 2012*

Ale. Two years later the pub changed hands, with the Jolly Roger Brewery moving to Worcester, but it has since closed. The Upton brewery became the Old Anchor Brewery, now also defunct.

In 1990 the pub was bought by Stuart McEwan, who ran it for the next 17 years. In 2007 the ground floor was revamped with the existing kitchen stripped out to increase restaurant capacity, and a new kitchen created in a storage area to the rear. The floods of that year hit the Anchor which was afterwards visited by Prince Charles and Camilla, Duchess of Cornwall, on a tour of the town. It was then sold to Guy Stevenson, of Pershore. At the end of 2011 it underwent further refurbishment, and reopened at the beginning of 2012.

In Lower High Street, formerly Bridge Street, stands another long established hostelry, the **Star Inn**, which was built in the 17th century and later became a posting house. It is mentioned in *Pigot's Directory* of 1822 but it was not until 1838, when Henry Bundy was the landlord, that it was described as a posting house. The *Prince Albert* coach stopped there twice daily on its journeys between Malvern and Cheltenham. The coaching services meant that in 1851 the Star and the White Lion were the two principal hotels in Upton. By 1855 there was a daily service to Worcester and *The Royal Mail* also stopped at the Star on its way from Malvern to Tewkesbury, Cheltenham and Worcester. But the coach trade was dealt the death blow with the building of a railway line and station at Upton in the 1860s, although in 1886 'Star Inn and Posting

*The Star Inn when run by Mr Bundy in the mid 1800s*

House' still appeared in huge letters across the side of the building. Mr. Bundy stayed at the pub until at least 1873, while Mr. G. Pemberton, who was also a veterinary surgeon, was there until the 1890s.

In the early 20th century, the proprietor Mr. C. Foster carried out structural alterations to the hotel, which was described in an advert in the *Upton on Severn News* of April 1902 as having 'Every accommodation for cyclists & Boating Parties. Billiards and ping-pong. Ordinary every Thursday at 1 - 1.30.

*Gentle flooding at the Star above in the early 1900s, and ever worsening floods in 1926 and 2007 (below right)*

Stabling'. In those days an 'ordinary' was a meal provided regularly at a fixed price. In 1916 Mrs. Clara Morgan was at the helm, with Mr. C.J. Bradshaw as proprietor in 1922 and James Cooper as proprietor in 1926, when the property was badly flooded. For most of the second half of the 20th century, the inn was run by the Barden family.

In 1975 members of the Croome and West Warwickshire Hunt met outside the Star Hotel for their Christmas holiday meet. Owned by Fownes, the Worcester-based hotel group, the inn was sold in 2001 to Rick Price and Carol Hobden, having been devastated by floods the year before and still in need of a lot of renovation work. In 2002 the hotel was renamed the Star Inn, its original name, and a year later it was bought by Penn Street Taverns, of Birmingham.

In February 2011 an outside bar, decking and summer furniture, valued at nearly £30,000, were destroyed in a fire which, fortunately, did not affect the main building. A man was arrested on suspicion of arson. The hotel/inn has 17 bedrooms and there are no fewer than four bars – the public bar with games area, lounge bar with comfortable armchairs, one in the functions room and a bar outside in the beer garden. There are two dining rooms.

Another pub existed in Bridge Street, previously known as **The Star and Horseshoes** and later called the **Nelson**, with Mr. J. 'Pumphrey' in charge in 1820 and Mr. William 'Pumfrey' in 1835, but it ceased trading in about 1840 when the **King's Head** was built. Since demolished, the building may have been sited where the public conveniences now stand.

When originally built in the 1840s, the present King's Head occupied a prime site on the main road leading to the bridge over the Severn and on to Worcester. The bridge was built of stone and was badly damaged during the Civil War. Although repaired, it became neglected and was eventually swept away by the floods of 1852. The next bridge was an iron structure which incorporated first a drawbridge and later a swing bridge. That too had to be replaced, but the new structure would not fit the site and had to be moved some 90 yards upstream, and a new approach road constructed. The only reminder of the pre-Second World War days are the old bridge abutments.

It seems that the King's Head was built on the site of an earlier hostelry of the same name; Martha Ruck was apparently the tenant in the early 18th century. In those days the old church, demolished later that century, in 1756, came close up to the inn, and carriages ran through an archway to stables at the rear. Luke Day is mentioned in *Robson's Commercial Directory* of 1838 as the landlord, followed in 1873 by Mr. J. Allsop, who was also a hay, coal and timber dealer. Tokens which could be exchanged for 3d worth of drink were available at this time.

At the turn of the century Joseph Turner was in charge, and was reported in the local paper as being summonsed by Worcester police court for 'furious driving' in High Street. PC Hawker said that Turner drove his pony and trap at a pace of 12 to 14 miles an hour, and did not stop when he held up his hand. John Buchanan, coachman to a Dr. Read, added that Turner was going 'like mad' and grazed the side of his wheel. In response, Turner said he was certain nobody could drive at 12 to 14 miles an hour. However, the magistrates found him guilty and fined him 10s with 25s costs.

The King's Head may have had a connection with a famous author in the 1920s and '30s. The Wodehouse Society is convinced P.G. Wodehouse, who had strong family connections with the area – one of his aunts was married to the vicar of Hanley Castle – based the Mulliner stories on an Upton pub where his amazing tales were told. Wodehouse called it the Anglers' Rest. After much debate the Society finally agreed that the pub in question was the King's Head.

For a period of nearly 60 years the King's Head was run by the Wilson family, first, Sam Wilson and then his son, Bob. Sam seems to have been a bit of a sportsman. At any rate, a huge white otter, on display in the Tudor House Museum in Worcester, is said to have been shot in a tree by Sam. Meanwhile his wife built up a reputation as a fine cook and held special dinner parties in the dining room, which is now the lounge bar. It was then full of stuffed animals – possibly shot by Sam!

After the Wilsons retired in the 1970s, the owners Whitbread carried out a major refurbishment including the creation of a large dining area by utilising the old skittle alley and enclosing the area where the coaches passed through, with the entrance becoming a smoked glass window and the top floor removed to leave a massive wooden beam stretching across the ceiling. A cattle shed at the back was transformed into the Riverside Bar, and the main bar area enhanced. Ian Lewis was the landlord for 17 years before it was taken over by Graham Bunn in 2000 with Enterprise Inns as owners.

Then in 2005 the King's Head was the centre of a shotgun siege as dramatic as any crime film. The story unfolds in the *Malvern Gazette* dated 21 July, when Upton-upon-Severn was

> ... brought to a standstill when a jilted lover walked into a pub brandishing a shot gun. Armed police wearing flak-jackets went to the scene and lined the waterfront. They trained their guns on the door of the King's Head, as gunshots rang out repeatedly from inside. Police blocked traffic from entering the town. Boats approaching on the Severn were turned back. People were ordered to stay inside their homes and ambulances were put on stand by.
>
> The drama began at 1.40 pm when Tim Bayliss, said to be suffering from depression, walked into the King's Head and shouted 'Don't move or I'll shoot'. Customers leapt from their seats and ran as Bayliss waved his gun towards them. Then he took a shoe off, sat on a chair, rested his toe on the trigger and aimed the gun towards his face. Landlord Grahame Bunn's wife Claire was upstairs at the time. Mr. Bunn crept back away from the bar, where Bayliss was sitting, and ordered his stocktaker David Thompson out of the pub. Then he ran upstairs to fetch Mrs. Bunn. Together, they ran outside through a back door and called the police. A shaken Mr. Bunn said Bayliss had been a regular at the pub for five years. 'I think he's very depressed because he's just split up with his girlfriend and he's got diabetes,' he said. 'I was terrified. This sort of think just doesn't happen here.'
>
> Armed police quickly arrived at the scene. By then, Bayliss was alone inside the pub, with everyone safely evacuated. When a police negotiator shouted for Bayliss – thought to be in his 20s – to answer the pub's phone, Bayliss walked out of the pub door, pointing the shotgun into his mouth. He crouched briefly by the pub A-board then walked

back in again. Soon afterwards, onlookers heard a shot ring out from the pub. Bayliss, initially dressed in blue jeans, and later wearing navy shorts and barefoot, appeared five more times at the door, with the gun pointing at his mouth or throat. Witnesses said they had heard a shot ring out from the pub every 10 minutes in a two hour period.

At 6.50 pm Bayliss emerged from the pub once again, crouched behind a car and appeared to be talking to a policeman nearby. He later gave himself up unharmed.

All the shooting took place in the Riverside Bar with Bayliss firing shots at two doors, one with glass, the ceiling disco ball, bottles behind the bar, and the fruit machine.

In July 2007 Prince Charles and Camilla, Duchess of Cornwall, visited the King's Head during their tour of the flood-hit town. Work on a glass-topped flood wall and associated landscaping, part of a major flood protection project for the Waterside, started in September 2011 and was finished in mid 2012.

The traditional Christmas Eve Hunt in 2010 took place on foot rather than on horseback because of the icy and snowy conditions, with the Croome and West Warwickshire Hunt meeting outside the King's Head where a brass band played carols.

**The Plough**, by the bridge and overlooking the river, was operating as a beerhouse in at least 1835 when John Pumphrey was described as a beer retailer. In the 1850s it was known as **God Speed the Plough**, with John and

*The King's Head in 2012*

*The Plough in the 1850s, on the day that the new bridge was opened*

his wife Hannah at the helm. On Hannah's death in 1880 at the age of 82, a tribute to her appeared in the parish magazine: 'There could not fail to be general and sincere mourning for one who was of so loving and motherly a nature, who had so deep a fund of sympathy and whose skilled and valued aid was always at the command of her neighbours.' The 1881 census shows that Mr. G. Harrison was the landlord, followed in 1901 by Mr. H. Harrison. In 1922 James Cowen took over as beer retailer.

*Severe floods affect The Plough*

*The Plough during the floods of 2002 (left), and in the dry in 2012 (right)*

Up until the end of the 1970s, the Plough was still serving only beer and cider. The bar used to be on the other side of the main entrance and part of the back of the pub that is now used as a cellar lay under the cemetery. An open yard at the back has been built over and an old well where the pool table now stands has been filled in and covered. Two columns serve as reminders of where the original back wall used to be.

The Marston-owned pub has been plagued over the years by flooding, being engulfed by floods in 2002 whilst in 2007 the water rose over the counter to a height of about four feet. The present landlord, Rob Baker, who runs it with his partner Katherine Langridge, hopes the refurbished bar area and new bar counter will escape any further damage now that the new flood defence wall has been erected.

During excavation work by the end of the present bridge, more than 30 skeletons were discovered from an extension, in use from 1835 to 1865, to the old church's main graveyard. It should not be a surprise therefore to learn that several ghost stories are connected to the pub. As soon as the new landlords arrived in 2010, their 2½-year-old son was found to be talking to a soldier cooking pigeons. The figure was wearing Army uniform and had his gun. Then, in a corner of the bar, a little girl with long blonde hair, wearing a bonnet and a pinafore, was seen by some customers and was heard crying at night. Other apparitions were also seen.

Just round the corner in Church Street used to be the **Wheatsheaf** in what is now the first of the Church cottages facing the roundabout. *Pigot's Directory* of 1822 lists the Wheatsheaf; at that time Mr. J. Tinkler was the landlord. Mr. T. Tinkler, possibly the son, took over in about 1835 and remained there until

*The two-storey building was once the Wheatsheaf*

the 1850s. He was also described as a basket maker. Other publicans took over, with Mr. J. Hicken the last one before it ceased trading in about 1890.

The oldest pub sited on the river is the 17th- or 18th- century **Swan Hotel**, which was once a typical bargee's tavern with its own wharf and warehouse. However, it does not seem to be listed until 1862 when John Harlow was the landlord, followed by Mr. J. Bibbs in 1884. Mr. Harlow was back again in 1892. In 1911 Thomas Harrod, manager of the Swan, who kept a journal and scrapbook, received the following complimentary postcard: 'Have arrived safe after a fine ride. Enjoyed Holiday grandly, exactly like coming from Home to Home. Shall highly recommend Swan Inn for staying at. Yours, A.S. Fletcher.' In 1922 Mr. P.C. Clements was in charge.

Originally three cottages and a blacksmith's shop, the pub, which is separate from the hotel with its own entrance, comprises two oak-beamed bars and a restaurant, and was a traditional mug house where bargees were given a 'mug' of beer to seal a verbal contract. The later hotel building was added at right angles to the pub in the 19th century, and the old warehouse was converted into the Barn Bar, available for use on special occasions. The Severn Way, after crossing the river to the west bank by way of the town's bridge, passes the Swan's front door.

The hotel once had nine en-suite rooms, but now is restricted to five. Riverside moorings are available. Long-serving previous landlords were Peter and Sue Davis, who were there for about 30 years. Another previous landlord for about four or five years was Kevin Barry, the ex-Chelsea player and uncle of Gareth, the England and Aston Villa and more recently Manchester City

*A gathering of scouts in front of the Swan Inn*

player. The property, owned by Marston's, was severely damaged during the floods of July 2007 and when the present licensees, Ralph and Sue Thompson, came it required a major refurbishment. They just reopened the bar to start with. It was closed again in 2010 for six weeks while more work was carried out.

There were several ancient inns in Dunns Lane, one of the favourite haunts of bargees visiting Upton, but they all ceased trading a long time

*The Swan engulfed by floods in 2007*

*The Severn Trow and Barley Mow are both seen in this 1857 picture from the Illustrated London News showing celebrations on Restoration Day (29th May)*

ago. The **Severn Trow**, at No. 21, opened in the 1830s with Mr. H. Doughty, landlord in 1835, staying there until the 1840s. Mr. J. Griffin was there in the 1860s and 1870s and Mr. C. Pumfrey in the 1880s, when it closed. The other main pub was the **Barley Mow,** which also opened in the 1830s with Mr. W. Gurney at the helm; Mr. Gurney was also there in the 1840s when the lane was called Grey Street, having been known as Queen Street in the 1820s. Other landlords included Mr. H. Hodges, who was there in the 1880s followed by Mr. A. Richards, who was also a lessee of the Gas Works and a mineral manufacturer, and Mr. W. McCubbin, who was there in 1901. It managed to survive an arson attack by the

*The building that was once the Severn Trow*

landlord in 1906, but became redundant in the late 1920s. An even earlier pub was the **Boat,** which ceased trading in the 1830s and was replaced by the Barley Mow.

**The Black Swan** was in existence in the 1820s when Mr. T. Crees, who was also a coal merchant, was in charge. Mr. E. Cottrill, who was landlord in the 1850s, was also a coal merchant. Mr. W. Brooks was the last landlord when the pub ceased trading in the 1870s. It was sometimes known as the **White Swan** and may have continued trading as the **Swan** when John Harlow was in charge.

In London Lane, between the Anchor and the White Lion, where once were warehouses and workshops, there used to be a pub called the **Comet** which was trading at the turn of the 19th century with Mr. T. Edwards in charge, but it closed in 1829.

In Brown Square at No. 2, hidden by massive industrial gates, is a grand house which was once a much smaller building and known as the **Spotted Cow**. It was a short-lived beerhouse, run in the 1860s and '70s by John Siers, who was also a farmer of 40 acres and employer of two labourers. Still to be seen today is a trap door with steep steps leading down to a cellar where the cider or beer would have been stored. And in one of the sections of a long row of outbuildings is a wooden hatch-way which nowadays goes through to the next-door garden. In the courtyard was a pond and a tree with circular seating.

The house, originally built in 1820, was bought in 1890 by James Pumfrey, a master builder. Having no fewer than 12 children, he added an extra storey to the house, which he also later extended to one side. When he left the house to his son, Charles, a conveyance of 1901 states that the property was 'formerly a public house known by the name and sign of Spotted Cow'. As well as being a builder's yard, the premises were also used as a dairy and coal merchants with the coal being transported by horse and cart.

*The Spotted Cow still retains the bracket from which was suspended the inn sign, just visible protruding from the front near corner of the building*

Not far away in the School Lane or Berrow Fields area was another transitory inn called the **Brewers Arms,** mentioned in 1855 but not thereafter.

*Two views of the derelict Royal Oak*

It is sad to see a pub which has ceased trading. It is even sadder to see a pub which is not only closed but in a state of neglect, almost criminally so. Unfortunately, this is the case with the **Royal Oak** in the old Pig Market, apparently abandoned by its owners and just left to slowly rot and die. Part of the roof of this sprawling, still impressive building looks as if it is about to cave in at any moment, whilst windows are boarded up with the frames rotting and paint peeling. The Royal Oak name can still be seen on the wall above the entrance and also '... ery', probably referring to a brewery. In a side lane an old wrought-iron bracket stretches to the far wall, but the sign itself is long gone.

It was first recorded as a pub in 1835 and for the rest of the century was run by first the Cook family and then the Prices. Mr. G. Cook, landlord from about 1850 to the 1870s, was described as a builder, carpenter and joiner. In 1901, when the inn was shown as being in Court Street, Mr. G. Price was also described as a builder.

It closed as a public house in 1970 and the premises, which are listed, were bought by a doctor who converted them into flats, in which someone was still living in 2011.

Nearby is the Old Court House, home of the County Court for a few years in the 19th century before it was moved to Malvern. On the other side was the site of the chapel where John Wesley preached in 1770.

In New Street there used to be two inns, **The Bell**, easily recognisable today as a tearoom, and **The Black Boy**, which has been demolished. According to a plaque displayed on the front of the building, the Bell was built in 1668 and seems to have been first recorded as licensed premises in 1835 when William Cleevely was landlord, a position he retained until the late 1840s. It was occupied by Mrs. Helen Thompson in 1868 and 1873. She may be the H.E. Thompson on the beer token made available to customers to exchange for beer up to the value of three old pennies. Alternatively, according to John Whitmore in his book *Worcestershire Inn Tokens*, she may have succeeded her deceased husband (whose Christian name also started with an H), which was the most frequent way women obtained innkeeper's licences in Victorian times, but if so his occupation must have been short lived in every sense, since the 1864 directory lists A. Harris. On the reverse side of the token were the words 'Ales, wines & spirits/check' and 3D (three pence) with laurel sprays.

From 1881 to 1901 the landlord was William Oakley, who was also a painter and plumber, succeeded by Edward Oakley in 1916. The photograph below, taken in about 1920, shows that E.J. Oakley was still the landlord and that the inn produced home brewed ales. To the right of the main entrance was the bar and smoke room, while a sign above a side entrance advertised Oddfellows Lodge and Foresters Court. According to *Stevens Annual* for 1922, the Bell was now a hotel with Mr. Parkes as licensed victualler and playing host to the Oddfellows and Foresters, and also the Angling Association. The Bell lost its licence in the early 1970s and in 1975 became Severn Antique Galleries, later a tearoom, then a drawing studio and in 2003 back to being a tearoom,

*The Bell c.1920*

or coffee and tea restaurant known as Bell House. The old copper bell sign, with its clapper, is long since gone, but inside the premises the present owner has on display a collection of about 450 miniature bells in glass, porcelain and brass.

The building next door, Julie Ann – which sells separates and lingerie – was once part of the pub, as was the Captain's Retreat, a first-floor flat with an entrance in between the two. The oak timber-framed property still has a cellar with a ramp from the street, and there is a courtyard at the back where people used to sit and drink. There used to be a well, but it is now closed up.

On the site of what is now Collinghurst House, a block of flats, was once the **Black Boy** inn, probably named after Charles II, who was given the nickname by his mother because of the darkness of his skin and eyes. In 1820 the landlord was Mr. W. Clevely, followed in 1835 by Mr. T. Pumfrey. A succession of landlords followed, with Mr. J.R. Back listed in the 1901 census. The pub survived until 1929 and was later demolished. The lane to one side of the block of flats is still referred to by some as 'Black Boy Alley'.

*The one-time Bell, as an antique gallery in 1975 (top) and in 2012*

On the way out of Upton at Hook Common there was the **Virgin Tavern**, according to the census of 1871, kept by William Clarke, aged 70, who was blind in one eye, and his wife. His daughter and four grandchildren lived with them. The name may be a reference to Elizabeth I, popularly known as the Virgin Queen.

*The Rose and Crown in 1911*

At Newbridge Green, on the road from Upton to Longdon, stands the ancient half-timbered **Drum and Monkey**, formerly the **Rose and Crown** inn, which was probably built in the 17th century, but later rebuilt, with the barn at the rear being even older, dating from about 1530. It was originally a bakery run by John Colston in 1840, later taken over by another baker, William Fawke, and his wife, Ann, in 1851. He was also described as a 'beerhouse keeper' and 'beer retailer'. On his death, in 1871, Mrs. Fawke continued both trades with the help of her children, John, Harry and Ada. They made bread in the bakery, which became the skittle alley, made their own stout, and ran a little grocery shop. She died in the pub in 1915 followed by Ada and Harry, leaving John to run it on his own. As the *Upton News* reported, John Fawke latterly had 'led the life of an intermittent recluse, for although the licence was renewed annually the "house" was very often not open to receive customers'.

John's eccentricities are described by Margaret Bramford in her book, *Upton-upon-Severn Recollections (Voices from the Past)*: 'Old John Fawke, in the early 1930s, lived, elderly and alone, amid the cobwebs and dust of the unkempt and eerie tavern, lit only by oil lamps. Winifred, his neighbour, took him meals. Old John had a yellow, wrinkled face and resembled a monkey. "He only needs a drum," customers would comment' – monkeys who would beat a drum then being a common form of entertainment.

On his death in 1933 at the age of 75, John Fawke left an estate valued at £4,500 with probate granted to his nephew, Frederick, of London, who was not interested in the business. The Rose and Crown, 'a seven-day beerhouse with modern bakehouse, pasture, orchard and nearly three acres of land', was

*The Drum and Monkey in 2012*

therefore sold at auction, the buyer being Jack Simmons of Birmingham, at a price of £900. During his tenure, the bakery was converted into a skittle alley, the kitchen used as tea rooms and a full licence was obtained. The Chescoes took over the licence in 1940 and the name was changed to The Drum and Monkey, which was already its nickname. According to Miss Bramford there are two connected stories about the choice of name. The first is about John Fawke resembling a monkey and the other is about musical acts involving a drum and monkey, sometimes performed by locals on a green opposite the pub.

And Edith Chescoe's explanation? 'During World War II, when we ran the pub, we did not get our ration of beer for the pub, one thirsty week. It went by mistake to the Rose and Crown in Severn Stoke. So Dad said "Why don't we call this pub by its nickname, the Drum and Monkey, to distinguish it from the other Rose and Crown".' However, the Rose and Crown sign is shown in a photograph taken in 1954, although in 1961 the sign is halved vertically with the Drum and Monkey on one half and the Rose and Crown on the other. The present sign, with a prominent Drum and Monkey, was painted by Miss Winnington, later Mrs. Pat Unwin of Longdon Hall, an artist who specialised in pub signs. The Chescoes stayed at the pub until 1963.

Later the inn was run by Peter Moore, until 1994, during which time he carried out extensive work on the barn converting it into two restaurants, now called the Mallards and the Mews, with a combined seating of 120 or about 200 buffet style. With a courtyard entrance, the area also has conference and meeting facilities. The pub itself, set in about four acres of land, is open plan with extensions carried out over the years. Above the main fireplace one can still see a segment of the original wattle and daub. The present owner is Howard Hill-Lines, who bought the property in 2006, having run no fewer than 15 pubs during his career including the Farmers Arms at Wellington Heath and Hunters Inn at Buckbury.

# Bibliography

**General Works**
Bradford, Anne *Ghosts, Murders & Scandals of Worcestershire* (2010)
Gaut, R.C. *History of Worcestershire Agriculture*
Gwilliam, Bill *Worcestershire's Hidden Past* (1991)
Lloyd, David *A History of Worcestershire* (1993)
Palmer, Roy *The Folklore of Worcestershire* (2005)

**Malvern**
*A Description of Malvern, including guide to Drives, Rides, Walks & Excursions* (1825)
Burrow, Edward J. *Malvern Illustrated* (1895)
Chambers, John *A General History of Malvern – a Guide* (1823)
Covins, Frederick *Malvern Between the Wars – a Reminiscence* (1981)
*Cross's Illustrated Hand-book to Malvern – a book for visitors* (c.1881)
Drake, Daphne *The Story of Malvern Link* (1989)
Edminson, Vera L. *Ancient Misericords in the Priory Church Great Malvern* (1996)
Goodbury, Valerie *West Malvern* (1994)
Griffiths, Alan & Joyce *Great Malvern – a photographic history of your town* (2001)
Holt, Gill (ed) *Malvern Voices Wartime – an Oral History* (2003)
Hurle, Pamela *Bygone Malvern* (1989)
　　*The Malverns* (1992)
　　*Malvern Girls College, A Centenary History* (1993)
Hurle, Pamela & John Winsor *Portrait of Malvern* (1985)
Iles, Brian *Malvern Through Time* (2009)
Keynes, Randal *Annie's Box* (2002)
Knight, Miss E.M. *The West Malvern Book* (1959)
Moody, Catherine *The Silhouette of Malvern* (1953)
Smith, Brian S. *A History of Malvern* (1964)
Smith, Keith *Around Malvern in Old Photographs* (1989)
　　*Around Malvern, The Archive Photographs Series* (1995)
Southall, Mary *A Description of Malvern* (1822)
Waite, Vincent *Malvern Country* (1968)

**Villages**

Ballard, Stephen *History of Colwall* (1997)
Bramford, Margaret Upton-Upon-Severn Recollections (Voices from the Past), (2005)
Fare, Malcolm *The Hanleys* (2010)
Godsell, Elsie *Reflection on Colwall* (1989)
    *A Short History of Colwall Village* (1993)
    *Collwall Village Past and Present* (1994)
Guarlford History Group *The Guarlford Story* (2005)
Gwilliam, H.W. *Pixham Ferry* (1982)
Hunt, Wynell M. *Cradley – a Village History* (2002)
Hurle, Pamela *Upton* (1979)
Lawson, Emily *The Nation in the Parish, Records of Upton-on-Severn* (1884)
Neve, Nicholas *Colwall Village Society* (2002)
Scot, Malcolm *The Book of Leigh & Bransford* (2002)
Spencer, Ralph *The Old Community – a Short History of Mathon*
Suckley Local History Society *Aspects of Suckley* (2006)
Tidball, Elizabeth & Rosemary McCulloch *Guarlford History*
Upton Town Council *The Story of Upton-upon-Severn* (2006)
Williams, Dorothy E. *The Lygons of Madresfield Court* (2001)
Women's Institute *Hotels & Inns in Colwall* (1973)

**Inns and Taverns**

Bradford, Anne *Haunted Pubs & Hotels of Worcestershire* (1996)
CAMRA *Real Ale around the Malvern Hills* (1996 and 2006)
Collis, Anthony *The Inn Signs and Pub Names of Worcestershire* (2008)
Dunkling, Leslie & Gordon Wright *A Dictionary of Pub Names* (1987)
Eisel, John and Ron Shoesmith *The Pubs of Bromyard, Ledbury and East Herefordshire* (2003)
Gwilliam, H.W. *A Gazetteer of Old Public Houses and Inns in Worcestershire* (*c.*1990)
Hackwood, Frederick W. *Inns, Ales & Drinking Customs of Old England* (1909)
Haydon, Peter *Beer & Britannia* (1994)
Turner, Keith & Jan Dobrzynski *Worcestershire's Historic Pubs* (2007)
Whitmore, John *Worcestershire Inn Tokens* (1988)
Wilkinson, Simon *Upton-upon-Severn, Public Houses – Past & Present* (2007)
Woodcock, Roy *Adventurous Pub Walks in Worcestershire* (2006)

**Journals and Newspapers etc.**
*Lascelles' Directory*
*Kelly's Directory*
*Robson's Commercial Directory*
*Pigot's Directory*
*Bentley's Directory*
*Malvern Advertiser*
*Malvern Gazette*
*Upton News*
*Berrows Worcester Journal*
*Pint Taken* (Worcestershire CAMRA newsletter)

# Index of People

AC/DC  173
Adamson, Sue  118-119
Adelaide, Queen  42
Alderman, T.  132
Allen, Charles & Lilla  215-216
    R.O.  7
Allsop, J.  242
Allsopp, Julie  70
Amelia, Queen  48
Andrew, D.R.  54
Andrews family  158
Anson, Harry  102
Anthony, George  190
Archer family  26
    Edward  27, 42
    John  27, 40
    Thomas  109
    William  50-51
Artopp, Fred  202
Ashmore, Thomas  94
Astaire, Adele  134
Atkins, Denis  142
Atkinson, Bernard  201
Attreed, William  33
Avery, Ted  135

Bache, Harry  229
Back, J.R.  253
Badham, Fred & Elizabeth  145
Baker, Amelia  99
    Rob  246
Bailey, James  119
    Peter  150
    Peter & Eunice  167, 223
    Tim  19-20
Baines, Charles  94
Bains, George  103
    Marinder  45

Baldry, Arthur/Terry & Dawn  103
Baldwin, E.  236
    Stanley  114
Balfour, A.J.  114
Ballard, Stephen  165
Banner, Walter & Harriet  216
    Bannister, Roger  32
Barden family  241
Barker, John & Joan, Diane  204-205
Barlow, Rod & Belinda, Maxwell  208
Baron, Rev. N.S.P.  111
Barrett Browning, Elizabeth  166
Barron, Chris  120
Barry, Kevin  247
Bartlett, Geoff & Carrie  82, 89
Baylis, Khamala  78
Bayliss, Tim  243-244
Beard, J.  37, 39
    Polly  209
Benbow, J.  122
    Richard  122
Beauchamp, Henry, 4th Earl  55
Bennett, Jack & Sylvia  195
    R.  94
Berry, Edward  180
    Thomas  71
    William  72
Best, John & Katherine, Mary  234
Bevan, PC  137
Bibbs, J.  247
Bicheno, Mr. & Mrs. Alfred  117
Biddle, Rob & Mary  157
    family  158
Bidwell, Edward  103
Bird, John & Margaret  153
Bissett, Mr.  125
Blackburn, Clifford  72
Blackwood, Francis J.  15

Blackwood-Wileman, R.W.  15
Blake, Albert  134
Boehm, Helen  52
Boords, Andrew  10
Boot, Jesse  114
Bosley, Albert  36
Boswell, James  5
Boucher, Mr. & Mrs. Matthew, Thomas  215
Bourne, James & Lucy  105
Boycott, Dave & Barbara  77-78
   Pat  78
Brewer, William  68
Bond, Fred  68
Bowden, Jonathan  225
Bowers, Charles  167
   W.  108
Brace, A.  135
   Chris  78
Bradley, 'Slingum'  145
Bradshaw, Charles  233
   C.J.  241
Bresclani, Mr. & Mrs. Mario  93
Bridges, Charlie  229
   Frank  72
   Robert  114
   Thomas  167
Broad, James  18
Brooks, Michael  87
   W.  250
Brown, Mr.  207
Browne, John  227-228
   Thomas  228
Browning, William  137
Bruorton, G.  230
   H.  230
Buchanan, John  242
Budden, J.R.  236
Bullock, Richard, William, Thomas & John  158
   William  103
Bullus, David, Samuel, & Louisa  90
Bundy, Henry  239-240
Bunn, Graham & Claire  243
Burgess, Percy  210
Burke, Brian and Pamela  188

Burrow, Edward  114
Burston, Stanhope  139
Burton, William  57
Butcher, David  20
Byng, John  5
   Col. John  235
Byron, Lord  114

Cairns, Jim & Michelle  211
Cameron, Mr. & Mrs.  102
Campbell, Dennis  69
Campbell-Bannerman, Sir Henry  114
Capstick, Dick & Pam  141
Carr, Brian & Melissa  223
Carroll, Lewis  203
Cave Brown Cave, Roland  15, 51, 165, 167
Chadwick, Steve  85, 90
Chapple family  56
   Charles  120
Charlwood, Edwin  232
Cherry, Brian  135
Chescoe, Edith  255
Child, Richard  203
Choi, Michael  99
Clarke, Ken & Maureen  210-211
   Mary  36
   William  253
Clark-King, Rev. Ellen  173
Clarkson, Kay  238
   Walter  136
Clements, P.C.  247
Cleevely, William  252
Clevely, W.  253
Clewer, Dennis & Sybil  199-200
   Ernest & Laura  88, 90
Cliffe family  222
Clifford, John  113
Colbert, Mrs.  109
Cole, G.H.  99
Coles, James  204
Collins, Dave  91
Collis, Thomas  171
Colston, John  254
Comerford, Brian  28
Cook, G.  251

J. 232
  T.K. 122
Cooke, Albert 123
  John 230
  Matthew 182
  Sally 214
  Thomas 122
Cooper, James 167, 229, 241
  Mr. 139, 140
Copson, Alfred, James 196
Corbett, Gladys & Percy 107
Costello, Bill 200
Cotterell, Archibald 75
Cottrell, Dennis 114-115
Cottrill, E. 250
Cotton, J. 83
Cowen, James 245
Cowles, Isaac 136-137
Crangle, Karl 71
Crees, T. 250
Cridland, Les 202
Crook, Douglas 103
Croft, Steve 187
Cross, Eleanor 96
Cuddon, James 213
Curnock, Ann 196

**D**alby, M. 230
Daly, Stephanie 120
Dance, Miss 135
Daniels, Mark 185
Danniell, Michael & Joanna 231
Danny, a pig farmer 88
Darwin, Annie 26, 29
  Charles 26
Davidson, Jim 32
Davies, Haydn & Sheila 138
  Henry & Frances 200-201
  Jack & Doris 75, 84, 101
Davis, Francis 158
  Les 184
  Mr. & Mrs. 195
  Peter & Sue 247
  Rose & Peter 103
Dawe, Ted 223
Dawes, Alison 181

Day, Luke 232, 242
de la Mare, Walter 114
de la Roche, Mazo 166
Deamer, David & Barbara 237
Dean, Frank 84, 85
Dee, James 82
  John 227
Deegan, Anne & Gerry 87
Denman, H.W. 36
Deykes, John 37
  Samuel 23
Dixey, Dr. H.E. 7, 16
Donohue, Sue 197
Doughty, H. 249
Downing, Alison & Richard 45
Downs, Joseph 23
Drake, Ernest 108
Dudley, Clive 214
Dugard, John 50
Dumas, Comte 42
Duncan, Cecil 16
Dunn, James 68, 75
  Percy & Mary 70
Dunne, Frank 91
  Jimmy 91
Dutson, William 82

**E**ast, Steve 76-77
Eberal, Theophilus & Sarah 210
Edgar, King 1
Edmunds, William 202
Edwards, Mr. & Mrs. 197
  T. 250
  William 212
Eeles, E.H. 159
Ekin, Ted & Barbara 117
Elgar, Alice & G. 238
  Edward 130
  Margaret 192
Ellis, Charles 184
Elliston, David 182
  Harold 73
Elms, Mr. & Mrs. Francis 150
  Southwell 150
Elmslie, E.W. 63, 80
Elton, Idris & Margaret 170

Emms, Mr. & Mrs. Peter  127
Erskine, Joe  127
Essington, Mary  127
   Samuel  124
   Admiral William  125
Esterhazy, Prince and Princess  42
Ethelbert, King of Kent  1
Evans, Charles  75
   Chris  83
   Fiona & Keith  173
   May  127
   Thomas  94

Fass, Michael  19
Fawke, William & Ann, Ada & Harry,
   John  254-255
Ferguson, Dr. John  22, 60, 61
Fielders, E.  55
Fielding, Henry  235
Finch, Henry  186
   Neil  90
Fiskins, James  36
Flack, Sheila & David  161
Fleetwood, Richard  174
Flower, Col Sir Fordham  69
Flux, Frederick  143
Foden family  20
Foley family  22, 23
   Lady Emily  22, 27
Foord, Ben  134
   Nugent  143
Forrester, Richard  90
Foster, C.  240
   George  83
Foulston, Joy  235
Fowler, Thomas  136
Franklin, Alice  101
Freeland, Edward & Emily  113
Frost, Basil & Elizabeth  169
Fryer, David & Carole  182

Gale, Widow  207
Gandolphi, John Vincent  127
Gardner, Albert & Ada  210, 211
Garmston, Ted  72-73
Gatfield, Samuel  234

George, Jack  124
   Wallace E.  196
Gilding, Thomas  172
Gillon, Terry  51
Goldsby, Fiona & Ron  198
Goode, John  139
Goodhew, Giles  178
Goodman, Pauline  201
Gordon, Noelle  127
Gore, Dr. Charles  114
Gough, Kenneth  133
Gould, Harriette  132
   Paddy  32
   Ron  31, 32
Grainger, G.  192
Grant, Leonard  88
Green, Charles  178
   Joan & Rowland, Dennis, Wendy
   174-175
   John  33
Grice, Daniel  132
Griffin, J.  249
   Sally & Neil  150
   PC  85
   Police Sergeant  204
   William  210
Griffith, Arthur Troyte  119
Griffiths, Dave  86
   James  122
   John  220
   William  190
Grubb, Archie  218
Gull, Aamer  45
Gully, Dr. James  22, 26, 46-47, 63
Gurney, W.  232, 249

Hadrin, William  148
Hale, Ron & Betty  140
Hall, Charles  180
   John  236
   John & Ann  234
   William (Alfrick)  206
   William (Guarlford)  139
Hancock E.  231
   Thomas  231
Hankins, Martin  223

Hanson, Lawrence  124
   Walter  124, 127
Hargreaves, Richard & Connie  140
Harlow, John  247, 250
Harris, A.  252
   Charles  34
   James  109
Harrison, G., H.  245
   William(s)  40, 52
Harrod, Thomas  247
Harrop, Arthur  86
   John Ward  17, 100
Harry, Mrs. Frank  101
Haslam, Mark  154
Hatch, Mr. & Mrs. Leslie  222-223
Hawker, PC  242
Hawkes, Alex  219-220
Hawtin, Bert  145
Hawthornthwaite, Julian  20
Hayes, Tom  223
Haynes, Robert & Nellie  93
   W.  38
Hayward, Edward  85
   Mr. & Mrs. Samuel  113
Henry VI, King  10
Henshaw, Dave  19
Heppenstall, Rev. L.D.  109-110
Herbert, Arthur  127
Hewer, G.  96
Hewitt, Thomas William  102
Hicken, J.  247
Hickinbotham, James  84
Hickman, Steve  31
Hicks, J.  82
Higgins, Frank  163
Hill, Albert & Caroline  79
   E.  159
   H.  233
   Herbert & Sarah  84
   Thomas Rowley  210
   Thomas William  210
   Timothy  212
   William  88
   William & Elizabeth  233
Hillard, George & Vanessa  118
Hilliard, William  55

Hill-Lines, Howard  256
Hobbs, William  226
Hobden, Carol  241
Hodges, George  186
   H.  249
Hodson, John & Vivienne  161
Holden, Ann  105
Holland, Frank  105
Honywood, Lady  61
Hopper, William  158
Hornyold, Thomas  127
Horton, Emily  169
Hossack, John Gutzmer  210
Howard, Mrs. Wm  140
Howes, Roger & Mary  103
Hughes, Beattie  163
   Edward & Helen  139
   John (Colwall)  170
   John (Cradley)  218
   Joseph & Sarah  146
Hurrell, John  85
Huskisson, William  122
Hyde, Fred & Violet  140

Ine, King of Wessex  1
Inge, Dean  114
Ingram, Annie  180
Israel, Henry  91
Ironmonger, Duncan  20, 73, 98, 154, 167

Jackson, Sir Barry  30
   Supt. E.T.  186
   Stan  140
James, Harold  70
   Robert  109
Jenkins, David  150
   Dilwyn & Christine, Philip & Caroline  223
Jethcott, Alan & Jean  203
Jolley, John  35
Jones, Fred & Fanny  180
   Herbert  30
   James  30
   James & Caroline  145
   Julia  127
   Kate  174

Mark & Sue  140
Martin & Sheila  133
Wally & Daisy  54, 83
Wally  85
William  91
Jonson, Ben  224
Jowett, Dr. Benjamin  114

**K**ale, T.  238
Kelton, Tony  120
Kendall, David  56
Kennedy, Nigel  112, 117
Kent, Duchess of  42
Kerby, William & Mary  184
Keyes, R.J.  232
Kilford, Rex, & Evelyn  80
King, Henry  172
Kings, Richard  145
Knapton, George & Dinah  93
Knight, Dame Laura  30, 42, 168
   Harold  42
Knot, Alfred  184
Knott, William  109

Lamb, Haydn & Susan  163
Lancaster, Kathleen  43
Lane, Edith  124
   H.  30
   Thomas  30, 67
   Thomas (of the Moodkee)  102
   William  77, 85
Langridge, Katherine  246
Laughton, John  231
Lawrence, James  220
   Nancy & Freda  225
   Sarah Jane & Geoffrey  213-214
   T.E.  30
   T.H.  155
   William  220
Lear, John & Chris  237
Lechmere, Anthony  145
   Sir Edmund  148
Lee, John  135
   J.W.  30
   Terry  173
Leighton, Richard  54

Lenham, Capt. Jack  132
Lennard, Mark  201
Lesley 'the Black Widow'  229
Letties, Joanne  196
Lewis, C.S.  35
   Ian  243
   Thomas  117
   V.  137
L'Huiller, John & Barbara  97
Limerick, H.  75
Lind, Jenny  181
Lloyd, Thomas  224
Lofting, Antony  223
Long, Don & Eileen  117
Longley, Charles  114
Lovell, Mr. & Mrs. B.  49
Lowis, Harry  28
Ludlow, PC  67
Luffman, John  105
Luxmore, Rev. Charles  217
Lynch, Brian  78, 201
Lyndhurst, Nicholas  32

**M**acdonnell, Mr. A.Y.C.
   & Mrs. E.B.  109
Manley, Reginald & Mrs. N.R.  51
Mansell, H.T.  105
Marie Amelie, Queen  42
Markham, Jervis  175
Marshall, A.  145
   John  120
Marston, Trevor  118-119
Martin, R.  114
   William  114
Masefield, John  171
Mason, F.H.  110
   Jimmy  87
Masters, John  238
Matthews, George  38
Maund, Arch  192
   Donald & Corinne  75-76
May of Teck, Princess  26
McCann, Cecil  67
   Geoffrey  75
McCluskie, Brian  20
McCubbin, W.  249

McEwan, Stuart  239
McHale, Mr. & Mrs. Bernard  49
Mellings, Henry  225
Mence, William  39
Merriman, C.  94
Millner, John  130
Mitchell, Gertrude  43
Moerschell, Frederick  38, 66
Moore, Peter  255
Moran, Owen  72
Morgan, Ann  189-190
    Clara  241
    Peter  69
Morris, C.  82
    Josiah  99
    Thomas  92
Moseley, Oswald  135
Mossop, Mr. & Mrs. A.I.  101
Myddleton Biddulph, Richard  180

Nash, Edmund  172
Nesbitt, Ian  169
Newsome/Neesam, J.  45
Newson, Rev. Frederick  1412
    Steve  86
Nicholls, Sue  44
Nightingale, Florence  21
Noctor, Bernard & Ivy  131
Norbury, Peter  19, 20
Normandy, Dr.  11
North, Horace & Annie  137-138
Nott, George  215

Oakley, C.  30
    Edward  233, 252
    William  252
O'Driscoll, Pat & Marie  44
O'Rourke, Colm 'Mad'  229
Ody, Elizabeth  202
Oliver, Geoffrey  186
    Jack  184
    W.C. & Lily  85
Orgee, Harvey  174
    Henry  18, 101, 213
    Thomas  174
Orleans, Duke of  48

Osborne, Ozzie  88, 221
Ovenden, Muriel  230
Owen, Gordon & Jacqueline  151

Pagan, Robin  28
Page, Ann  229
    G.  229
    W.  33, 229
Paine, Frank  53
Parker, James  222
Parkes, Mr.  252
Parrish, Billy  180
Parsons, Geoffrey  81
    James  94, 225
Paton, George  169
Pattin, John & Sue  128
Paul, Graham & Claire  76
Pedlingham, Charles  174
    Tom & Alice  171
Pemberton, G.  240
Perry, John, Lyn  117
Peters, Del & Jane  89
Phillips, James  114
    Walter  203
    William  167
Phipps, Alfred  67
Pinchbeck, David & Gillian  152
Pitt, Edmund  116
Plowden, Edmund  224
Pocket, Peter  180
Porter, Emma  91
Potter, Joe  154
Powell, Bill  140
    Thomas  74
Pratt, Joseph & Mary, William  144
Pressdee, Lucy  210
Price, Bill  196
    D.  153
    G.  251
    Richard  135
    Rick  241
Probert, E.  30
Probin, Derek & Averill  120
Prosser, George & Susannah  158
Pryse, William  207
Pudge, Henry  150

Pugh, Deborah & Tony  151
   James & Sarah  67
Pullen, John  169
Pumphrey/Pumfrey C.  249
   Charles  250
   J. & M.  242
   James  250
   John & Hannah  244-245
   T.  253

**R**andall, Ian  78
Rashleigh, H.G.  15
Ravenhill, John  222
   Thomas  222, 224
Rawlins, Charlie  153
Rayner, W.J.  80
Redding, Elizabeth & Thomas  210
Redfern, David & Lesley  189
Reece, J.T.  233
Reeve, D.K.  127
Reeves, Esca  28
   William  83
Rellie, William  114
   Mrs.  115
Reynolds, Edward  103
   Fred & Doris  158, 159
   Reg  105
Ricardo, Florence  47
Richards, A.  249
   Mrs. & son Mr. R.  50
Roberts, Fred & Ethel, George & Sheila,
   Sue, Dave  146-147
   George  39
   Martin & Caroline  201
Robinson, Colin  112
   Gerald & Mal  189
Rodgman, Alfred, Harry, Wally  184
Rogers, William  171
Romney, Mr.  148
Ross, Mr. & Mrs. Michael  128
Rowe, Tim, Simon, Anni  225
Ruck, Martha  242
   Samuel  116
Rudd, David  135
   Frank  72, 134
Rushton, Joseph  225

Russell, Mrs.  128
Ryland, W.H.  14

**S**anderlands, Samuel  234
Sanger, Mr. & Mrs.  178
Sankey, Andrew  20
Scales, Prunella  32
Schneider, L.  51
Scott, Keith & Elizabeth  170
Scott-Bowden, Col. & Mrs.  168
Scudamore, Michael  167
Selassie, Haile  51
Shaw, George Bernard  30
Sheen, Joseph  139
Shenstone, William  5
Sherwood, Albert  148
Shiers, Edgar  83
Shirley, Carl and Melanie  35
Siddons, Sarah  235
Siers, John  250
Simmons, Gordon & Ann  155
   Jack  255
Singleton, Col. Michael  174
Sinnick, Jane  122
Slade, David  186
Smith, D.M.  127
   Denis & Dorothy  167
   Harry  132
   H. Percy  167, 173
   Murray & Christine  214
   Pat & Barry  157
   Thomas  171
   Vernon  186
   Mrs. Walter  124
   Walter  132
   William  148
Soden, George, Paul  238
   Paul and Martin  20
South, John  202
Southall, David  49
Southgate, Tom  53-54
Southwood, Ralph  57
Spawton, W.  120
Spiers, PC  67
Spurrier, William  224
Stafford, Frederick  80

Staunton, Luke  222
   PC  67
Steer, R.A.  108
   William  130
Stevenson, Guy  239
   H.W.  37
Stewart, Carolyn  150
Stimson, Mark  112
Stimpson, Donna  87
Stuart, James  153
Stubbs, Jeff  87
Sudds, W.  187
Sutch, E.T.  127
Sutton, Jeremy & Roger  58
Symonds, William  236

Talboys, Mr. & Mrs.  123
Taylor, Joe  105
   Mr.  94
   W.  85
Temple, Dr. William  114
Tennyson, Arthur  92
Thackeray, Trevor  186
Thatcher, Frank  16
Thomas, Bob & Iris  133
   Helen and Nigel  29
   Howard  139
   Lewis  91
   William  224, 230
Thompson, David  243
   Helen  252
   Ralph & Sue  248
Tinkler, J., T.  246
Tipping, Blackford & Ada  42
   H.B.  39
Todd, Arthur  93
Tolkien, J.R.  35
Tomlinson family  143
Tovey, William  236
Trigg family  34
   Edwin  34
   Gladys  34, 56
   Harold  34, 56
   Thomas  34, 68, 109
Turberville, J.  236
   Richard  228

Turle, Henry  116
Turner, John  191
   Joseph  242
Tussaud, Victor  127
Tyler, J.H.  13
Tyndall, Juliet  142

Underhill, Ted  39

Vivian, Andrew  148
   John  148

Wade, Nathaniel  82
Waechter, Lady  205
Wagstaff, Alfred  82
Walker, Roland  207
Wall, Dr. John  21
   Robert  225
Wallis, Ellen, Frank & Robert  33
Wallimans family  28
Walter, Louisa, John  212
Walton, Canon Murray  111
Warrener, Dave and Sue  36
Watkins, William, Hannah  210
Watley, Henry  83
Watson, Bill  74
Weir, Michael  142
Weston, Fred  195
   Wally  134-135
Whitby, Gary  192
White, Charles  131
   Geoffrey  103
   George  131
   Ray & Queenie, Glen & Anna  216-217
Wigginton, Frederick  150
Wilder, Samuel  83
   William  83
Wilkes, Peter  155
Wilkinson, Tony  39
Williams, Andy  214
   Dene  196
   Elsie  220
   Lynda  192
   Mal  196
Williamson, Bert & Maude  220, 221

Willis, E.  39
Wilson, Dr. James  21, 40, 60-61
   H.  81
   Sam, Bob  243
Withey, Robert & Bridget  237
Wodehouse, P.G.  242
Wood, Tony & Lynne, & Bill  69
   Peter  117
   Thomas  210
Woodbridge, James & Anne Maria  213
Woodhouse, John, Alexander  219
Woods, Peter  102
Woodward, David  221
Wormington, Thomas  86
Wright, Abby  132

**Y**app, J.  225
   John  212
   Richard  219
Yorke, Mike & Helen, Enid  150
Young, Annie  127
   Mrs. Henry  48

# Index of Hotel, Inn & Pub Names

Abbey Hotel, Great Malvern  50-52
Admiral Benbow, West Malvern – see Hornyold Arms Hotel
Albion/Albion Vaults, North Malvern  104
Anchor, Malvern Link  87-90
Anchor, Welland  151-152
Angel, Great Malvern  66
Archer's Royal Kent and Foley Arms Hotel – see Foley Arms Hotel
Ark Inn, North Malvern  100-101
Ashbury House Hotel, North Malvern  102

Bakery, Great Malvern  54
Bakery Inn, Malvern Link  54, 82-83
Barley Mow, Upton  249-250
Bear and Ragged Staff, Bransford Bridge  191-193
Beauchamp Arms, Malvern Link  85-86
Beauchamp Hotel, Great Malvern – see Great Malvern Hotel
Beauchamp Vaults, Great Malvern  58
Bell, Upton  251-253
Bell Inn, Mathon  224-226
Belle Vue Hotel, Great Malvern  36-39, 40, 41
Belvoir, North Malvern  100-101
Black Boy, Upton  251, 253
Black Horse Inn, Upper Welland  154
Black Swan, Upton  250
Bluebell Inn, Barnards Green  136-138
Bluebell, Leigh  201
Blue Bell, Callow End  196-198
Boat, Upton  250
Boat, Pixham  197
Bowling Green, Bowling Green  186
Brewers Arms, West Malvern  116-119

Brewers Arms, Upton  250
Bridge Inn, Leigh  201
British Camp  3, 178-182
Bucks House, Colwall  171
Bull's Head, Cradley  217-218
Byeways, Longley Green  208-209

Carpenters Arms, Malvern Link  92-93
Case is Altered, Mathon  224
Cavalry Arms, Barnards Green  131-132
Chase Inn, Upper Colwall  20, 166-167
Cherry Tree, West Malvern  119
Church Ale House, Colwall  175-176
Cliffe Arms, Mathon  222-224
Coach and Horses, Hanley Swan  142-144
Cob and Castle, Great Malvern  66
Colwall Park Hotel, Colwall  167-169, 171
Comet, Upton  250
Cottage in the Wood, West Malvern  127-128
County Hotel, Great Malvern  21, 23, 60-63
Coventry Arms, Powick  186-187
Cowleigh Arms, North Malvern  103-104
Cross Keys, North Malvern  104-106
Cross Keys, Suckley  210-211
Cross Keys, Upton  232
Crown, Bowling Green  185-186
Crown, Suckley  209
Crown/Old Crown, Upton – see Little Upton Muggery
Crown Hotel, Great Malvern  5, 39-40, 41
Crown Inn, Colwall  169-170
Crown Inn, Cradley  220-222
Crowne/King's Arms/Queen's Arms, Upton  234

**D**og and Pheasant, Colwall  171
Downs Hotel – see Foley Arms Hotel
Drum and Money, Newbridge Green  254-256
Duke of York, Rye Street  161

**E**dward G's, Great Malvern  39
Essington Hotel, West Malvern  124-127
Ewe and Lamb, Callow End  – see Old Bush
Ewe and Lamb, Hanley Swan  145
Express Inn, Malvern Link  19, 86-87

**F**armers Arms, Birtsmorton  161-163
Farmers Arms, Longdon  163-164
Feathers, Castlemorton  155
Fermor Arms, Great Malvern  52-54
Fir Tree Inn, Malvern Link  82, 83-85
Fish, Upton  232-233
Foley Arms Hotel, Great Malvern  23-29, 38
Foresters Arms, Barnards Green  133-135
Fox, Bransford Bridge  190-191
Fox and Hounds, Mathon  – see Bell Inn, Mathon
Fox and Hounds, West Malvern  113-116
Fountain Inn, Barnards Green  132-133

**G**as Tavern, Barnards Green  – see New Gas Tavern
Gate Hands Well, Suckley  211-212
Gloster Arms, Malvern Link  90-91
God Speed the Plough, Upton  – see Plough, Upton
Great Malvern Hotel, Great Malvern  55-58, 59
Green Dragon, Guarlford  139-141

**H**alf Moon, Leigh  201
Halfway House, Bastonford  187-188
Hanley Quay, Hanley Castle  148
Happy Jack, West Malvern  109
Hare & Hounds, Hanley Castle  146
Hawthorn Inn, Upper Welland  153-154
Herefordshire House, West Malvern  119-120

Hole in the Wall, Great Malvern – see Fermor Arms
Hope Pole, Colwall  171
Hornyold Arms Hotel, West Malvern  122-125
Horse & Groom, Colwall  – see Horse & Jockey
Horse & Jockey, Colwall  172-173

**I**mperial, West Malvern  119
Imperial Hotel, Great Malvern  22, 38, 63-66
Imperial Tap, Great Malvern  66
Inn at Upton  – see White Lion Hotel
Inn at Welland  151-152

**K**ing's Arms/Crowne/Queen's Arms, Upton  234
King's Head, Upton  242-244

**L**amb Inn, West Malvern  34, 109-112
Langland Arms, Barnards Green  135
le Taverne, Great Malvern  33
Little Upton Muggery, Upton  229-230
Lodge Inn, Castlemorton  158-160
Lord Nelson, West Malvern  130
Lygon Arms, Malvern Link Top  34, 67-69

**M**agpie, Callow End  197
Malvern Hills Hotel, , British Camp  178-182
Malvern Link Hotel, Malvern Link  22, 80-81
Marlbank Inn, Welland  151
Moor End Cross, Mathon  226
Morgan, Barnards Green  131-132
Morgan, Malvern Link Top  67-69
Mount, Colwall  171
Mount Inn, West Malvern  113
Mount Pleasant Hotel, Great Malvern  40-45

**N**ag's Head, Malvern Link Top  20, 71-74
Nelson, Longley Green  208
Nelson, Upton  242

New Gas Tavern, Barnards Green  135-136
New Inn, Alfrick  – see Wobbly Wheel
New Inn, Cradley  – see Stable
New Inn, Great Malvern – see Crown Hotel
New Inn, Malvern Link  92
New Inn, Malvern Wells – see Railway Inn, Malvern Wells
New Inn, Storridge  202-203
New Inn, Suckley  212
New Recruit, Malvern Link Top – see Retired Soldier
North Malvern, North Malvern  100-101

Oak, Mathon  226
Oddfellows Arms, Colwall  – see Horse & Jockey
Oddfellows Arms, Malvern Link  91
Oddfellows Arms, Malvern Link Top  74
Old Bush, Callow End  194-195
Olde Anchor Inn, Upton  20, 237-239
Oliver's, Great Malvern  39
Oxford Arms Hotel, Malvern Link Top  75

Peter Pocket's, British Camp  178-182
Pheasant Inn, Welland  149-150
Pixham Ferry Inn, Pixham  197
Plough, Longdon  162-163
Plough, Suckley  209
Plough, Upton  244-246
Plough and Harrow, Guarlford  141-142
Plough Inn, Castlemorton  157-158
Plume of Feathers, Castlemorton  155
Portobello Inn, Malvern Link  79-80
Pound House, Alfrick  207
Prancing Pony, Stifford's Bridge  – see Seven Stars
Prince of Wales, Malvern Link Top  77-78
Priors Croft, Great Malvern  58-60

Queen's Arms/Crowne/King's Arms, Upton  234
Quiet Woman, Suckley  212

Railway Hotel, Malvern Link – see Malvern Link Hotel
Railway Inn, Malvern Link  81-82
Railway Inn, Malvern Wells  121-122
Red Cow, Upton  230-231
Red Lion, Powick  183-185
Red Lion, Stifford's Bridge  212-214
Red Lion Hotel, Great Malvern  30-32
Redan, West Malvern  107-109
Residential Hotel Ltd, Great Malvern  39
Retired Soldier, Malvern Link Top  13, 75-77
Robin Hood, Castlemorton  156-157
Rock Inn, West Malvern  119
Rose and Crown, Newbridge Green  – see Drum and Monkey
Rose and Crown, West Malvern  119
Rough Leasow, Longley Green  209
Royal Kent and Coburg Arms – see Foley Arms Hotel
Royal Malvern Hotel, Great Malvern  – see Great Malvern Hotel
Royal Oak, Colwall  171
Royal Oak, Leigh Sinton  200-202
Royal Oak, Malvern Link  79, 93-95, 206
Royal Oak, Upton  251

Saracen's Head, Suckley – see Cross keys, Suckley
Seven Stars, Stifford's Bridge  215-217
Severn Stars, Upton  231
Severn Trow, Upton  249
Seville House, Longley Green  209
Somers Arms, Leigh Sinton  19, 199-200
Spotted Cow, Upton  250
Square & Compasses, Callow End  197
Stable, Cradley  218
Stanhope Cottage, Great Malvern  36
Star Inn, North Malvern  99-100
Swan, Alfrick  204
Swan, Callow End  197
Swan, Newland  20
Swan, Welland  3
Swan Hotel, Upton  247-248
Swan Inn, Hanley Swan  142-144
Swan Inn, Newland  95-98

Talbot, Great Malvern  66
Talbot Head Hotel, Upton  233-234
Three Horseshoes, Poolbrook  138-139
Three Kings Inn, Hanley Castle  145-147
Three Nuns, Colletts Green  188-190
Trundle Inn, Cradley  – see Cliffe Arms
Tudor Hotel, Great Malvern  21, 45-49
Tyre Hill Inn, Hanley Swan  148

Unicorn, Upton  232-233,
Unicorn Inn, Great Malvern  3, 32-36, 236
Unicorn Commercial Hotel – see Unicorn Inn, Great Malvern

Vault/Vaults Inn, Malvern Link Top – see Wine and Spirits Vaults
Vaults, Hollybush  160
Vernon Arms, Powick  186
Virgin Tavern, Hook Common  253

Wellington Inn, Claines Pitch  176-178
Wells House, West Malvern  129-130
Westminster Arms Hotel, West Malvern  113-116
Wheatsheaf, Upton  246-247
White Horse Hotel, Great Malvern  29-30
White Lion Hotel, Upton  237
White Lion Inn, Great Malvern  45
White Swan, Upton  250
Whitehall Inn, Rushwick  197-198
Wine and Spirit Vaults, Malvern Link Top  70-71
Wobbly Wood, Alfrick  206-207
Wyche Inn, West Malvern  119-12

Ye Boars Head, Great Malvern  66
Ye Olde Robin Hood, Castlemorton – see Robin Hood
Yellow Lion, Powick  186
Yew Tree, Callow Green  174-175

# Index of Breweries

**A**llen Brothers Brewery  12, 13, 15, 16, 68, 225
Arnold Bennet & Co  17

**B**ailey's Brewing Company  19-20
Berkeley's Brewery  19
Brompton Steam Brewery  12

**H**illiar & Bennett  17
Homphreys Brewery  19

**J**olly Roger Brewery  20, 238-239
Jones & Davis Brewery  70

**L**ewis Clarke & Co  83, 113, 202, 210
Link Brewery  17

**M**alvern Chase Brewery  19-20
Malvern Hill Brewery  17
Malvern Hills Brewery (MHB)  20, 94

**N**orth Malvern Brewery  18

**O**ld Anchor Brewery  20
Old Brewery  19

**R**oyal Malvern Well Brewery  17, 18
Royal Well Brewery  12, 13-17, 36, 88, 225

**S**t. George's Brewery  20, 94
Star Inn, Upton  239-242
Star and Horseshoes, Upton  242
Spreckley's Brewery  83, 120, 145, 167, 207

**T**ank Brewery  101

**W**alkers and Homfrays  86
William Essington Webb's brewery  19
William Ivey's brewery  19
Wye Valley Brewery  132

*Also from Logaston Press*

# The Story of Worcester

*by* Pat Hughes & Annette Leech

Here are gathered many tales of the city and its inhabitants over the centuries: events and personalities from visiting monarchs to food riots, from a friar who was found up to no good in the Cardinal's Hat, to crowds flocking to see an amazing learned dog who could 'read, write and keep accounts'. Trades and tradesmen, crime and punishment, building and rebuilding, the pattern of the streets and the ever present great River Severn, the ebb and flow of generations of Worcester families and the arrival and departure of many visitors, welcome and unwelcome: the city seems to appear before our very eyes. Whether caught up on the fringes of the Wars of the Roses or besieged in the Civil War, Worcester keeps going – and growing, as its traditional trades are joined by the arrival of newer industries.

The story tells of both the rich and the poor, city officials and felons condemned to transportation, the idle and the industrious. After years of research, historians Pat Hughes and Annette Leech have many tales to tell, from early experiments with wind and wave power to the flourishing of Happy George and Hallelujah Lily, all gleaned from their extensive research among the city's archives, and illustrated with a wealth of photographs, paintings, drawings and plans.

This is history brought to life through the words and deeds of those long gone, and provides an inspiration to look for the past in Worcester's ancient street names, its mediaeval and later buildings, and even in its parks and open spaces.

320 pages with 140 colour and 90 black and white illustrations.
Paperback.   Price £15

ISBN 978 1 906663 57 3

*Also from Logaston Press*

# Mercia
# The Anglo-Saxon Kingdom of Central England

*by* Sarah Zaluckyj

Of the three great Anglo-Saxon kingdoms in Britain before the advent of 'England' — Northumbria, Mercia and Wessex — Mercia has long deserved its own history. Northumbria had Bede, Wessex had the Anglo-Saxon Chronicle, but Mercia has largely to be explored through the eyes of others.

This book attempts to redress this gap. Using the fragmentary chronicles that refer to the kingdom, inferring from lost sources utilized by later medieval chroniclers, extracting information from the charters, letters and other documents of the period and incorporating the growing amount of information gained from archaeological excavations carried out across the breadth of Mercia, this book provides a study of how the kingdom emerged from the Dark Ages in the late 6th and early 7th centuries and grew into a power to be reckoned with by the popes in Rome and the Carolingian empire from the late 8th century, a position of strength from which it subsequently declined.

320 pages with over 180 photographs, plans, drawings and maps.
Paperback.   Price £14.95

ISBN: 978 1 906663 54 4

*Also from Logaston Press*

# The Mercian Maquis
## The Secret Resistance Organisation in Herefordshire and Worcestershire During World War II

*by* Bernard Lowry & Mick Wilks

For decades after the end of the Second World War little was known about the secretive organisation known as the Auxiliary Units. Formed in 1940, at the same time as the Home Guard, its members were recruited from amongst a tightly-knit farming community and from those in other reserved occupations. Organised into patrols of about half a dozen men and knowing their locality intimately, their role would have been to carry out acts of sabotage and terror behind the German invader's lines whilst the Regular Army regrouped for counter offensives.

Whilst the bulk of the patrols covered the coastal areas, this book details the Units' most inland operational area. The establishment, operation and function of the 12 patrols formed in Herefordshire and Worcestershire are fully explained, together with information on the even more shadowy world of the Special Duties spies and urban saboteurs.

From carefully camouflaged underground Operational Bases liberally supplied with explosives and arms and constructed in woodland on high ground, patrol members would have set out at night to harry the invader. This was to be done in the knowledge that they and their families risked summary execution if captured.

This book covers a period of little known local history now revealed through research of the few remaining documents and by interviewing surviving patrol members. Over a period of several years the authors have found or identified Operational Bases near Dinmore, Dinedor, Credenhill, Ross, Ledbury and Bromyard Downs in Herefordshire, and near Alfrick, Broadheath, Claines, Crowle, The Lenches and Overbury in Worcestershire.

160 pages, 70 black and white photos and plans.
Paperback   £10
ISBN 978 1 873827 97 0